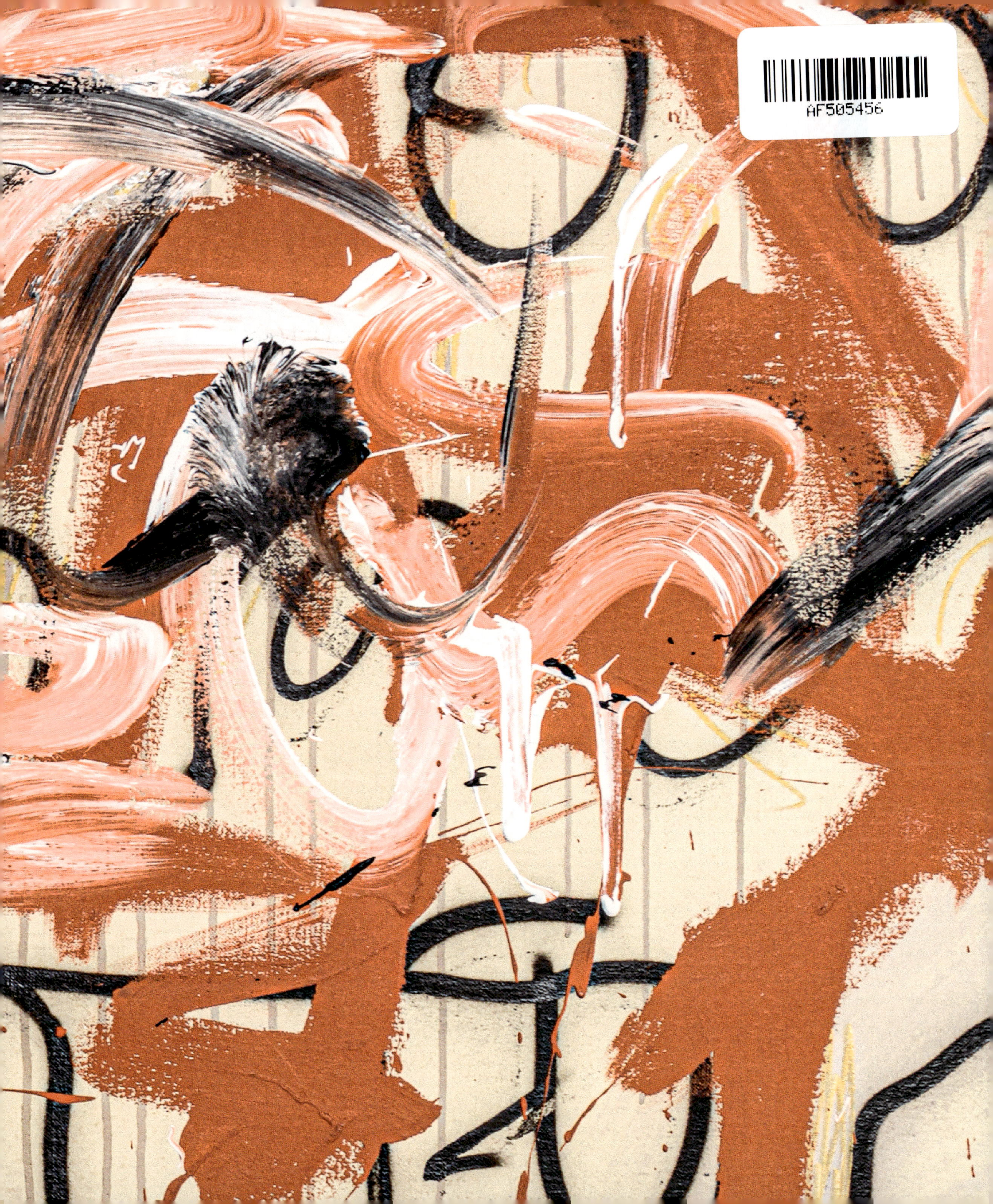
AF505456

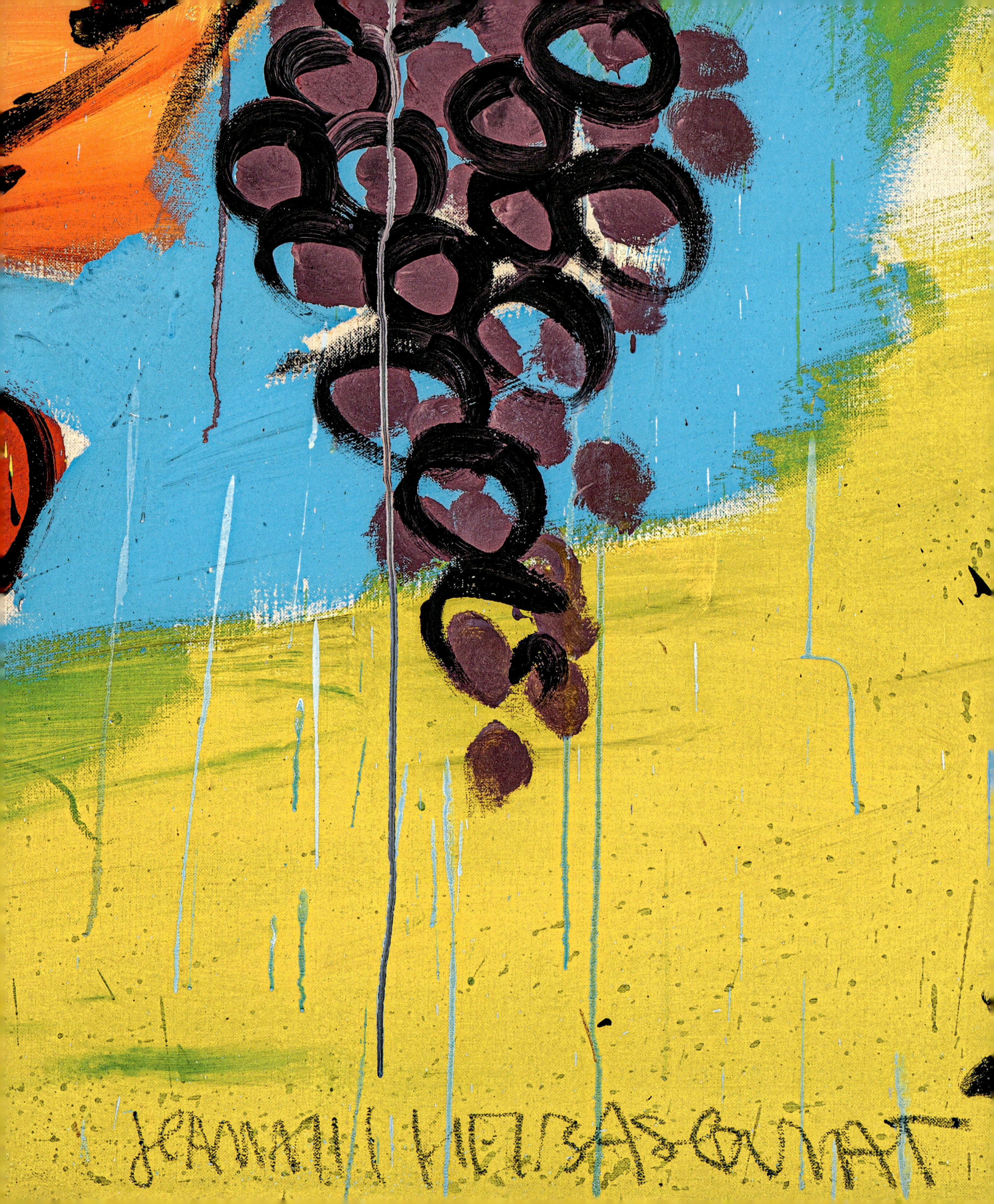
JEAN-MICHEL HELIOS BASQUIAT

Basquiat: The Modena Paintings

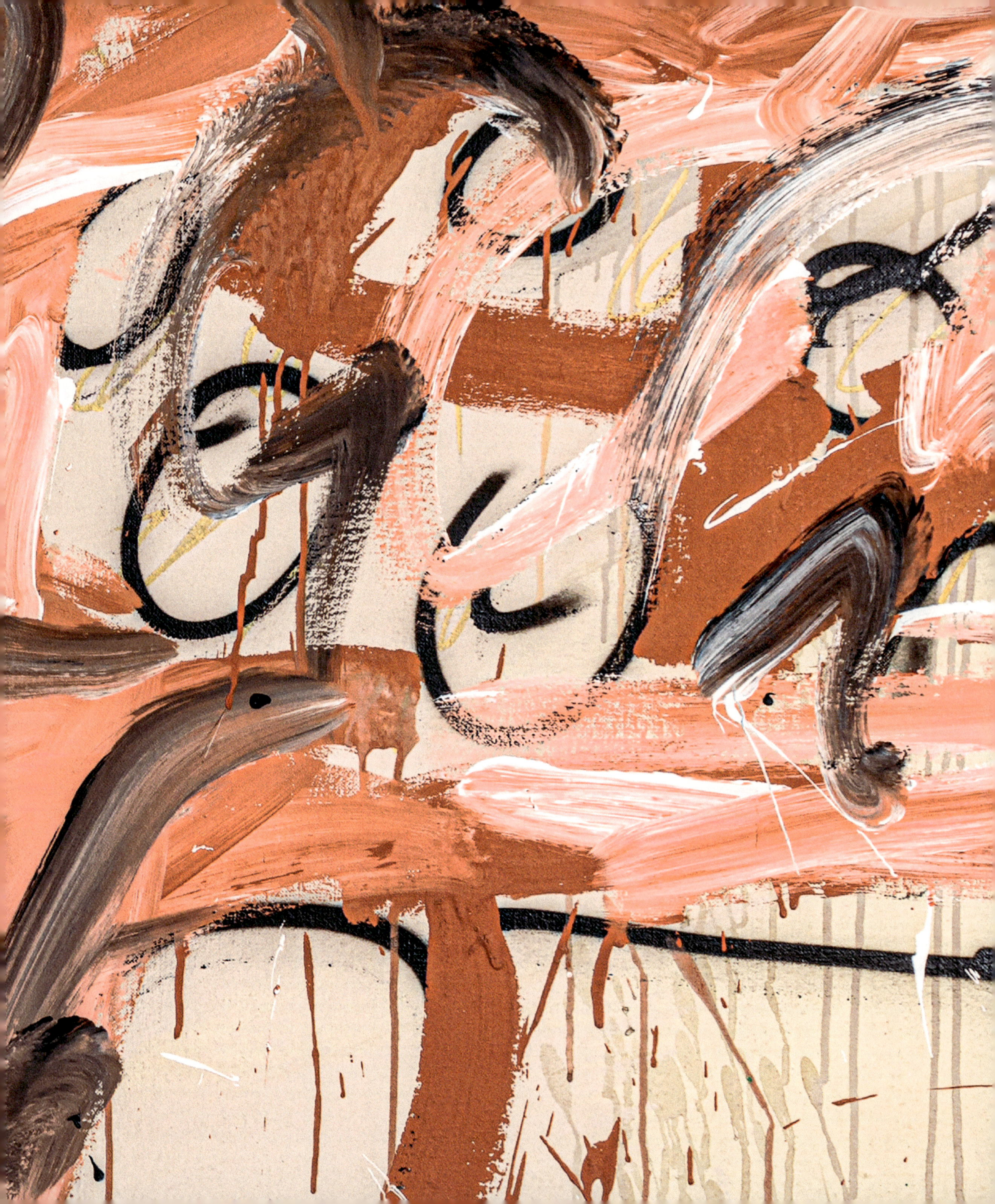

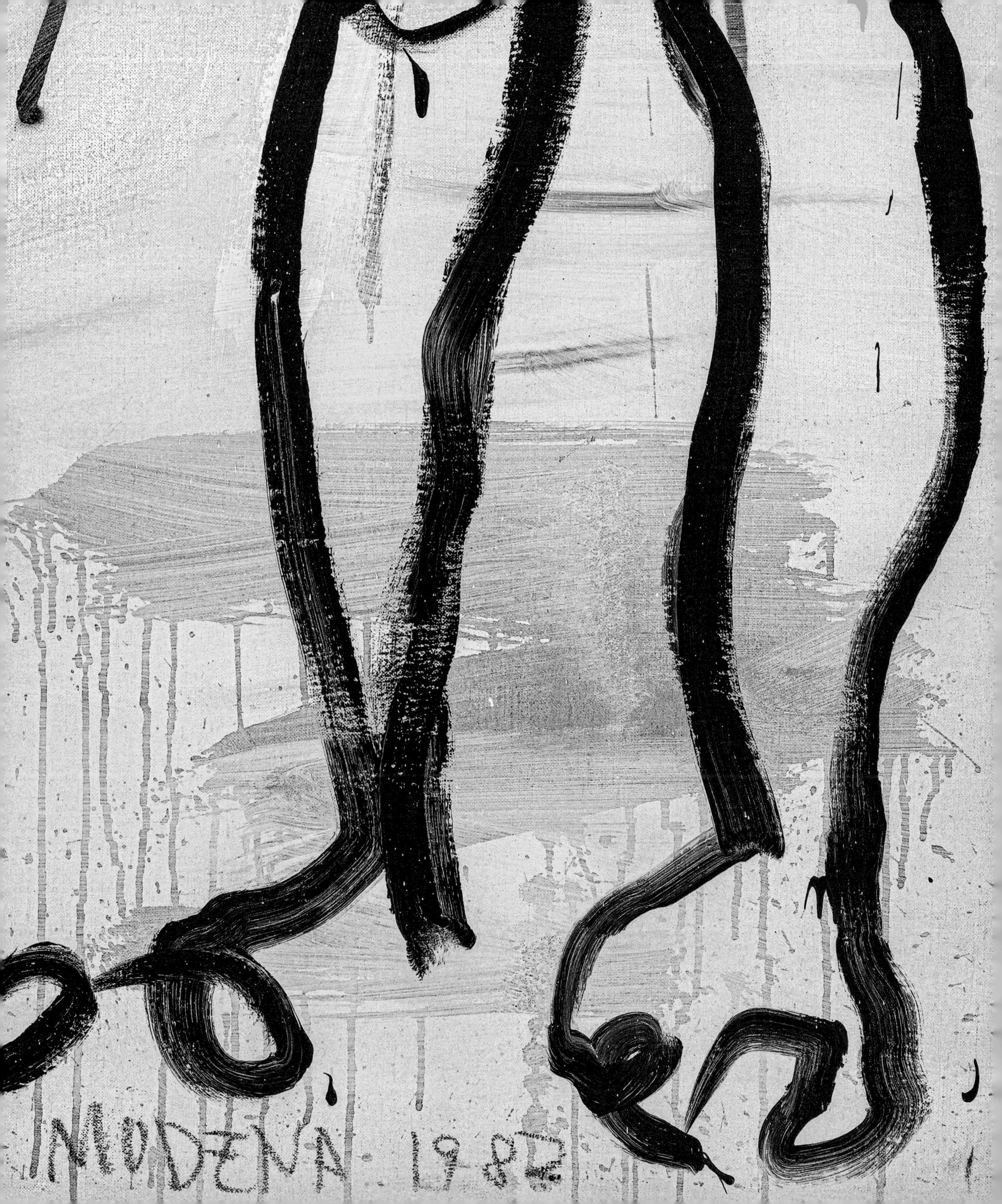
MODERN. 1988

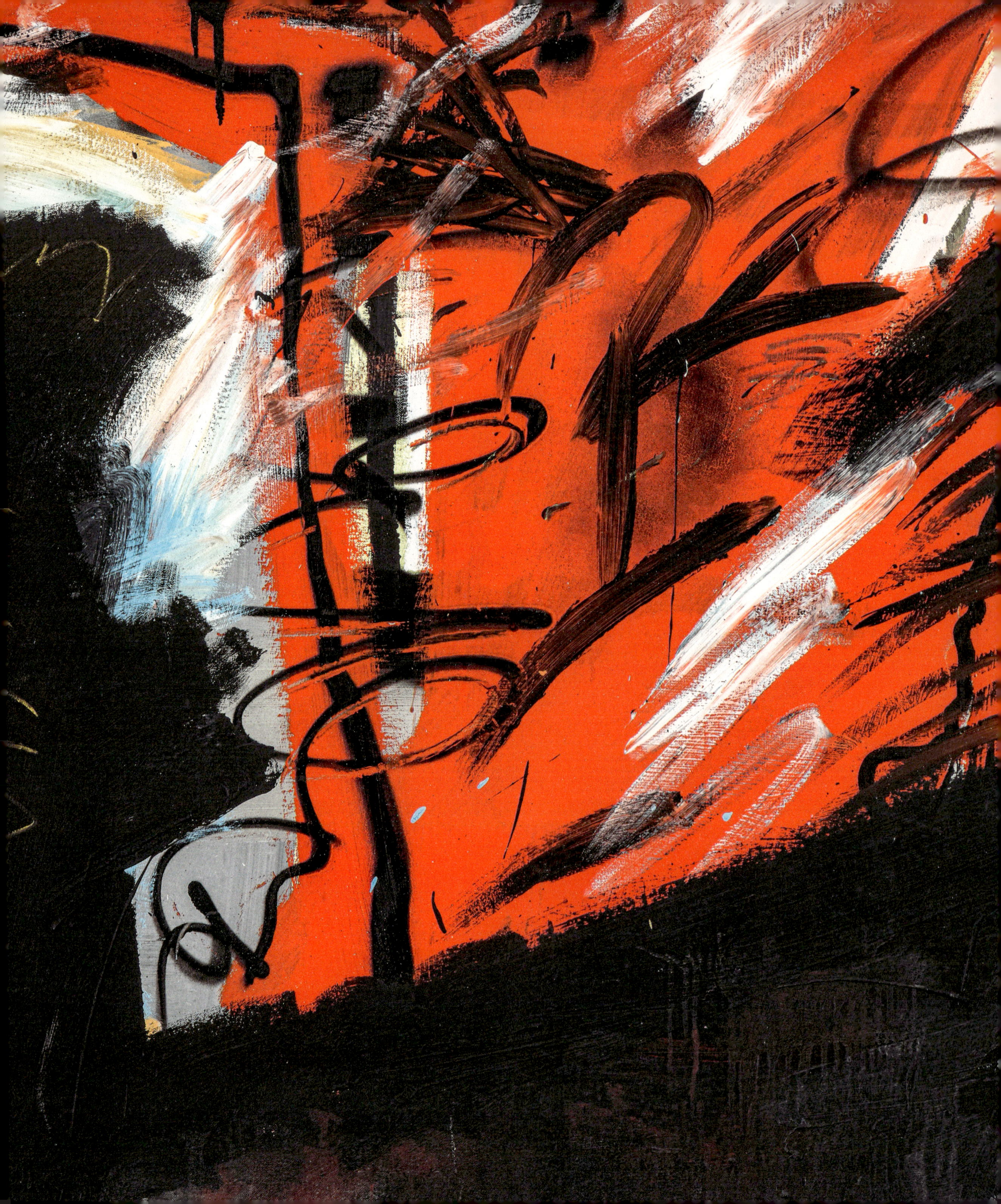

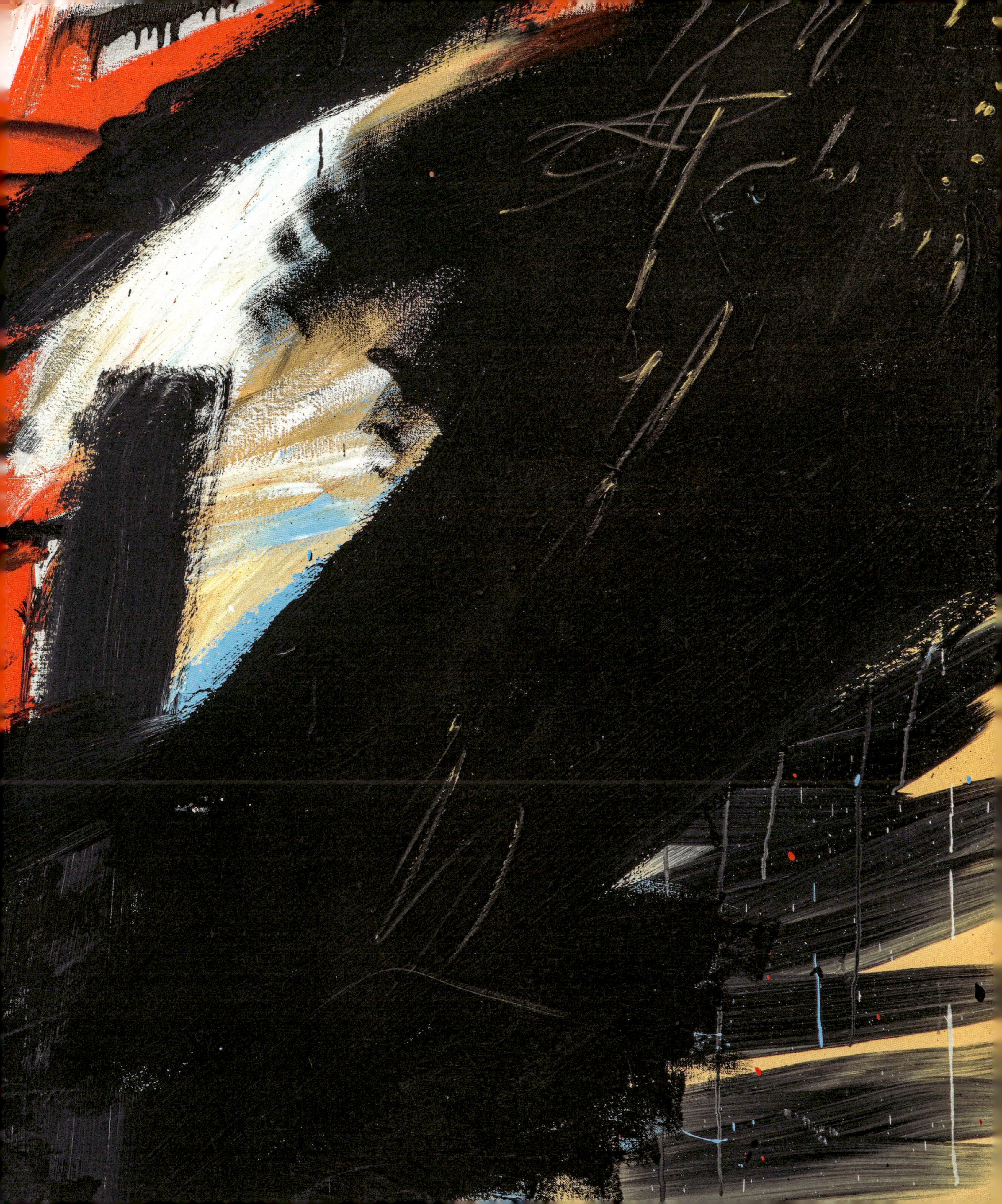

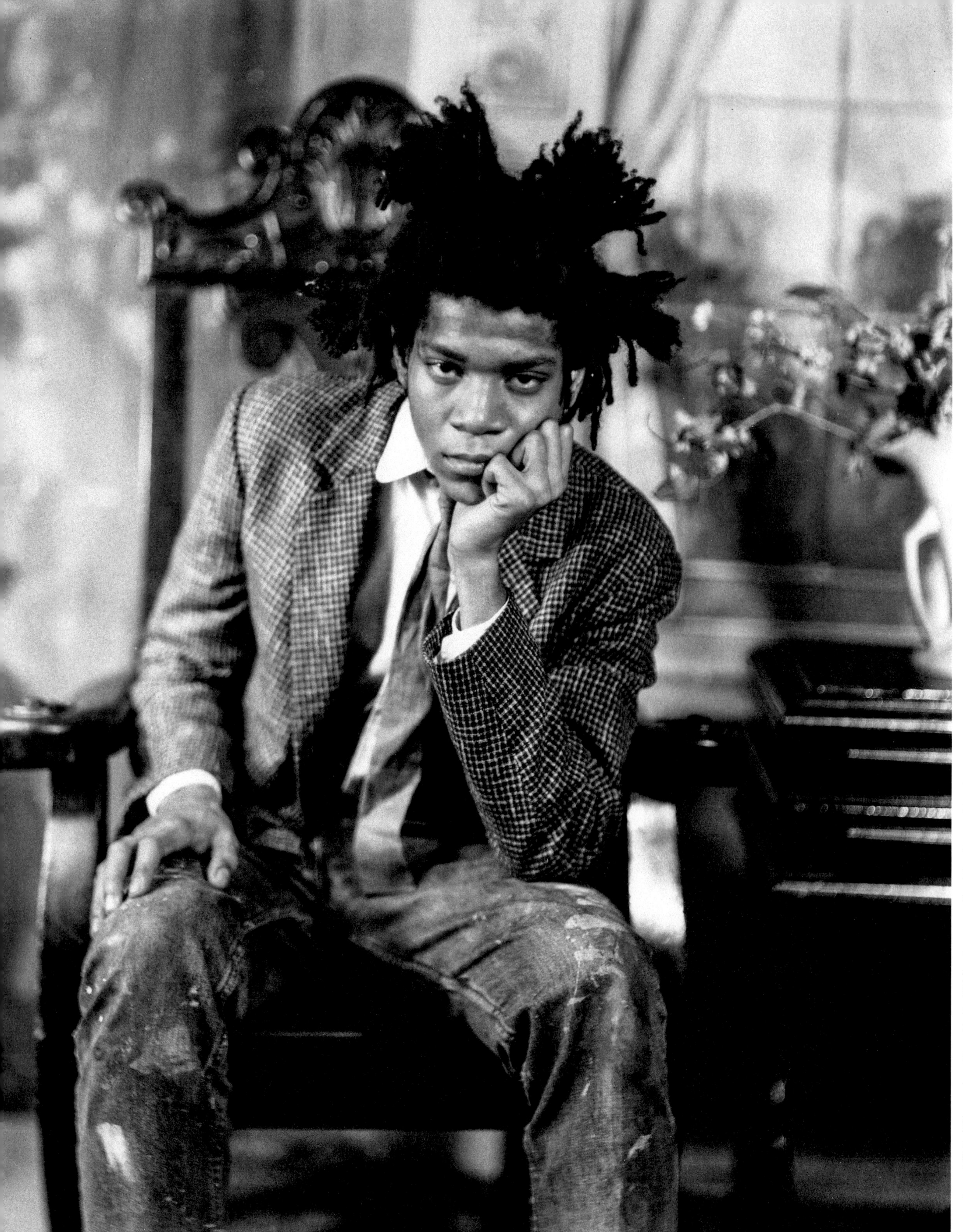

Jean-Michel Basquiat, New York, 1982, photographed by James Van Der Zee for the magazine *Interview* (January 1983 issue)

Basquiat
The Modena Paintings

Edited by Sam Keller and Iris Hasler
for the Fondation Beyeler

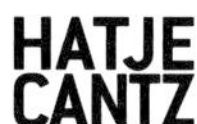

FONDATION **BEYELER**

Lenders

The Fondation Beyeler would like
to express its utmost thanks
to all of the lenders, who
contributed so significantly to
the success of the exhibition:

Aby Rosen Collection, New York
Nahmad Collection
Private collection, courtesy
    Galerie Bruno Bischofberger,
    Männedorf-Zurich, Switzerland
Private collection, Switzerland

as well as to all of the private
collectors who wish to remain
anonymous.

Partners

The exhibition and the catalogue
are generously supported by:

Beyeler-Stiftung
Hansjörg Wyss, Wyss Foundation
Thomas und Doris Ammann Stiftung

FX & Natasha de Mallmann
Annetta Grisard
L. + Th. La Roche-Stiftung

as well as further patrons who
prefer to remain anonymous.

For their continued support, the
Fondation Beyeler extends its sincere
appreciation to its partners:

Bayer
Novartis
UBS

accurART
Asuera Stiftung
AVINA Stiftung
Bank J. Safra Sarasin
BLKB
Gemeinde Riehen
GLOBUS
Kultur Basel-Stadt
La Prairie
Max Kohler Stiftung
Richard Mille
Rolls-Royce Motor Cars

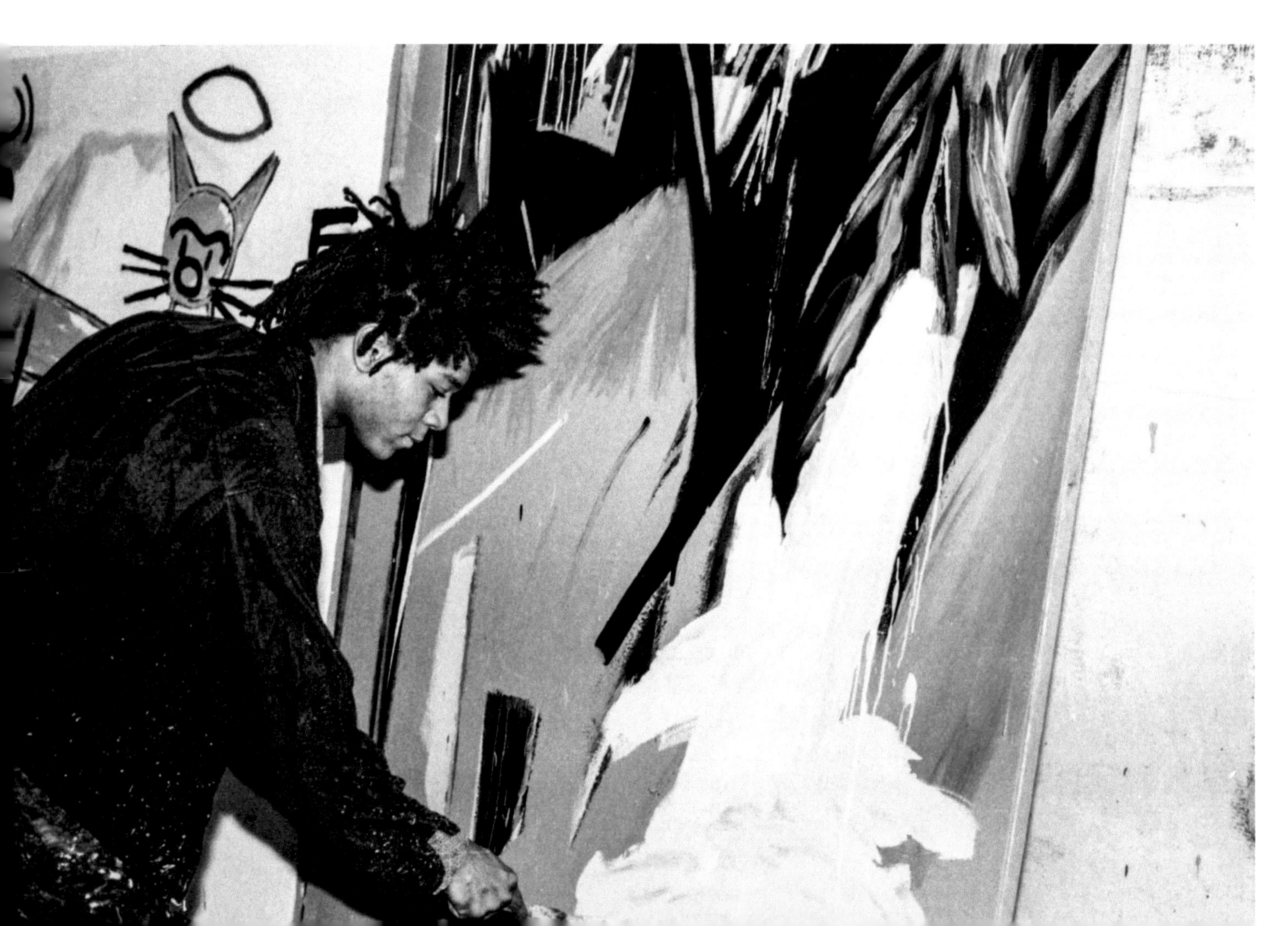

Jean-Michel Basquiat in his studio at the Annina Nosei Gallery, New York, 1982, photographed by Marion Busch

Foreword and Acknowledgments

Jean-Michel Basquiat (1960–1988) and the Fondation Beyeler are connected by a long common history. As early as 1983, soon after Basquiat's initial successes as an artist, Ernst Beyeler invited the young New York painter to contribute to a group exhibition titled *Expressive Malerei nach Picasso* at his legendary gallery in Basel. The presentation featured four paintings by Basquiat, and a reproduction of his *Philistines* (1982) adorned the cover of the catalogue. The Beyeler Collection includes one of his works, the drawing *Black Man* (1982), donated by the Collection Renard. In 2010 the Fondation Beyeler staged the largest and most significant European museum show to date of Basquiat's work. The present exhibition, *Basquiat: The Modena Paintings*, revisits his artistic oeuvre, turning this time to a particular group of pictures—hitherto not known in their entirety as such—comprising eight large-scale paintings created by Basquiat in Modena in 1982. The gallerist Emilio Mazzoli invited Basquiat, then just twenty-one years old, to stay in Modena and paint the pictures on-site for one of his first solo presentations. Although Basquiat worked in a frenzied burst of creativity, completing the paintings within just a few days, the project was cancelled before the show's opening. The eight pictures soon found their way into private collections around the world. Some of them are now among Basquiat's best-known and most valuable works. Even so, the "Modena Paintings" have never been exhibited together as a group. Here, for the first time, we have been able to assemble the entire cycle of pictures and—as envisaged by Basquiat in 1982—to present them together. This was the starting point of our own project, with the ambitious aim of realizing the original exhibition concept, over forty years after it was first outlined, and thus reappraising a significant episode in the history of contemporary art. In this connection, a number of further questions arose, such as: How did Basquiat come to be painting in Modena in the first place? Which eight works did he create there? Why exactly was the show abandoned?

A number of important interview partners and contemporary witnesses helped to answer these questions, among them Emilio Mazzoli, who is still running his gallery in Modena; Annina Nosei in New York, who as Basquiat's first dealer played a key role in furthering his career; and Bruno Bischofberger in Zurich, who represented the artist exclusively from the fall of 1982 onward and purchased

four of the Modena paintings before in turn selling them
to collectors.

As the son of a Haitian father and a mother whose
parents were from Puerto Rico, Basquiat became the first
Black artist to achieve a breakthrough in the White-dominated art world. He worked with Andy Warhol, Keith Haring,
Francesco Clemente, the singer Debbie Harry, and a range of
other artists and musicians. In the short span of less than
a decade, before his untimely death at the age of twenty-
seven, he created an extensive oeuvre, comprising over
1,000 paintings and objects as well as 3,000 works on paper.
Basquiat succeeded, moreover, in establishing a new approach
to painting. After the flourishing of Conceptual Art and
Minimalism in the 1960s and 1970s, he was a champion of the
shift to a figurative and expressive formal language in
the 1980s. In the Modena cycle, created at the start of his
brief career, the focus is on monumental figures, often
executed in black. The individual works share a number of
motifs and stylistic features, emphasizing the painterly
versus the graphic. The images, depicted on a large scale,
are less detailed and minutely drawn than in Basquiat's
later work. Teeming with skeletal silhouettes, comic-like
figures, commonplace objects, and poetic slogans, the
pictures combine motifs from contemporary pop culture,
cultural history, and everyday life, with references to
political and economic issues, delivering a critical
commentary on consumer society, injustice, and racism. Our
exhibition of the Modena paintings aims at complementing the
many retrospectives of Basquiat's oeuvre with a presentation
devoted to a central aspect of his early work and thereby
to promote a deeper understanding of his artistic legacy.

The cooperation of many supporters was essential to the
realization of this ambitious project. Our sincere and
express thanks are due to the Estate of Jean-Michel
Basquiat, in particular to Nora Fitzpatrick and the
artist's sisters, Lisane Basquiat and Jeanine Heriveaux,
and to David Stark, for their sympathetic interest in our
exhibition from the outset, as well as to the lenders, who
kindly agreed to entrust us with the precious works from
their collections. We are especially grateful to the art
dealers Bruno Bischofberger, Emilio Mazzoli, Annina Nosei,
Alberto Mugrabi, and Joe Nahmad, for their outstanding
services to Basquiat and his oeuvre and their crucial
support in mounting our show.

For assistance in financing the exhibition, the
Fondation Beyeler is indebted to the Beyeler-Stiftung, the
Wyss Foundation, and the Thomas und Doris Ammann Stiftung,

with the support of the Canton of Basel-Stadt and the
Municipality of Riehen. Our thanks are also due to
FX & Natasha de Mallmann and the L. + Th. La Roche-Stiftung,
and to a number of further sponsors who prefer to remain
anonymous. The exhibition catalogue was kindly subsidized
by Annetta Grisard.

We would like to thank the authors Dieter Buchhart,
Fiona Hesse, Michiko Kono, Regula Moser, Demetrio Paparoni,
and Jordana Moore Saggese for their enlightening catalogue
contributions, reconstructing the details of Basquiat's
stay in Italy and carefully examining each of the works
created in Modena in 1982. Christoph Steinegger devised
the visually impressive graphic concept for the catalogue,
published with the unfailing cooperation of Nicola von
Velsen and Richard Viktor Hagemann at Hatje Cantz Verlag
and production manager Christine Stäcker. The editorial
management of the catalogue was supervised with meticulous
care by Franziska Stegmann and Romina Del Principe.
Particular thanks are due to all of the above, and to the
copyeditor Joann Skrypzak-Davidsmeyer and the translators
John Ormrod and Caroline Higgitt.

The organization of the exhibition required the close
cooperation of many members of the Fondation Beyeler staff.
We are grateful to our colleagues in Exhibition Services
and Art Handling, Conservation, Education, Communication,
Sponsoring & Fundraising, the Director's Office, Guest &
VIP Relations, Events, the Art Shop, Technical Services
and IT, Accounting and Legal Services, and the Library, as
well as to our Managing Director Ulrike Erbslöh for their
passionate and professional commitment. Thanks are due
also to our external partners. We would like, finally, to
express our gratitude to several other individuals who have
contributed to the success of the presentation, especially
Paola Aeschlimann-Rebstein, Flore Auberjonois, Romain Brun,
Rupert Burgess, Sara Citarella, Jeffrey Deitch, Jean-Paul
Engelen, Kai Eric, Emily Evrard, Martin Furler Bassand,
Giulia Guaitoli, Fred Hoffman, Meiling Lee, Esty Neuman,
Scott Nussbaum, David Oakey, Petra Pearman, Silvia
Sokalski, Christian Stauffenegger, Céline Stössel, Giulia
Trabaldo Togna, Ryan VanGrack, Jami Vandine, Cecilia
Weaver, and Shauna Young.

We greatly hope that our visitors and readers will
find pleasure and enrichment in their encounter with an
art whose expressive power has stood the test of time and
remains as fascinating now as at the moment of its creation,
over forty years ago.

Sam Keller and Iris Hasler

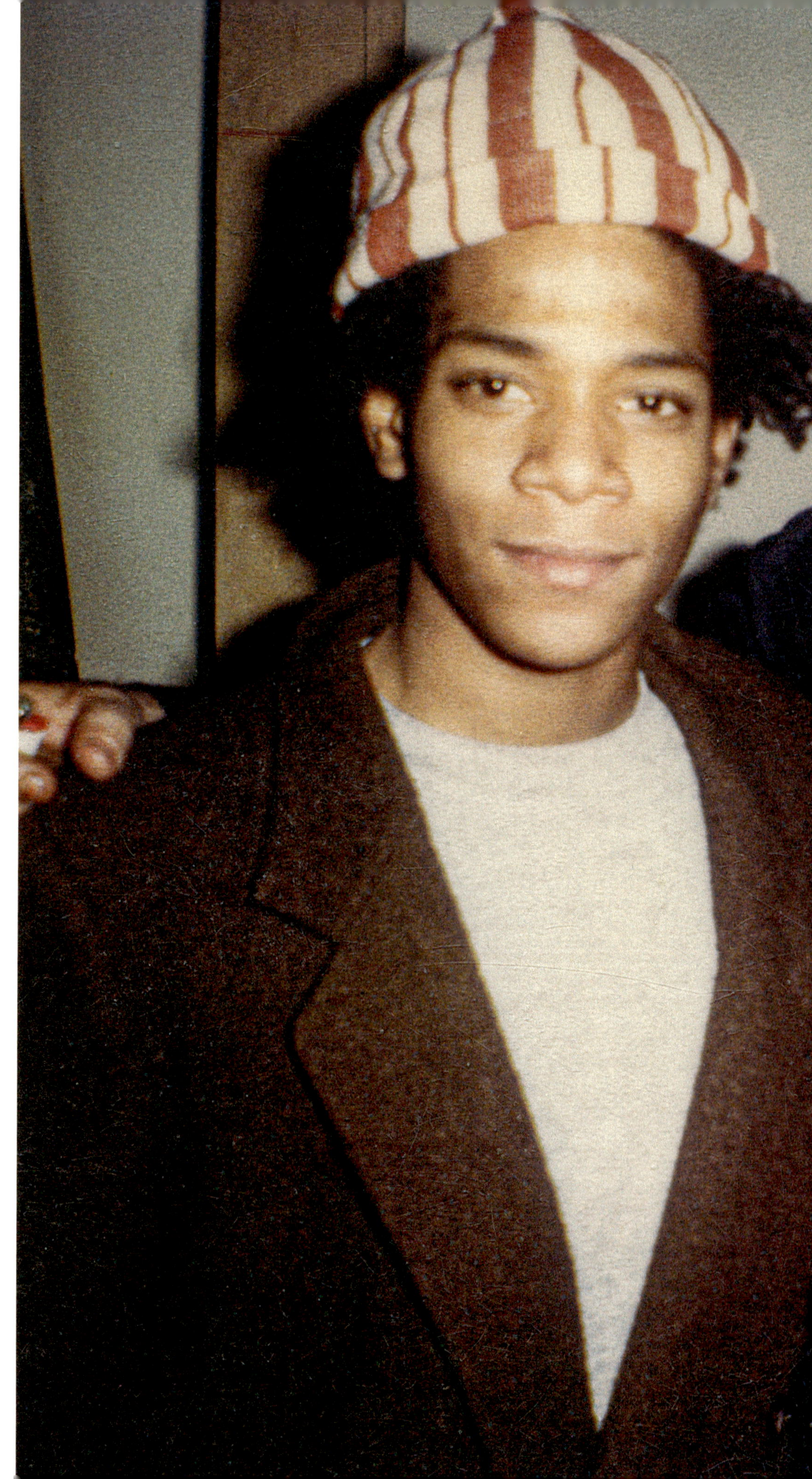

Jean-Michel Basquiat and Emilio Mazzoli, 1981, photographer unknown

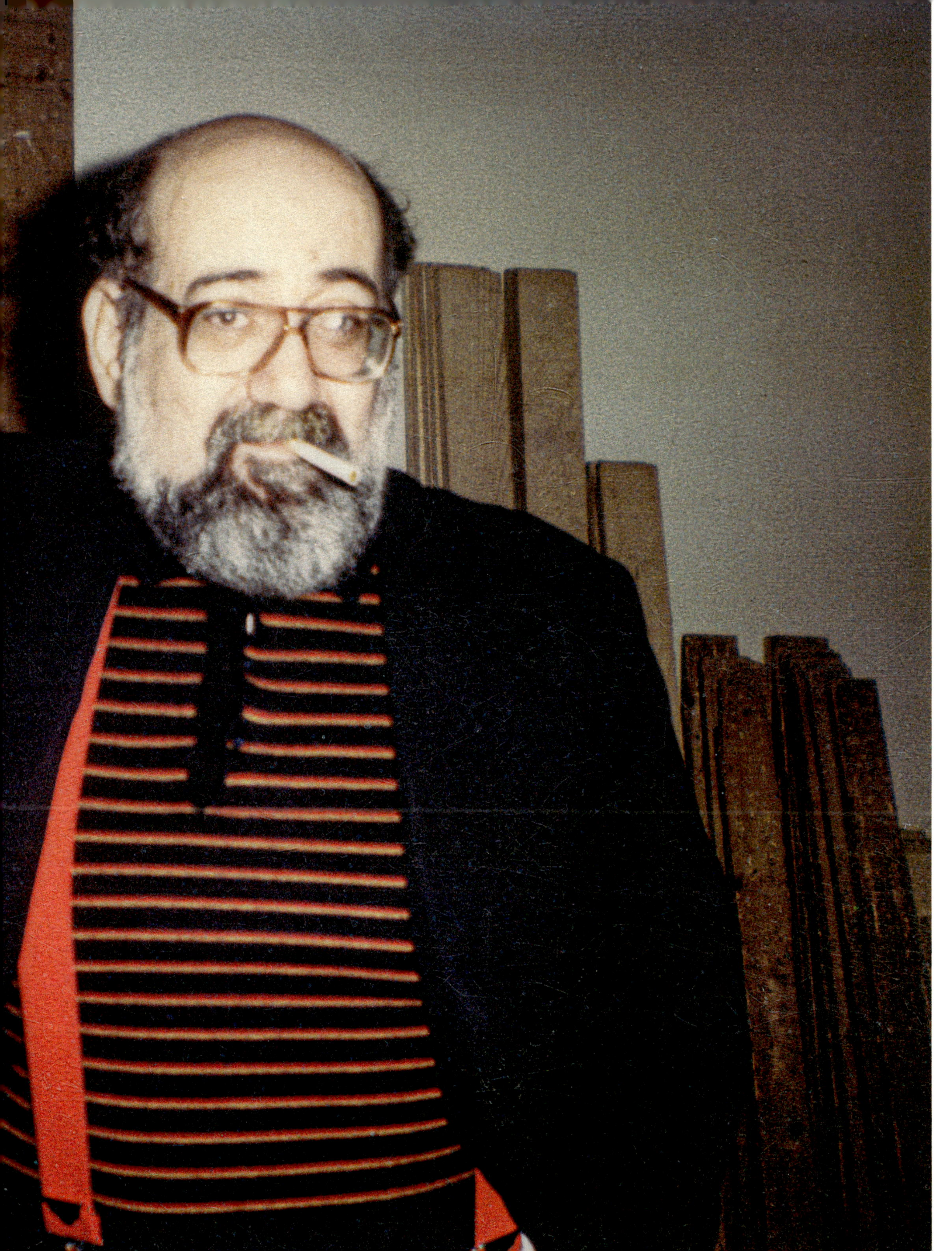

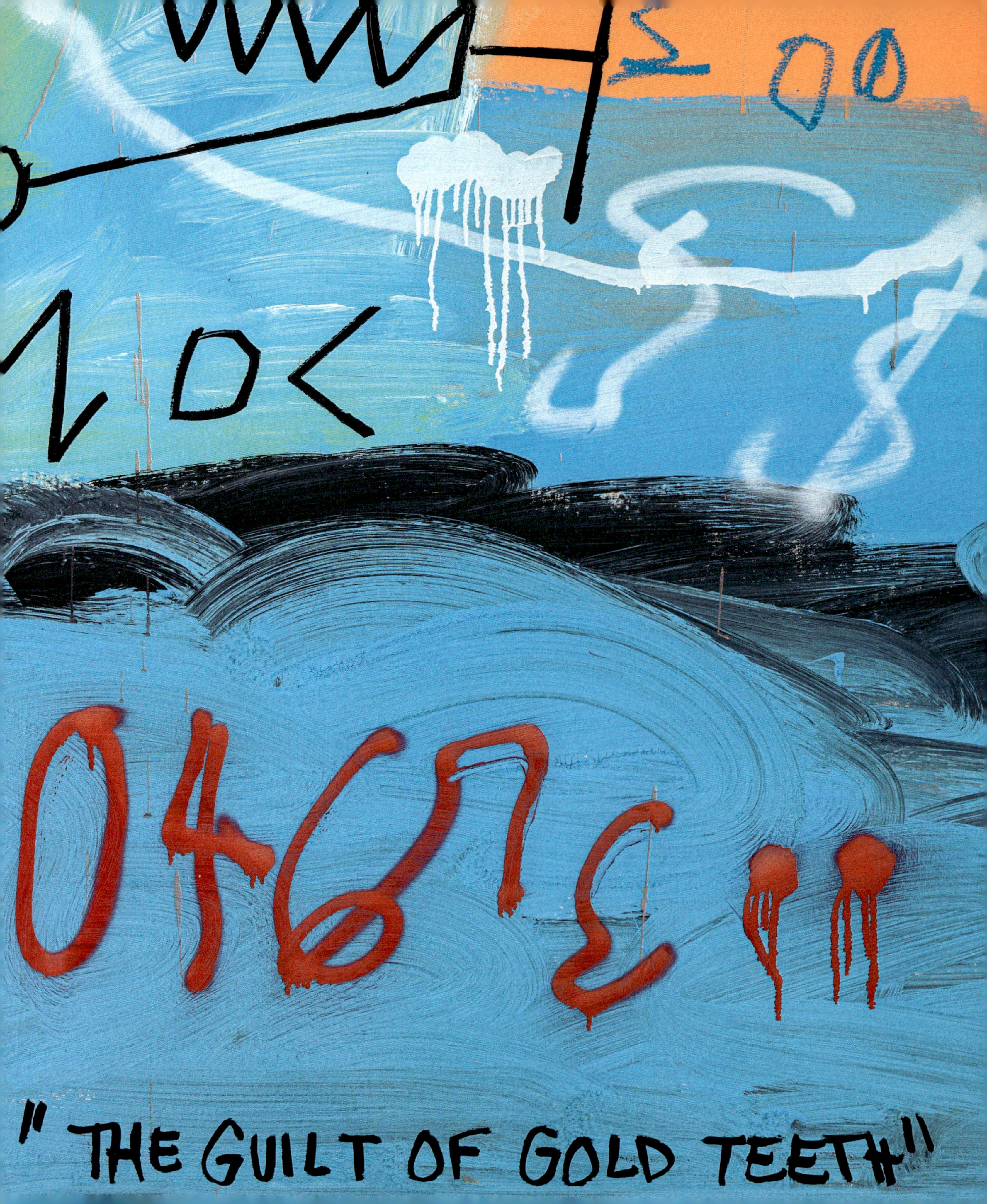
" THE GUILT OF GOLD TEETH "

Jean-Michel Basquiat in Modena

Iris Hasler

"Modena / Jean Michel Basquiat 1982" and "Jean Michel Basquiat Modena 1982": the signatures on the two canvases, instantly catching the eye, have a particular significance. They are inscribed in bold black capitals in the lower right-hand corner on the front of *The Guilt of Gold Teeth* and *Untitled (Woman with Roman Torso [Venus])* and set in fields of light color and thus included in the composition rather than being relegated to the back side of the canvas. In addition to his name and the year of execution, the artist identifies the place where the painting was made. It would thus seem that Modena, in the Italian province of Emilia-Romagna, held a particular significance for Jean-Michel Basquiat, the New York artist with his boundary-defying conception of art, his Haitian and Puerto Rican roots, his challenging personality, and his capacity for—even today—upsetting the White-dominated art world.

At the invitation of the art dealer Emilio Mazzoli, Basquiat spent several weeks in Modena in the summers of 1981 and 1982. At the time, the gallery's program was focused on Conceptual Art, Arte Povera, and the Transavanguardia movement. Mazzoli worked with artists such as Sandro Chia, Francesco Clemente, and Mimmo Paladino, who were based in Italy and New York.[1] It was the painter Chia who directed Mazzoli's attention to the young Basquiat when he made his first institutional appearance at the beginning of 1981 in the group exhibition *New York/New Wave*,[2] at P.S. 1 Contemporary Art Center in the Long Island City neighborhood of Queens. This venue, now known as MoMA PS1, was a showcase for the downtown Manhattan art and music scene in which Basquiat had become a prominent figure through his much-talked-about "SAMO" activities. Using this pseudonym, an abbreviation of "same old shit," Basquiat and his school friend Al Diaz roamed the gallery district in Lower Manhattan from 1977 to the early months of 1979, writing short and often witty poetic statements, at first in Magic Marker and then in spray paint, on the sides of buildings and in subways, and signing the result with the tag "SAMO©" **(see fig. p. 96)**.[3] Basquiat also wrote and drew prolifically in notebooks and on paper as well as painting on canvases, cabinets, and doors, using whatever material he had at hand. Oil stick, spray paint, and acrylic became his preferred media. For *New York/New Wave* he made twenty-three paintings and drawings, which—arranged on a single wall in a manner recalling a salon style hanging—were featured as one of the show's few examples of painting **(fig. 1)**. Mazzoli was not alone in his enthusiasm for the works. The Zurich art dealer Bruno Bischofberger and Annina Nosei, his New York colleague with Roman roots, also attended the opening, at Chia's recommendation. All three gallerists bought works from Diego Cortez, the exhibition's curator and an early supporter of Basquiat's art.[4]

C oncerning the role played by sponsors and intermediaries, Nosei explains: "When Sandro Chia saw the work of Jean-Michel Basquiat, its vivacious quality somehow summed up for him the American scene today. Sandro thought that if I gave a chance to so [*sic*] young an artist—which meant money—he might make more paintings and develop quite soon. I made the commitment, and the results were astonishing. Soon I was not alone in seeing Basquiat as one of the few Americans capable of handling urban subject matter, quoting without restraint, as de Kooning himself did."[5] Before he began working together with Nosei, however, Basquiat traveled to Modena in May 1981 for his first-ever solo exhibition. Cortez accompanied him, bringing with him the pictures Mazzoli had purchased

Fig. 1
Installation view of Jean-Michel Basquiat's works (left wall) in the exhibition *New York/New Wave*, P.S. 1, Long Island City, New York, 1981

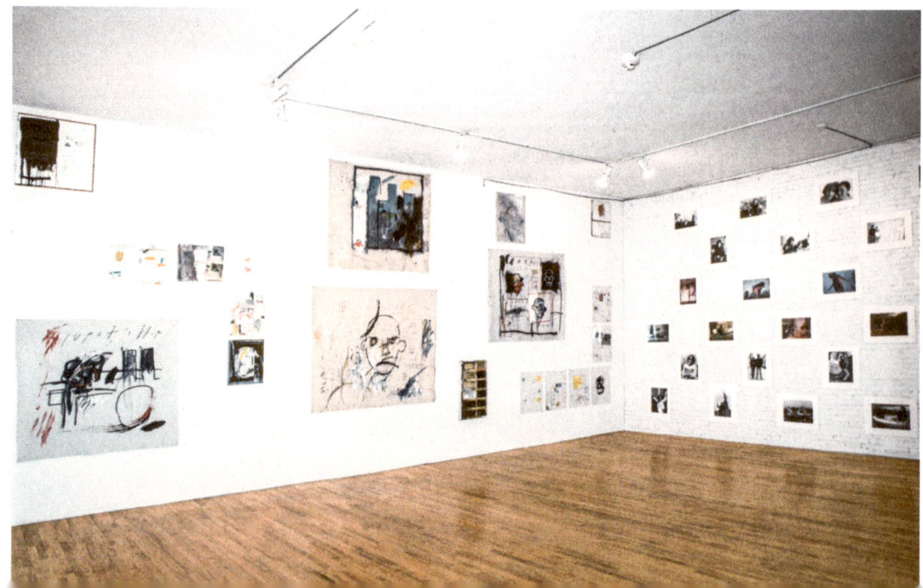

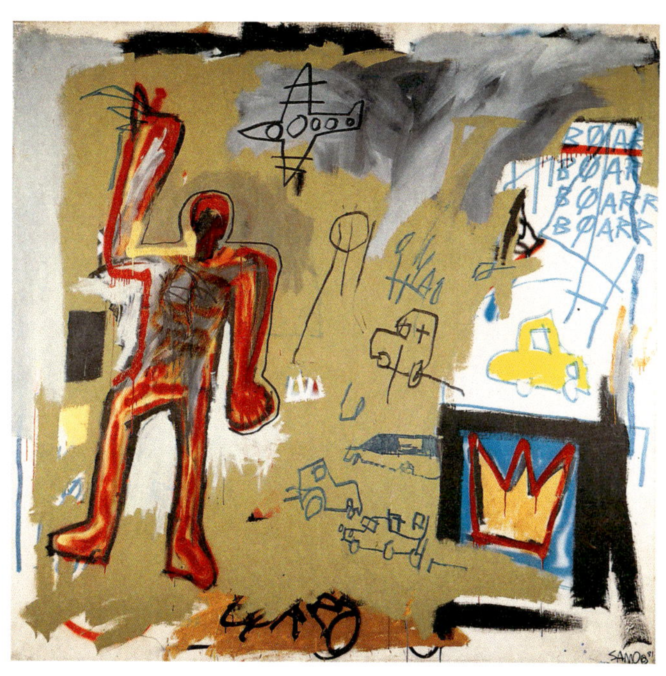

from the show in New York.[6] To fill the gallery space
of some one hundred square meters, Basquiat worked
on-site to paint a number of additional pictures measuring around 200 by 200 centimeters. *Untitled (Red Man)*
and *Untitled* **(fig. 2 and fig. p. 99)** feature motifs, such as auto-
mobiles, planes, and "skelly courts" from a children's
street game, that are omnipresent in Basquiat's early
work[7] but no longer found in the canvases he painted a
year later in Modena. The fact that the exhibition was
titled with the artist's name "SAMO," which Basquiat had
abandoned in 1979, was probably more in the interest of
the gallerist than the artist. The works on display were
also signed "SAMO 1981."[8] In the end, the show was a
disappointment: hardly anyone attended the opening,
and the paintings were eventually bought by Mazzoli's
friends and acquaintances as a personal favor to the
dealer.[9] Basquiat looked back with mixed feelings at his
stay in Modena, remarking: "It was fun because it was
the first time, but financially it was pretty stupid."[10]
Mazzoli paid him for the works; but later, when Basquiat
was more familiar with the art business, he may have
perceived the amount—reported to be 30,000 dollars—in
less euphoric terms than he initially had.[11] There was no
contract between the artist and the gallery or a formal
agreement regarding a fixed percentage of proceeds, but
that was a common practice at the time. For Basquiat,
the more significant outcome of this first solo exhibition was certainly his transition from making art in
public and private spaces to presenting it in galleries.

Fig. 2
*Untitled
(Red Man)*, 1981,
acrylic, oil
stick, and
spray paint
on canvas,
204.5 × 211 cm,
private
collection

Shortly thereafter, Basquiat's exhibition activity started to flourish. In late 1981 he participated in Nosei's group show *Public Address*, and she subsequently became his first dealer. Since Basquiat lacked a studio of his own, she made a workspace available in the basement of her gallery.[12] In April 1982 she organized his first solo exhibition there and then arranged for him to have a further show, at the gallery of Larry Gagosian in Los Angeles.[13] At the same time, the Italian curator Achille Bonito Oliva decided to include two paintings by Basquiat in his exhibition *Transavanguardia: Italia/America* at the Galleria Civica del Comune in Modena.[14]

In June, Basquiat returned to Modena, where plans for a second exhibition at Mazzoli's gallery were in hand, again with works to be painted on-site. This suggests that the experience of Basquiat's first show in Modena in 1981 was not so negative as to preclude a repetition: neither the artist nor the dealer dismissed the idea. Even so, Basquiat later spoke of his misgivings about the project. In a conversation with a journalist in 1985, he described the situation, saying: "They set it up for me so I'd have to make eight paintings in a week, for the show the next week. That was one of the things I didn't like. I made them in this big warehouse there. Annina, Mazzoli, and Bruno were there. It was like a factory, a sick factory. I hated it. I wanted to be a star, not a gallery mascot."[15]

In the Villaggio Artigiano—an industrial estate outside Modena—Mazzoli had rented a warehouse for the gallery's artists to use while on working visits to the town. The Rome-based artist Mario Schifano, for instance, repeatedly stayed in Modena, over a period of several years, to paint new pictures. Mazzoli prized this sort of direct exchange in front of the work in progress, unhampered by everyday concerns. Schifano was

"It was fun because it was the first time, but financially it was pretty stupid."

not in Modena when Basquiat arrived, but his work was in evidence at the studio in the form of both completed pictures and canvases that had been prepared but remained blank. Basquiat seems to have been impressed by, or at least interested in, the exceptional size of the blank canvases, which he used for his own work.[16] The cycle of works he created in Modena comprised eight paintings measuring at least 200 by 400 centimeters, a size far larger than that of the vast majority of his previous pictures.[17] The place name "Modena" in the signature on the back of each work makes it clear that the picture belongs to the group. In addition to these shared features, the works are linked by similarities in terms of their motifs and style. In the manner of a stage scene, all eight works are dominated by a monumental figure, often rendered in black and set against a background overlaid with broad, gestural brushstrokes. *Untitled (Angel)* **(cat. pp. 38–39)** and *Untitled (Devil)* **(cat. pp. 30–31)** have the effect of a diptych, presenting the titular figures of angel and devil as half-length portraits with arms raised. It is a pose that can be interpreted as at once imploring and triumphant; it not only recurs in other works from the Modena group but is also frequently found in Basquiat's oeuvre as a whole.[18] The rendering of the devil's skeleton with rough horizontal lines, and that of the skulls, with their deep eye-sockets and nose cavities, also characterize the figures in *Boy and Dog in a Johnnypump* **(cat. pp. 48–49)** and *The Field Next to the Other Road*[19] **(cat. pp. 72–73)**. The headdress on the skull, suggesting both a halo and a crown of thorns, is a further Basquiat trademark, appearing, for example, in *Untitled (Woman with Roman Torso [Venus])* **(cat. pp. 62–63)** and *Profit I* **(cat. pp. 54–55)**. The latter works, like *The Guilt of Gold Teeth* **(cat. pp. 66–67)**, show a greater density of scribbling, in Basquiat's typical style, than the other paintings in the group. *The Guilt of Gold Teeth* in particular, with its plethora of cryptic words, combinations of numbers, and dollar signs, anticipates later

works such as *Hollywood Africans*, from 1983 **(fig. 3)**. With
Untitled (Cowparts) **(cat. p. 42–43)**, showing an over-life-size
cow with a semi-paralyzed appearance and strikingly
round eyes, the circle is completed: the thick white
brushstrokes that accentuate the solid-black body in
Untitled (Angel) here outline the basic features of the
animal, caught in flagrante, as it were, in one of its
main occupations.

With the exception of *Profit I* and *The Guilt of
Gold Teeth*, in which the combination of acrylic, spray
paint, and oil stick establishes a dialogue with graphic
elements, the works in the group are characterized by
a painterly emphasis. The collaging of different images
and words, which otherwise typifies Basquiat's work,
is almost absent from the Modena pictures. The artist's
repertoire in Modena is generally less focused on
detail; the scale of the images is larger. Human and
animal bodies feature most prominently. Unlike the
earlier works, the Modena paintings are devoid of
car accidents, skylines, and night skies—impressions
that Basquiat took from the street and the immediate
surroundings of the city and transposed directly to
his pictures.[20]

In several of the eight paintings we find similar
colors, such as in the flat backgrounds or the vivid
red brushstrokes used to emphasize the figures. This
reflects Basquiat's method of working on two or more
canvases at once, since each layer of color had to dry
before he could apply the next.

Disagreements Result in Cancellation

After Basquiat had completed the eight paintings, the
exhibition project was nevertheless not pursued further.
This was due to an unfortunate clash of expectations.
Whereas Nosei, as Basquiat's dealer, wanted to receive
a percentage of the sales revenue, Mazzoli saw himself
as the artist's chief sponsor from the outset and conse-
quently sought to claim the credit not only for organ-

izing and financing the exhibition but also for Basquiat's ongoing development as an artist.[21] For his part, the painter was unhappy with the plans his dealers had set up for the production of new works, which made him feel like a mere puppet of the art market, or, as he put it, a "gallery mascot."

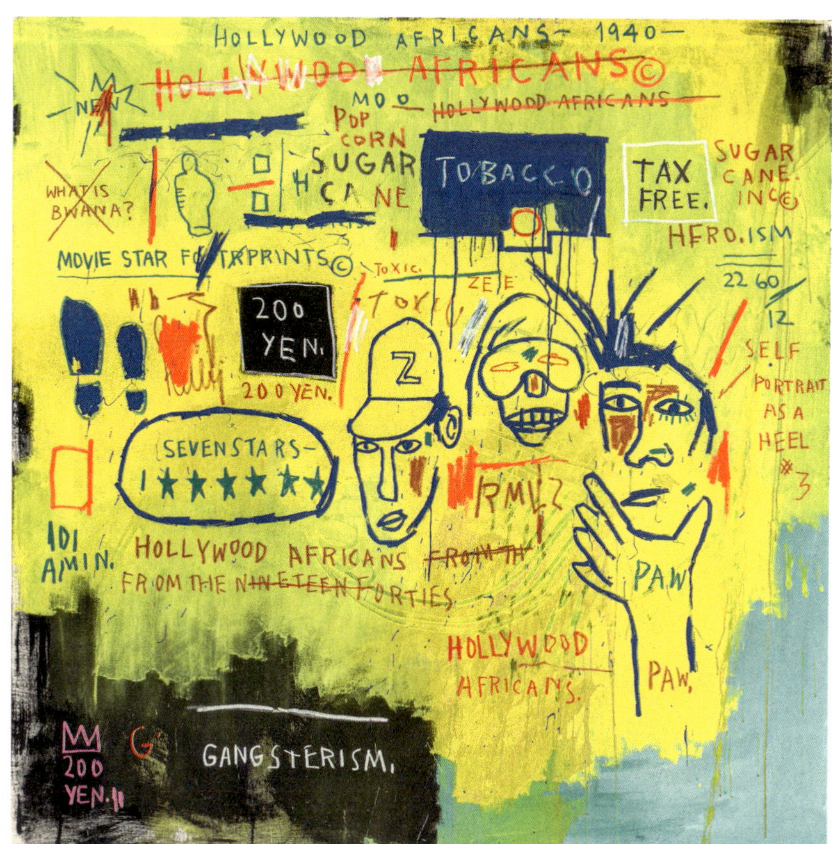

Hollywood Africans, 1983, acrylic and oil stick on canvas, 213.5 × 213.5 cm, Whitney Museum of American Art, New York

Contrary to Basquiat's recollection, Bruno Bischofberger was not involved in the exhibition plans or even present in Modena, as the Zurich gallery owner and Mazzoli have both reported.[22] Before Basquiat left, somewhat hastily, to return to New York, Mazzoli paid him for the eight paintings, which were never shown together in Modena.[23] With Annina Nosei acting as intermediary, Bischofberger bought four of the works: *Profit I, Boy and Dog in a Johnnypump, Untitled (Woman with Roman Torso [Venus])*, and *The Guilt of Gold Teeth*.[24] The other paintings found their way into various collections: *Untitled (Devil)*, for instance, went to Japan[25] and *The Field Next to the Other Road* was acquired by the dealer Mario Diacono,[26] who soon presented the work, in September 1982, as the sole exhibit in a show at his gallery in Rome.[27] The same month saw the opening of Basquiat's first of in total four solo exhibitions at the Galerie Bruno Bischofberger in Zurich that were mounted prior to the artist's death, in 1988. Of the works created in Modena in 1982, only *Profit I* was shown there.

The place name "Modena" is an integral part of the signature on all of these works. It is conceivable that it was the gallerist who came up with the idea to sign them this way. If not, what other reasons might there be that explain why the time Basquiat spent in Modena could

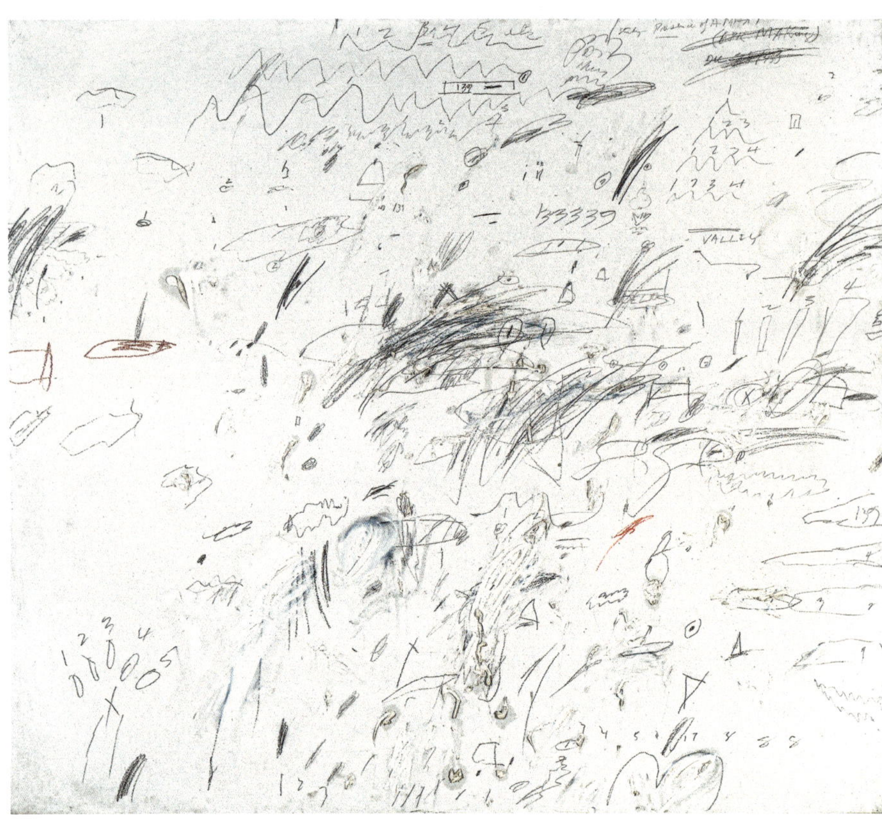

Cy Twombly,
*Study for
Presence of
a Myth*, 1959,
pencil, oil,
and colored
chalk on
canvas,
178 × 200 cm,
Kunstmuseum
Basel

have been so important to the artist? Mazzoli had invited him there in 1981 for his first-ever solo presentation, giving him an early and very welcome opportunity to show his work and opening the way to financial success. This was also Basquiat's first chance to travel to Europe, specifically to Italy, the adopted country of Cy Twombly, whose scraped and scratched canvases with elements of writing had a lasting influence on Basquiat's work **(fig. 4)**. Mazzoli's offer was tantamount to a public expression of recognition of his artistic activities in the context of a prestigious gallery, which the Galleria d'Arte Emilio Mazzoli certainly was at the time. Basquiat's deep desire for international art world fame—"I wanted to be a star," he said—may indeed have been satisfied by the invitations to Modena. Although the outcome of the journey in 1982 frustrated the high expectations of all those involved, the cancellation of the exhibition that year did nothing to impede Basquiat's rapidly growing success.

1) See the archive of the Galleria d'Arte Emilio Mazzoli, www.galleriamazzoli.com/en/exhib_mod.html (accessed February 16, 2023).

2) See Phoebe Hoban, *Basquiat: A Quick Killing in Art* (London, 1998), p. 75.

3) See M. Franklin Sirmans, "Chronology," in *Jean-Michel Basquiat*, ed. Richard Marshall, exh. cat. Whitney Museum of American Art, New York; The Menil Collection, Houston; Des Moines Art Center; Montgomery Museum of Fine Arts (New York, 1992), pp. 233-50, esp. pp. 234-36.

4) Cf. Hoban 1998 (see note 2), p. 73; Eric Fretz, *Jean-Michel Basquiat: A Biography* (Santa Barbara et al., 2010), p. 74.

5) Annina Nosei, in *The Art Dealers: The Powers Behind the Scene Tell How the Art World Really Works*, ed. Laura de Coppet and Alan Jones (New York, 1984), pp. 282-89, here p. 288.

6) Cf. Hoban 1998 (see note 2), p. 77; Fretz 2010 (see note 4), pp. 74-75.

7) See the catalogue of works in *Jean-Michel Basquiat*, ed. Galerie Enrico Navarra, 2 vols. (Paris, 2000), vol. 2, pp. 69-269, esp. pp. 70-94.

8) Cf. Fretz 2010 (see note 4), pp. 75-76.

9) Emilio Mazzoli, in conversation with the author, Modena, November 21, 2022.

10) Jean-Michel Basquiat, "Art: From Subways to Soho: Jean-Michel Basquiat," interview by Henry Geldzahler, *Interview* 13, no. 1 (January 1983), pp. 44-46, here p. 46; reprinted in Jordana Moore Saggese, ed., *The Jean-Michel Basquiat Reader: Writings, Interviews, and Critical Responses* (Oakland, 2021), pp. 32-38, here p. 35.

11) Cf. Hoban 1998 (see note 2), pp. 77-78.

12) Cf. Sirmans 1992 (see note 3), p. 239.

13) Cf. Fretz 2010 (see note 4), p. 93.

14) See the essay by Demetrio Paparoni in this catalogue, pp. 81-92.

15) Jean-Michel Basquiat, in conversation with Cathleen McGuigan, in "New Art, New Money: The Marketing of an American Artist," *The New York Times Magazine* (February 10, 1985), pp. 20-28, 32-35, 74, here p. 34; reprinted in Saggese 2021 (see note 10), pp. 119-27, here p. 123.

16) Emilio Mazzoli, in conversation with the author, Modena, November 21, 2022.

17) Most of Basquiat's canvases up to the beginning of 1982 were smaller than this, measuring at most 200 by 200 centimeters, with the exception of *Jimmy Best...*, (1981, 244 × 244 cm), *Per Capita* (1981, 203 × 381 cm), *Untitled* (1981 in Modena, 200.5 × 282 cm), *Untitled (Red Man)* (1981 in Modena, 204.5 × 211 cm), *Untitled* (1981 in Modena, 203 × 203 cm), and *Untitled* (1981, 218.5 × 264 cm).

18) See, for example, the works *The Ring* (1981), *Untitled (The Black Athlete)* (1982), *Asbestos* (1981-82), *Untitled (Saint)* (1982), *Red Savoy* (1983), and *Black Man* (1984).

19) The year written on the reverse of *The Field Next to the Other Road* remains uncertain. In the catalogue of works, the painting is dated 1981, but there is no mention of a signature. See Galerie Enrico Navarra 2000 (see note 7), pp. 90-91, no. 2. However, its dimensions (221 × 401.5 cm) and technique indicate that it belongs to the 1982 group of works. Emilio Mazzoli, in conversation with the author, Modena, November 21, 2022, also dated the picture to 1982, since the works from the previous year were all in smaller sizes. Moreover, the paintings made in Modena in 1981 had been signed "SAMO."

20) Cf. Richard Marshall, "Repelling Ghosts," in exh. cat. New York et al. 1992 (see note 3), pp. 15-27, here p. 16.

21) Emilio Mazzoli, in conversation with the author, Modena, November 21, 2022.

22) Bruno Bischofberger, in conversation with the author, Männedorf-Zurich, August 29, 2022; Emilio Mazzoli, in conversation with the author, Modena, November 21, 2022.

23) Cf. Fretz 2010 (see note 4), p. 94.

24) Bruno Bischofberger, in conversation with the author, Männedorf-Zurich, August 29, 2022.

25) See "Provenance" in the auction catalogue *20th Century & Contemporary Art Evening Sale: New York Auction*, Phillips, New York, May 18, 2022, Lot 12: Jean-Michel Basquiat, *Untitled*, www.phillips.com/detail/jean-michel-basquiat/NY010322/12 (accessed January 24, 2023).

26) See Charles Giuliano, "The Remarkable Mario Diacono," April 26, 2020, www.berkshirefinearts.com/04-26-2020_the-remarkable-mario-diacono.htm (accessed November 24, 2022).

27) Mario Diacono, *Jean-Michel Basquiat: Il campo vicino l'altra strada*, exh. broch. Galleria Mario Diacono (Rome, 1982).

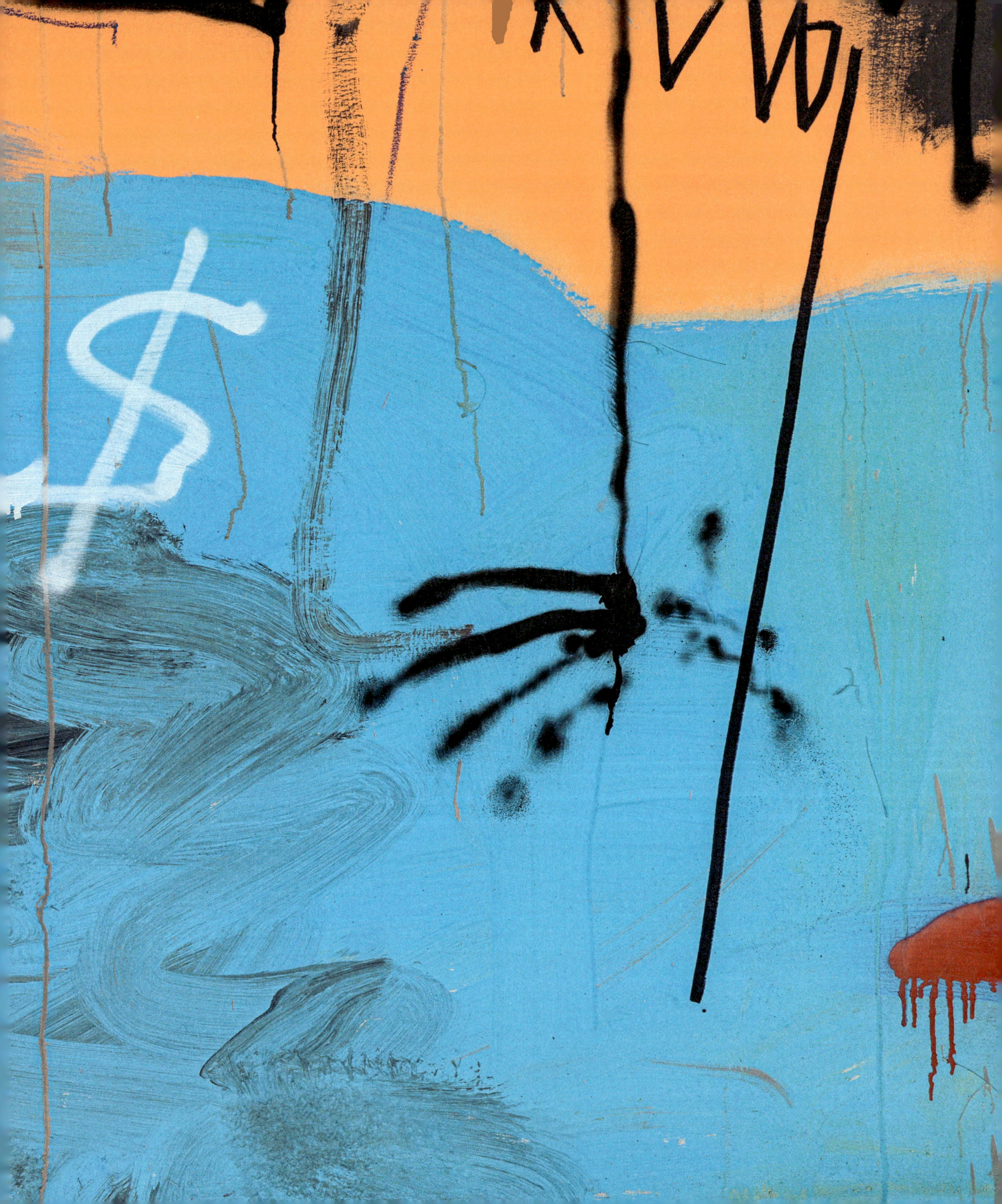

The Modena Paintings

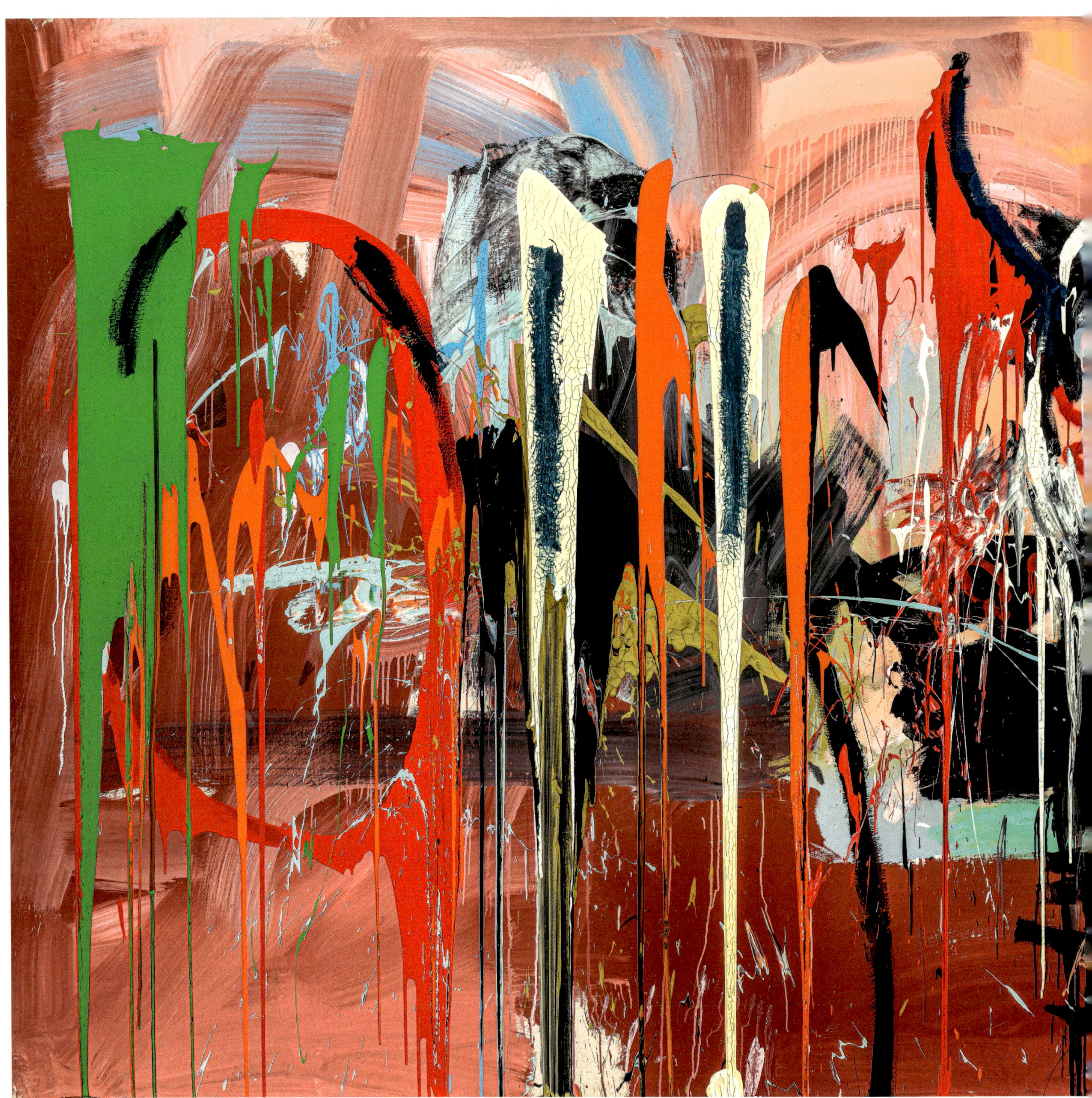

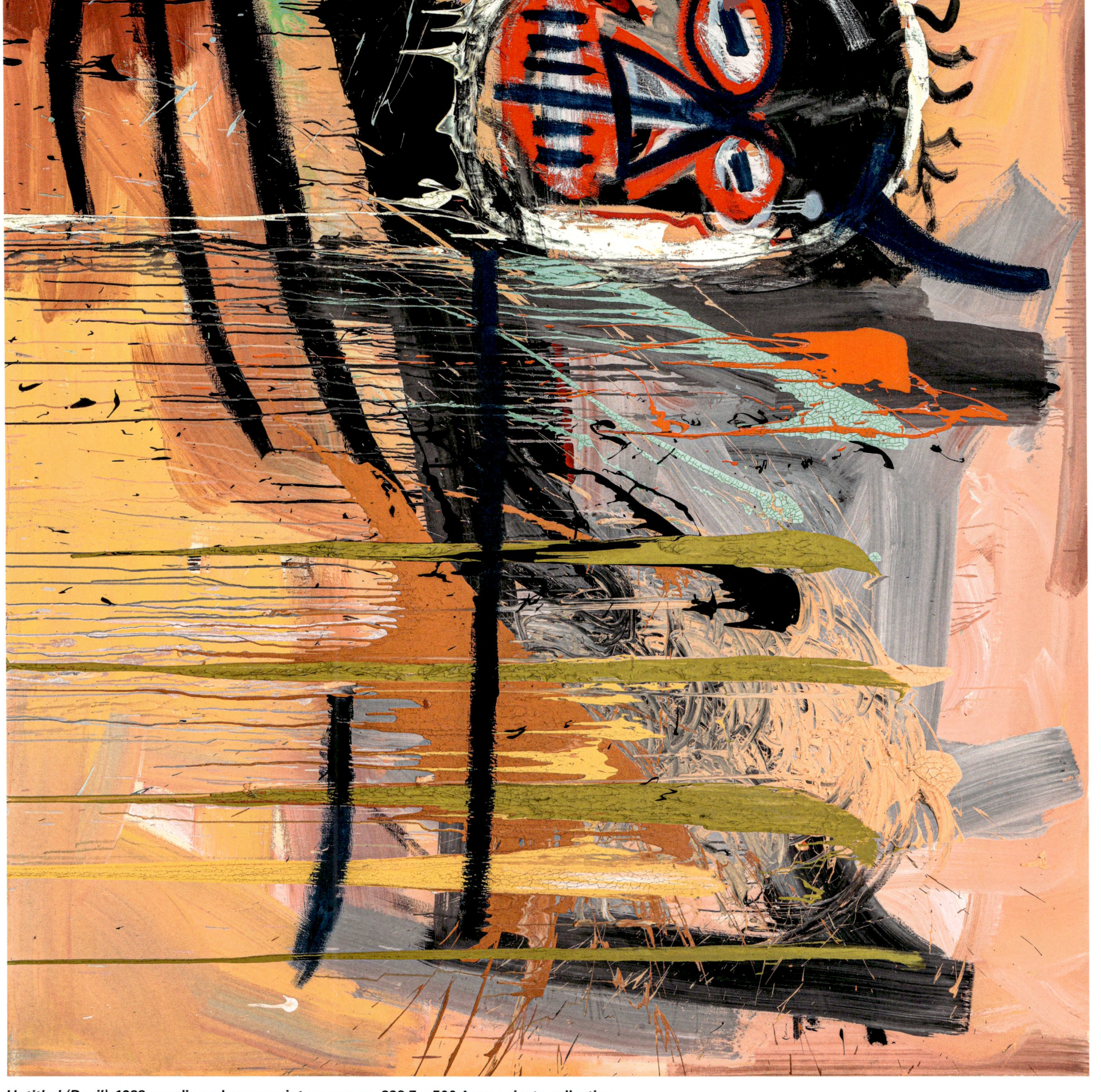

Untitled (Devil), 1982, acrylic and spray paint on canvas, 238.7 × 500.4 cm, private collection

Untitled (Devil)

In the early 1980s most conversations in the art world were somewhat obsessed with the status of expressive painting and, most particularly, its relevance in the context of Minimal and Conceptual artworks, which had dominated the 1960s and 1970s. Minimalist artists produced sculptures from everyday materials arranged in mathematical sequences, in order to avoid the influence of the artist's individual subjectivity. Conceptual artists focused their work on the processes of making, often restricting access to or destroying the finished "object" in an attempt to avoid the (capitalist) fetishization and the aestheticization of art. In their outright rejection of the previous, Abstract Expressionist generation's ontological search for meaning in the splattering and pouring of paint onto unprimed canvases, these artists—and the critics that surrounded them—publicly doubted the potential of expressive painting to answer the epistemological questions they privileged.

The emergence of Neo-Expressionism and its emphasis on bold colors, figuration, and gesture was unsettling for many critics, who expressed skepticism about the growing alliance between art and consumer culture. As discussed by the art historian Alison Pearlman, these critics "held that certain values—namely, artistic originality, the rarity of the object, and the beauty of the object—were the cornerstone of modern art's economic value and hence complicit with bourgeois interests."[1] Nevertheless, or precisely because of its socioeconomic significance, the Neo-Expressionist style of painting—such as that we see in *Untitled (Devil)*—was embraced by collectors and propelled young artists like Jean-Michel Basquiat to superstardom.

Among the painting's clearest ties to the Neo-Expressionist style is the presence of the drips of paint in yellow, turquoise, and olive green that run vertically down the surface of the canvas. We notice among the poured drips that the top of some lines correspond in width to the various brushes used by the artist; we can see an imprint of the paint-loaded brush that, when removed from the surface, left excess paint that dripped downward toward the bottom edge of the composition. These lines reveal the process of their creation as well as the presence of the artist, who has dripped, layered, and smeared the colors onto the canvas.

Basquiat's paint application recalls the mature works of the American artist Jackson Pollock (1912-1956), who dripped and splashed his way to art world infamy **(fig. 1)**. Basquiat's composition, however, is not a simple homage to his predecessor. We notice that the drips on the surface of his painting do not seamlessly blend into a patterned field of swirling color that defined Pollock's "all-over" style. Instead, Basquiat's drips are isolated in their careful application onto the peachy-red surface of the canvas. They seem frozen in time, constrained by the space of the rectangle rather than spilling over onto the sides. Here, it is

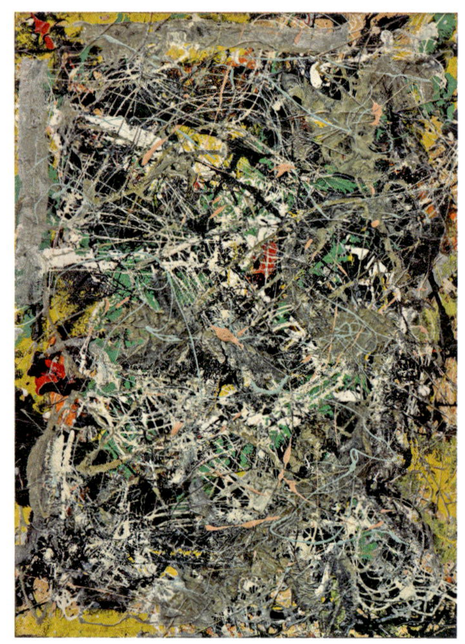

Jackson Pollock, *Untitled*, ca. 1949, paper, enamel paint, and aluminum paint on fiberboard, 78.7 × 57.5 cm, Fondation Beyeler, Riehen/Basel, Beyeler Collection

1) Alison Pearlman, *Unpackaging Art of the 1980s* (Chicago and London, 2003), p. 13.

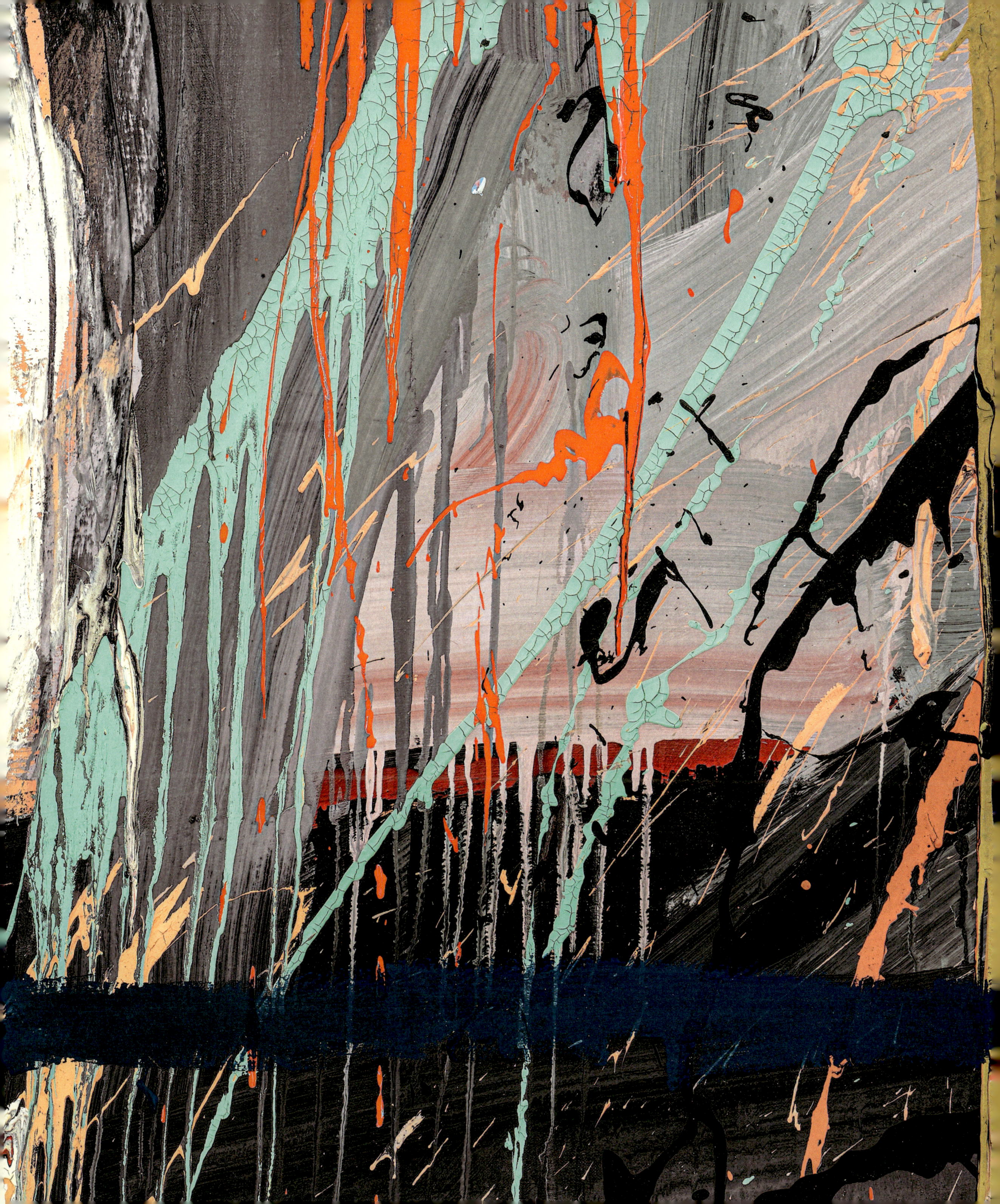

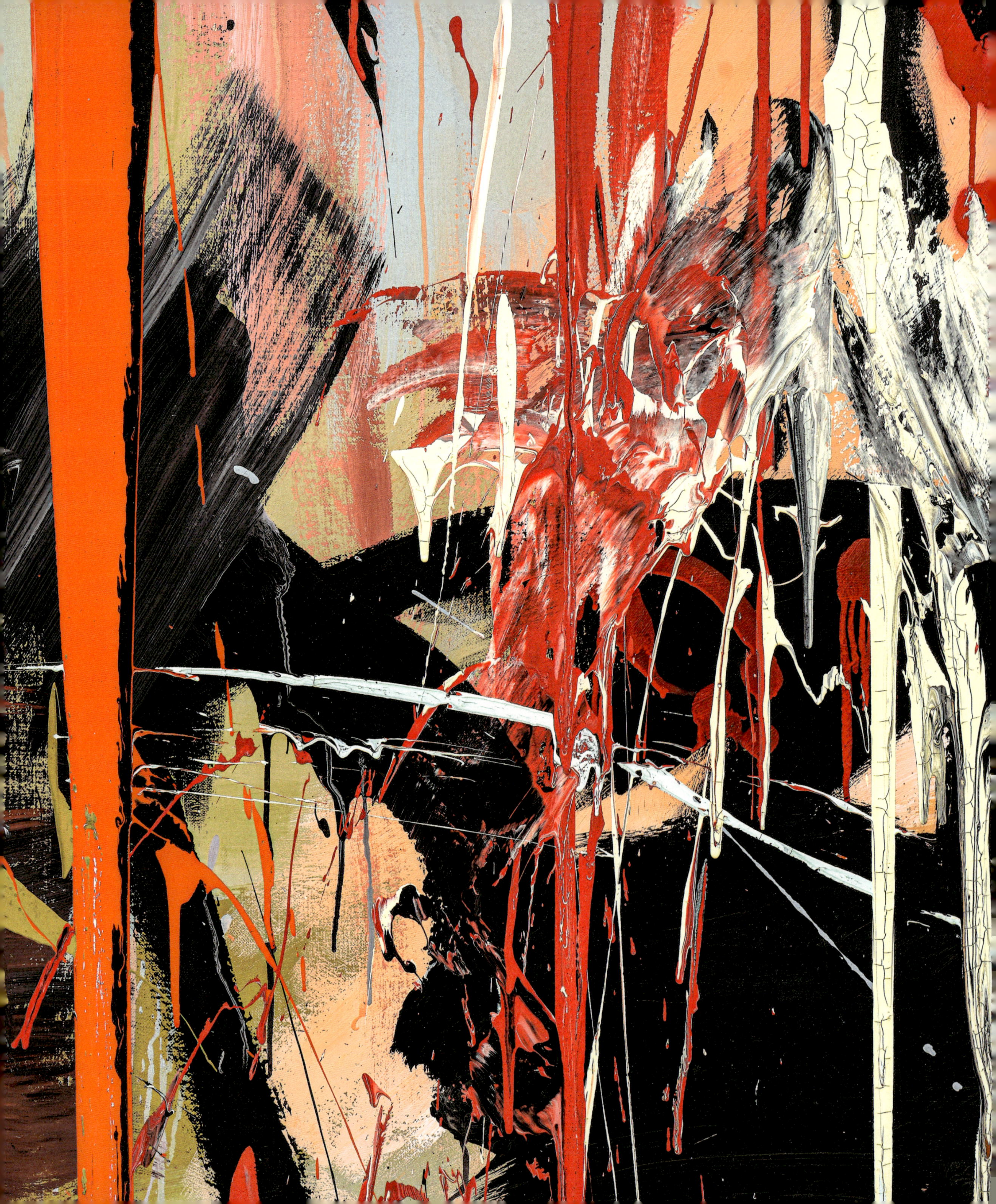

as if Basquiat is referencing Pollock (and Abstract Expressionist painting in general) via citation rather than adoption. He deploys the drip as a stylistic element rather than as an organizing principle.

We detect other forms of citation in *Untitled (Devil)* as well, most notably with the enormous head that occupies the center of the composition. To construct this figure, Basquiat first rendered a head and face in black with coiled hair framing the top of the head. Then, he applied a mask-like layer on top of the black face using red and blue paint. The eyes and nose have been radically abstracted to a composite of two circles and a triangle; the open mouth, with comically large red lips and white teeth, has been overlaid with six vertical stripes in dark blue. While we may be tempted to identify the source of this face as either an African mask—such as the horned buffalo masks of Burkina Faso **(fig. 2)**—or perhaps even the self-portraits of Pablo Picasso, which bear a striking similarity in their simplification of facial features, the head can be seen as a citation of both. In other words, Basquiat's conflation of African art and that of Picasso here carries with it the echoes of a modernist past that simultaneously denies the presence of Black people while explicitly relying upon their creative and expressive capacities. JORDANA MOORE SAGGESE

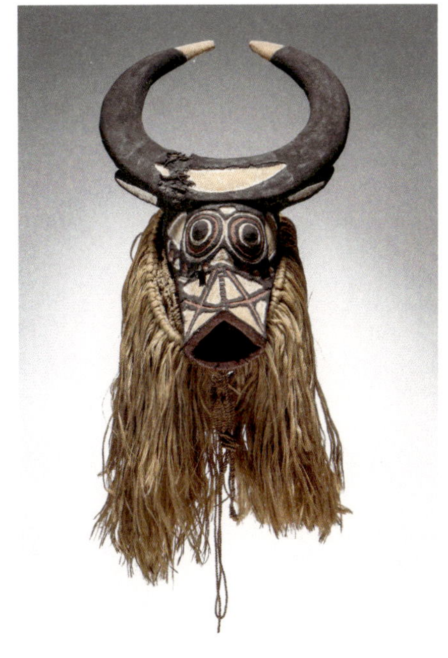

Fig. 2
Buffalo Mask, early to mid-19th century, West Africa, Burkina Faso, probably Bwa-people, wood, plant fibers, paint, and iron, height: 69.8 cm, Cleveland Museum of Art

Untitled (Angel)

Untitled (Angel) can be interpreted as the antithesis of *Untitled (Devil)*, in a relationship similar to that between *Irony of Negro Policeman* **(fig. 1)** and *La Hara* **(fig. 2)**. Both from 1981, the latter pair of opposites contrasts the "irony" inherent in the powerlessness of an African American police officer acting as law enforcer and agent of oppression in the 1980s with the brutal arbitrariness and menacing potential of the bloodthirsty White policeman. This dualism is also found in *Untitled (Angel)* and *Untitled (Devil)*, which form a kind of dialectical diptych, and is reflected in a whole range of visual and linguistic contrasts that play a part in Basquiat's work. These oppositions are especially striking in pictures such as *Dos Pajaros* (1985), showing the contrasting heads of two birds, marked "bueno" and "malo." In other works, the artist introduces verbal pairings such as "left" and "right," "famous" and "not famous," "salt" and "peppar" [*sic*], or "fake" and "real." And in *Both Poles* (1982) he presents two literally polar opposites. If we accept the posthumously added titles, referring to an "angel" and a "devil," these two paintings can be seen as depicting the conflict between good and evil in the most emphatic embodiment known to our culture. Basquiat thus on the one hand constructs an arc of tension with pairs of opposites that he on the other hand brings together again, like yin and yang, since they seem to be mutually dependent and form a whole only in combination.

The figure of the angel, like the cow in *Untitled (Cowparts)* and the devil in *Untitled (Devil)*, is rendered on a canvas-filling scale. With huge, staring eyes, shedding drips of red color from the pupils, the figure rears up like a monument, set slightly left of center against a background painted in whitish or reddish shades of ocher. The striking white and red contours of the skull-like head and the black body are drawn with broad brushstrokes. The body seems to dissolve into the lower edge of the picture, while the outstretched arms, with hands held high, extend all the way from the left to the right of the canvas. Floating above the skull is an attenuated halo, hastily applied with black spray paint. In contrast to the visually dominant halo in *Profit I*, with its aura of light and crown of thorns, the one above the head

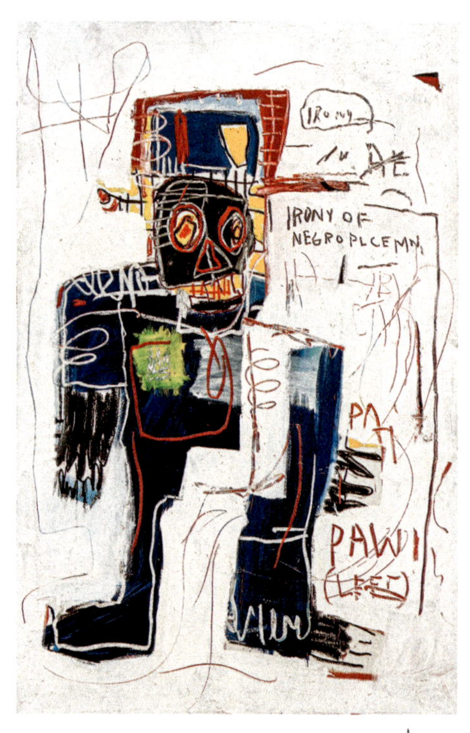

Fig. 1
Irony of Negro Policeman, 1981, acrylic and oil stick on wood, 183 × 122 cm, private collection

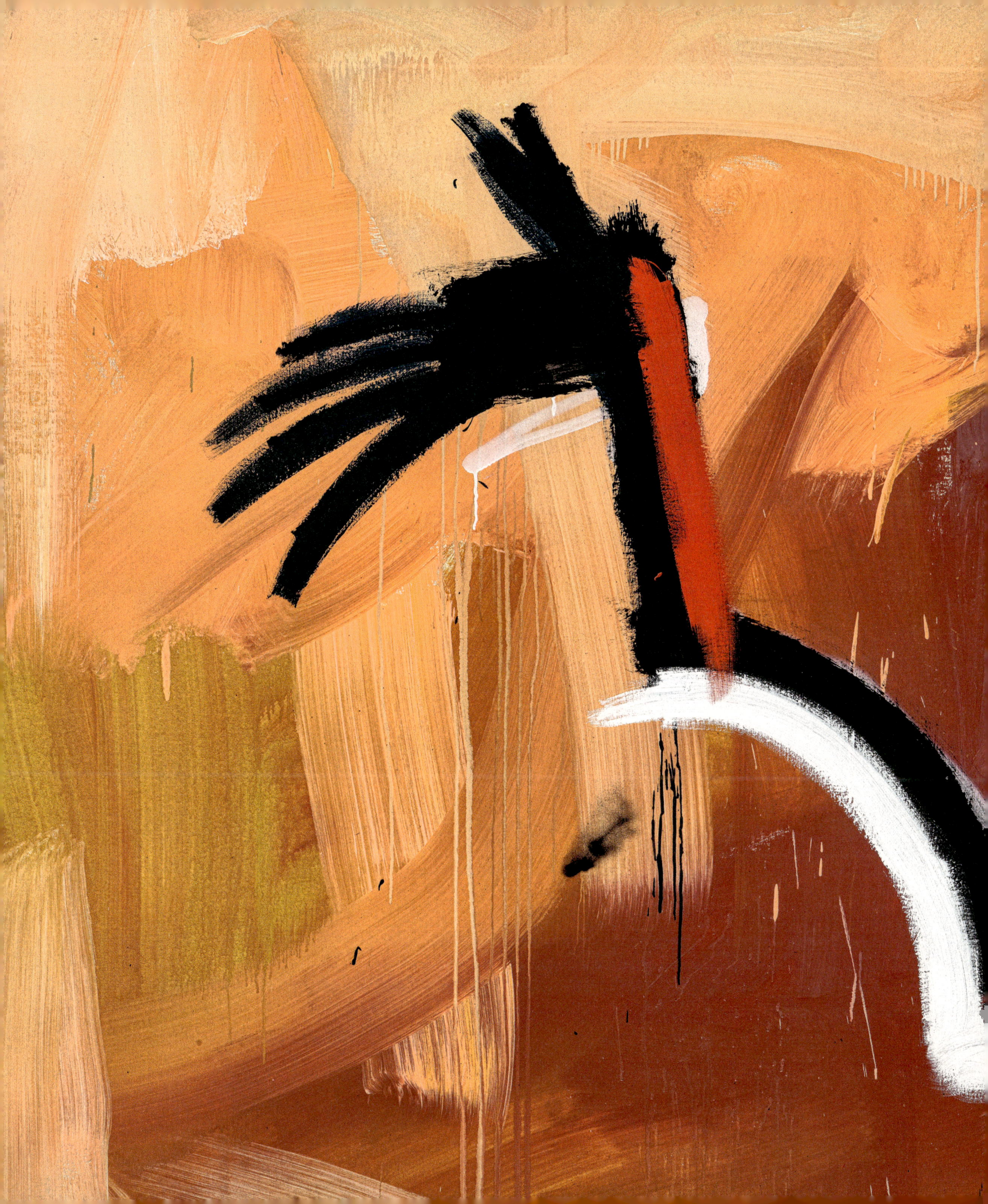

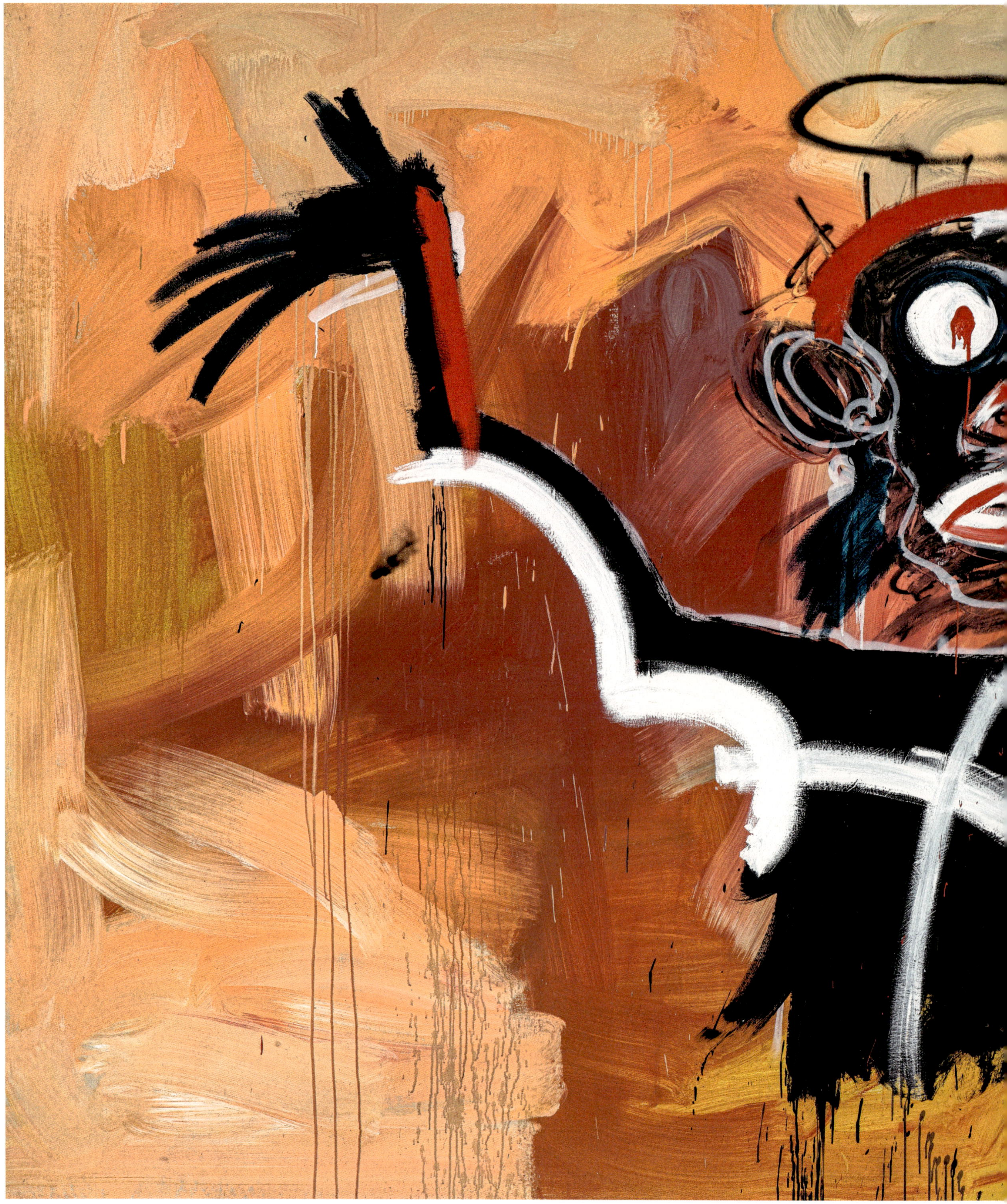

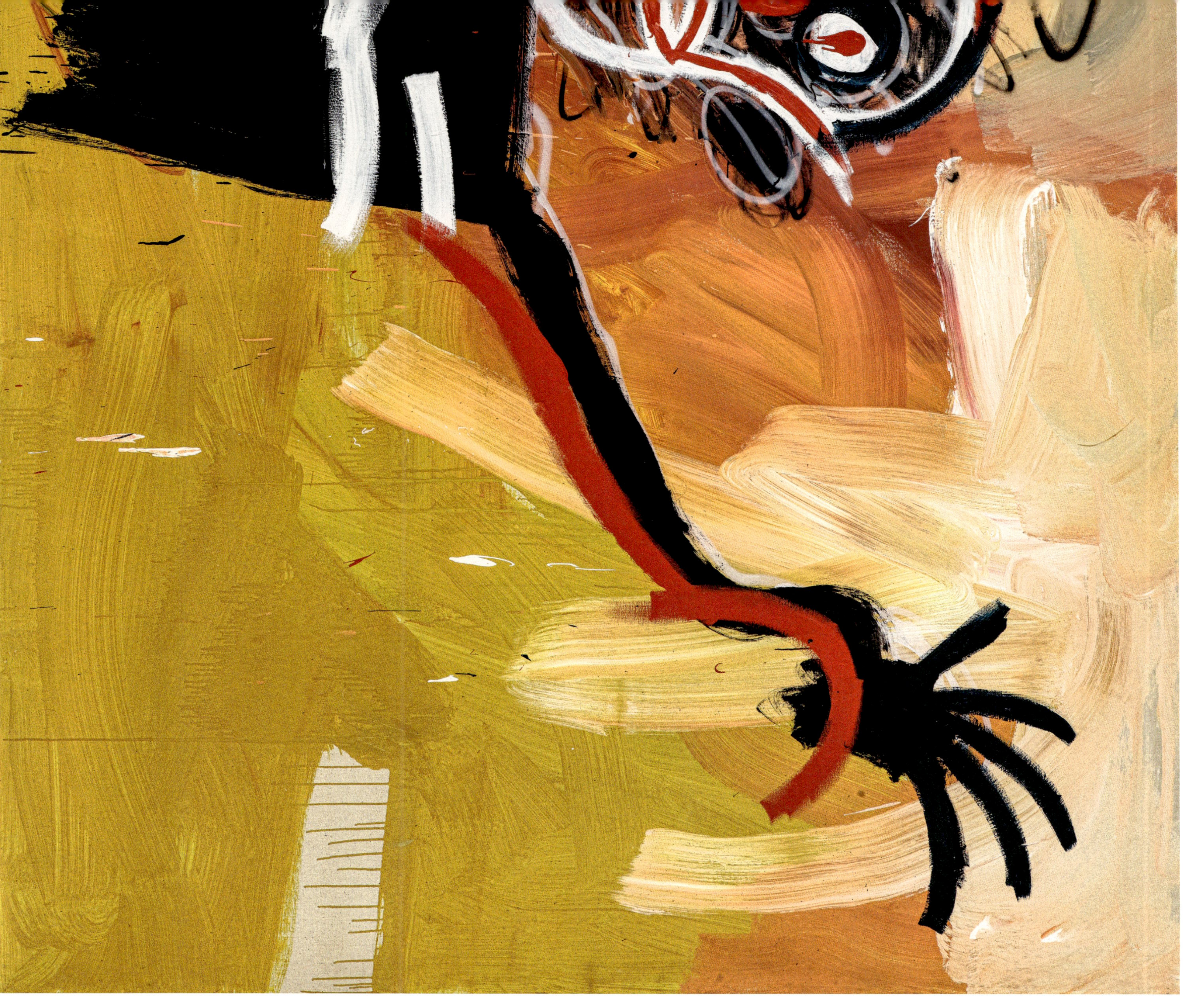

Untitled (Angel), 1982, acrylic and spray paint on canvas, 244 × 429 cm, private collection

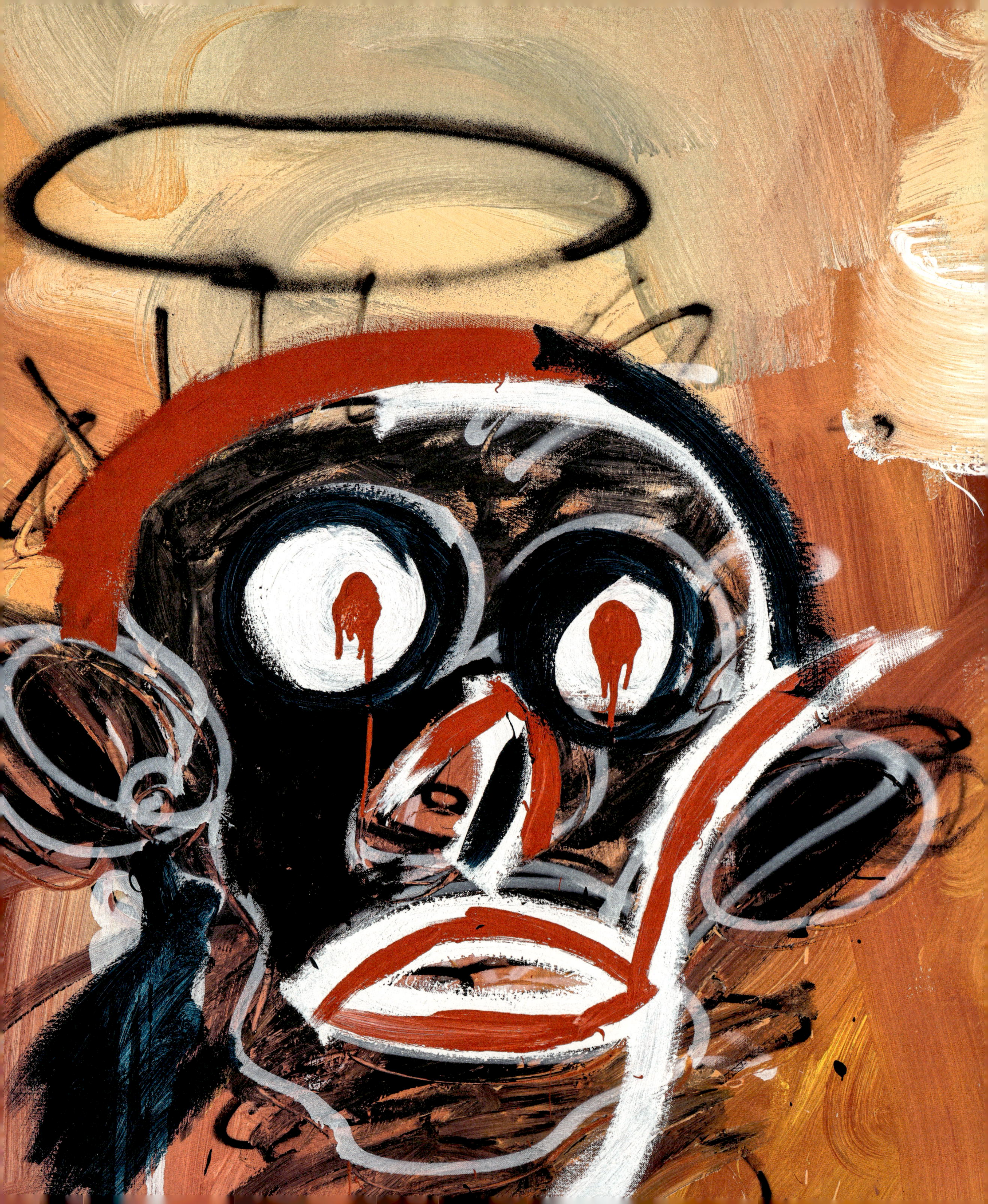

of the supposed angel seems to have been added almost incidentally, as a secondary attribute. The figure has the air of an avenging angel, menacing and poised to attack. The white line connecting the head with the body cuts straight through the torso and is transformed into a kind of wound by the additional line of red at the top of the skull. The aggressive appearance of the figure corresponds to a comment Basquiat later made about his art: "It's about 80 % anger."[1] This is not a charming, winged angel, but a creature that is damaged and damaging, resisting oppression with the utmost dynamism, determined to ensure that justice prevails. Thus "everything is dead in life," as Egon Schiele wrote in 1910.[2] The painting, whether speaking of racism, drugs, violence, genocide, or war, becomes a document of being, of human presence in a "life that has to be understood as an incessant weathering."[3] Here, tormented humanity finds the indelible sign of its existence.

DIETER BUCHHART

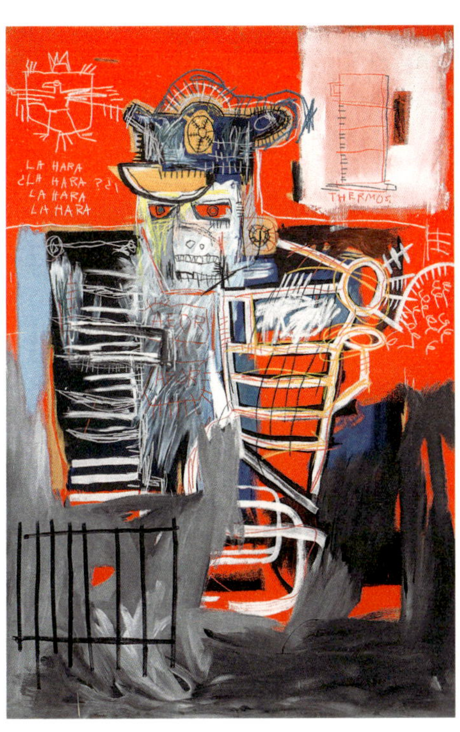

Fig. 2
La Hara, 1981, acrylic and oil stick on wood, 183 × 121.5 cm, private collection

1) Jean-Michel Basquiat, "Art: From Subways to Soho: Jean-Michel Basquiat," interview by Henry Geldzahler, *Interview* 13, no. 1 (January 1983), pp. 44–46, here p. 46; reprinted in Jordana Moore Saggese, ed., *The Jean-Michel Basquiat Reader: Writings, Interviews, and Critical Responses* (Oakland, 2021), pp. 32–38, here p. 38.

2) Egon Schiele, "Tannenwald," July 1910, Egon Schiele Datenbank der Autographen, http://www.schiele-dokumentation.at/browserecord.php?-action=browse&-recid=202280&-skip=134 (accessed February 27, 2023). This excerpt is published in English in Rudolf Leopold, introduction to *Egon Schiele: The Leopold Collection, Vienna*, ed. Magdalena Dabrowski (Cologne, 1997), p. 32.

3) Egon Schiele to Oskar Reichel, September 1911, in Christian M. Nebehay, *Egon Schiele, 1890–1918: Leben, Briefe, Gedichte* (Salzburg and Vienna, 1979), p. 184.

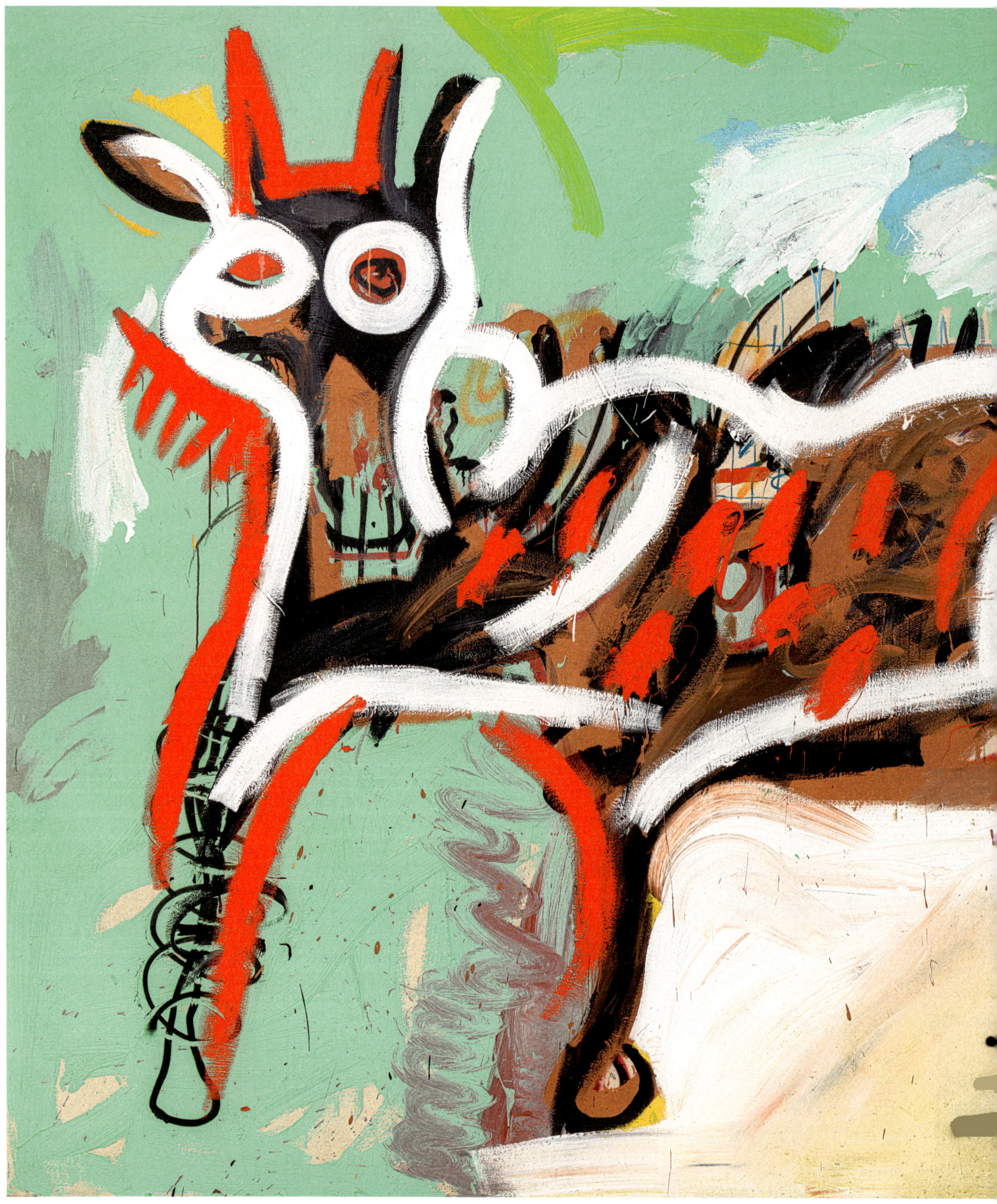

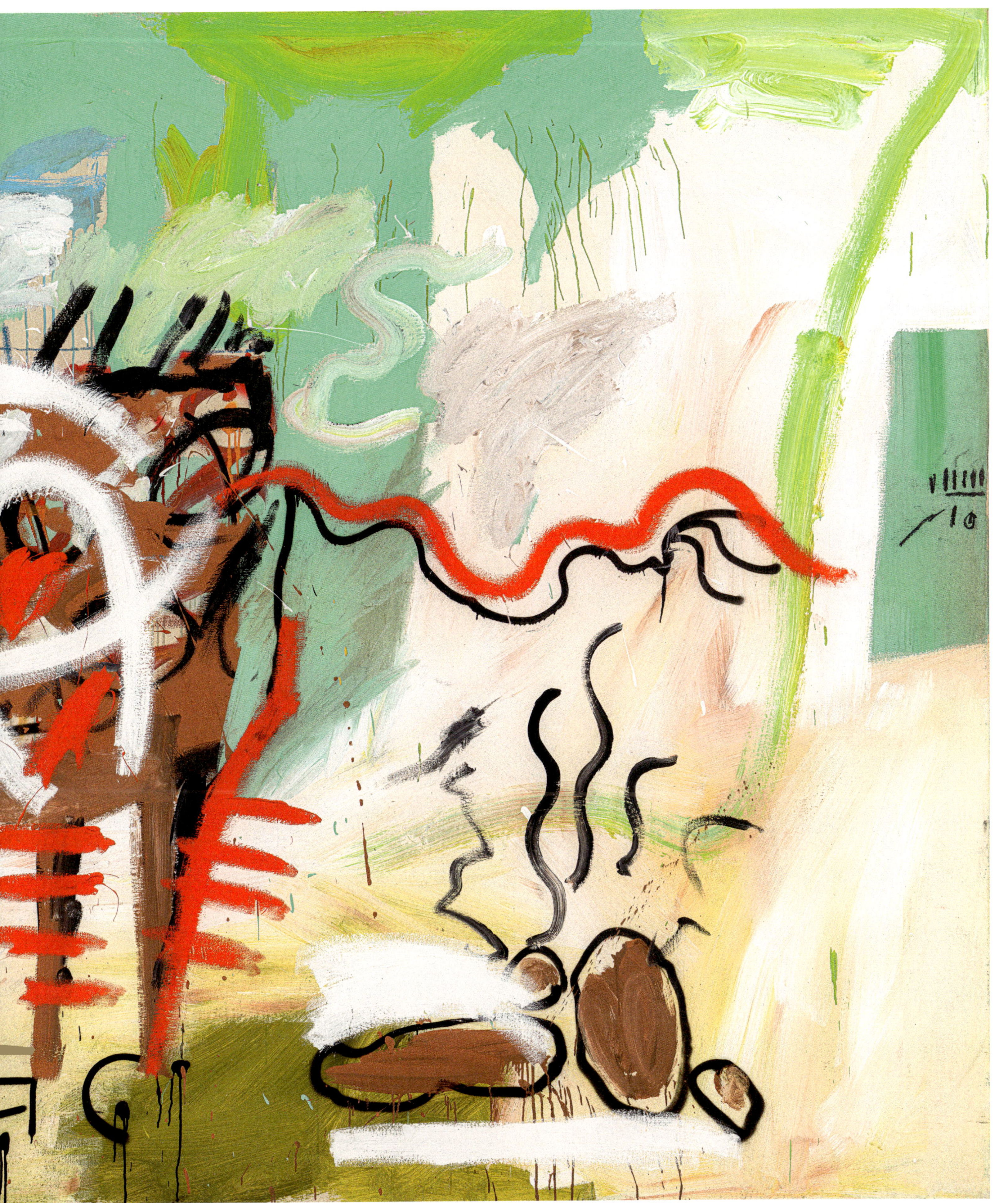

Untitled (Cowparts), 1982, acrylic, spray paint, and oil stick on canvas, 239.4 × 420 cm, Aby Rosen Collection, New York

Untitled (Cowparts)

The painting *Untitled (Cowparts)* oscillates between a gestural abstract background and the depiction of a vividly patterned cow. Thus, the large-scale work derives its visual appeal from the tension between different painting techniques and diverging speeds of execution. The cow, rendered with rapid, expressive brushstrokes and given a monumental size, abounds with vitality, while the green-and-white planes appear serene and self-contained, receding into the background and further emphasizing the plasticity of the motif. The image of the animal combines these two extremes: the cow is a calm and gentle creature, yet its gaze is boldly directed at the viewer, issuing a kind of coquettish challenge. Jean-Michel Basquiat knew how to combine drawing and painting. Like the white outline, the red and black lines of the skeleton are graphically conceived, allowing the color to dribble downward.

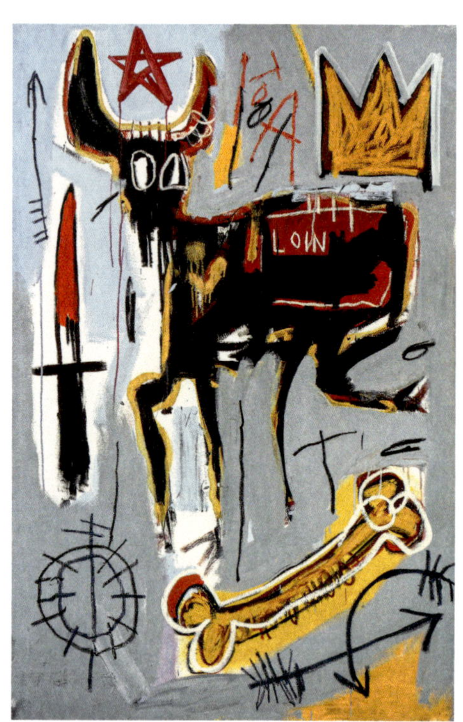

Loin, 1982, acrylic and oil stick on canvas, 183 × 122 cm, private collection

In *Untitled (Cowparts)* Basquiat's interest is focused on a single animal, the cow. While rather untypical for the artist, who often turned attention to the human body, in 1982 he did in fact paint a series of other creatures that fill the entire canvas, as in *Loin* **(fig. 1)** and *Part Wolf* or also *Red Rabbit*, in which a giant rabbit is depicted against a red background.

These animals are charged with symbolic significance, and the artist's engagement with them is just as emphatic as in his encounters with humans. The depiction of the cow could be understood as referring to art-historical precedents such as the *Yellow Cow* (1911) by Franz Marc, the cows of Jean Dubuffet **(fig. p. 76)**—brut and assertive—or Pablo Picasso's images of bulls. At the same time, the aesthetic is redolent of urban graffiti. Basquiat, moreover, has clearly retained the humor of his earlier street art. Perhaps deliberately, He endows the animal with human features, approaching the motif in a way that reflects his customary wit and irony. And the sight of the excrement, still steaming and palpably humming, is almost bound to elicit a smile from the viewer.

The white contour line, opaquely applied and echoing the style of *Untitled (Angel)*, is not the sole indication that the work belongs to the Modena series. The artist's

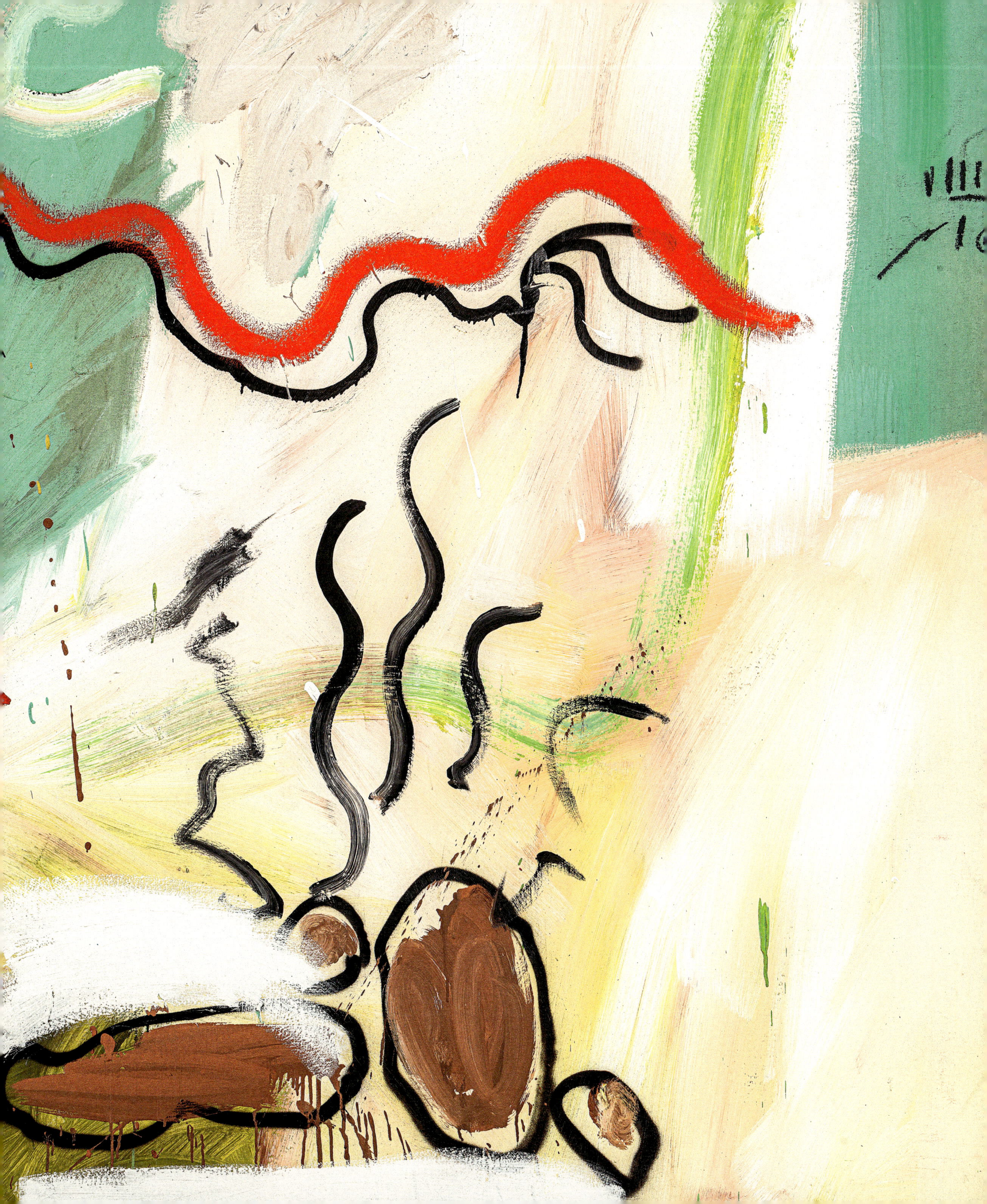

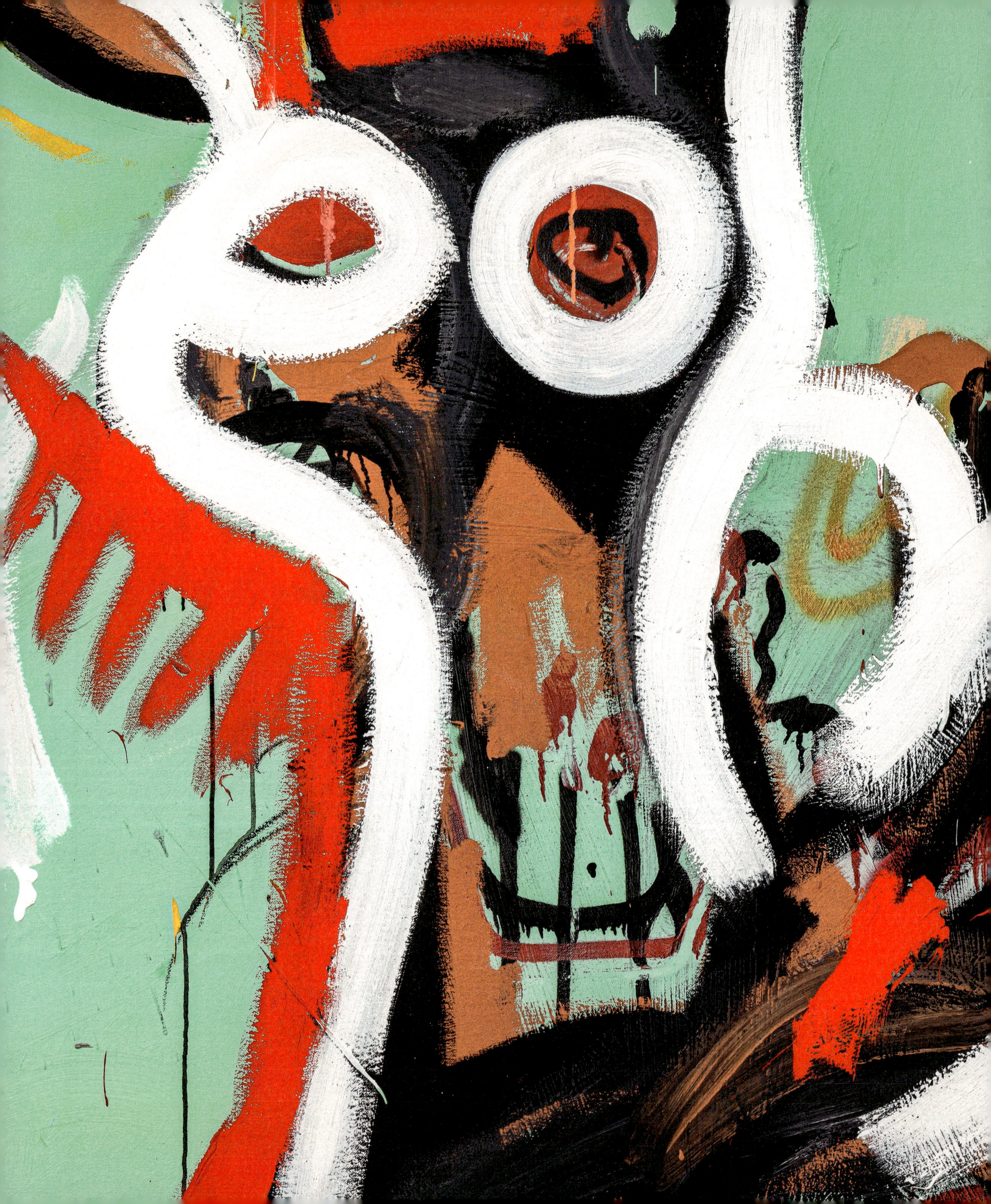

signature on the back of the canvas and the inscription "Modena 1982" were just discovered during the preparations for the current exhibition.

Dispensing with enigmatic inscriptions and numerological games, Basquiat painted this work in a transitional phase. Only a set of tally marks, placed centrally, can be seen at the right edge of the picture. In *Untitled (Cowparts)* a further intriguing element emerges: the semi-visible underdrawing in the upper part of the cow's body. Here, the turquoise background is missing, revealing a grid pattern on the exposed painting ground, showing signs of a preliminary compositional activity not apparent elsewhere in the picture. Basquiat often applied colors in a succession of layers, creating pictorial elements and then partly obscuring them. This also occurs in the Modena painting *Profit I*, where the red figure was subsequently overpainted with patches of black. This shows that Basquiat created his works in an ongoing process, skillfully using gaps and empty spaces to develop a field of free association.

Quite deliberately, the artist left traces that point to the corrections he made while working on the painting, without removing all evidence of the previous state. Thus, he reveals the possibility of a second, underlying pictorial reality, and signals a change of rhythm. Lydia Yee has aptly compared Basquiat's technique with that of a DJ.[1] Basquiat—himself a DJ—generally listened to music while he painted, and evidently found it a source of inspiration. In this picture, too, he used the musical technique of sampling, giving rise to a spontaneously orchestrated, almost intoxicating, and at the same time percussive painting. It is as if this larger-than-life cow, with its spellbinding gaze and fresh deposit of cow patties, were standing in front of us with all its physicality and liveliness.

REGULA MOSER

1) Lydia Yee, "Breaking and Entering," in *One Planet under a Groove: Hip Hop and Contemporary Art*, exh. cat. The Bronx Museum of the Arts, New York; Walker Art Center, Minneapolis; Spelman College Museum of Fine Art, Atlanta (New York, 2001), pp. 15–23, here p. 19.

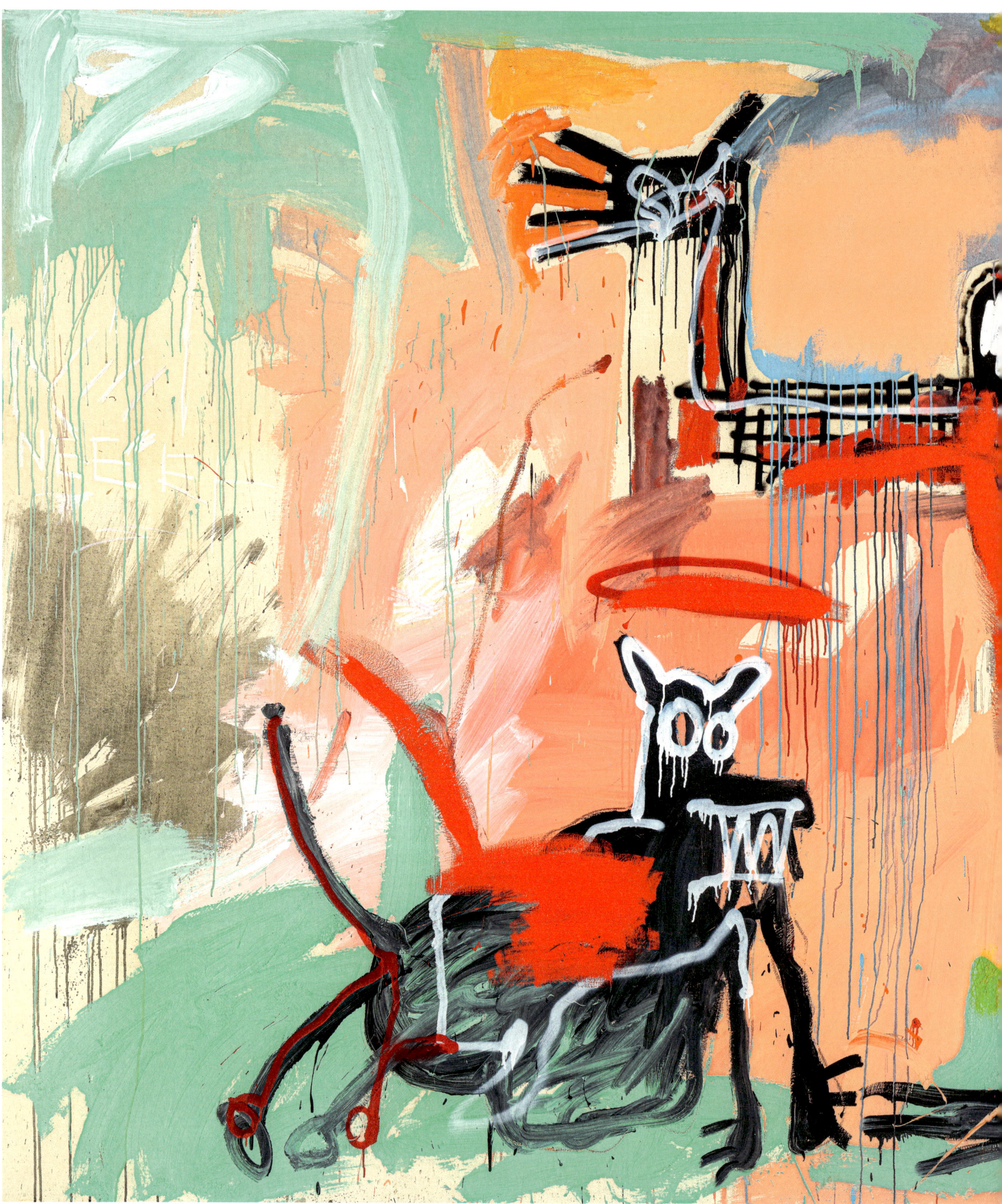

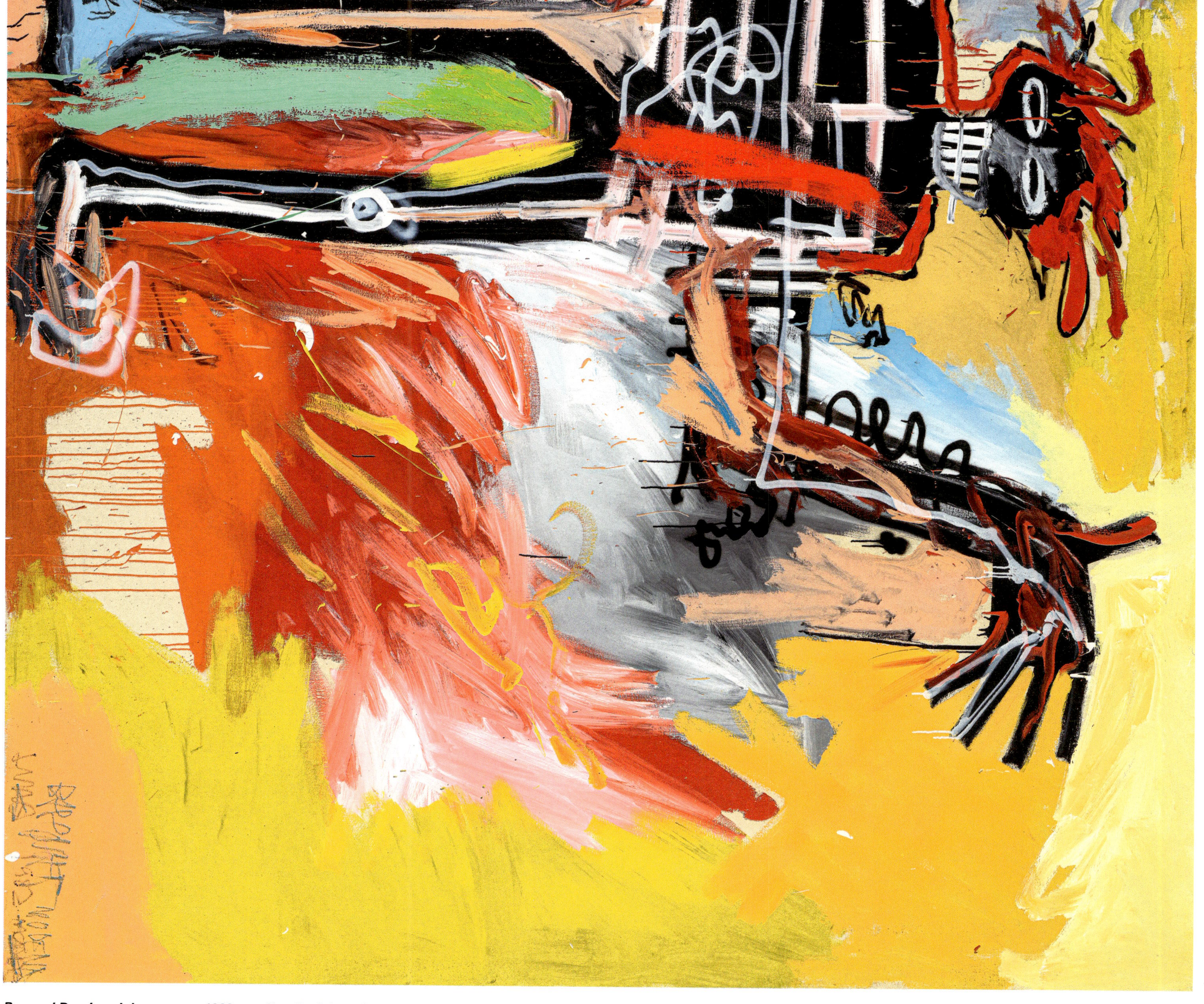

Boy and Dog in a Johnnypump, 1982, acrylic, oil stick, and spray paint on canvas, 240 x 420.4 cm, private collection

Boy and Dog in a Johnnypump

A human figure and a dog are depicted against a background comprising patches of bright color. The bodies of the person and the dog are black. The animal's eyes and teeth, and the outlines of its head and rump, are delineated in white; its back legs and tail are highlighted with red, and a patch of red, like a halo, is placed above its head. Lines of a lighter color represent the skeleton and internal organs of the human figure, whose shoulders and head are bordered in red, repeated in the color of the hair that sticks out in untamed strands. The eyes are denoted by two ellipses; the teeth and mouth are sketched in white. The hands are raised, with fingers outspread. At the left edge of the picture, we see a group of letters whose meaning remains a mystery.

The title conveys some information about the scene, telling us that the human figure is a boy, playing with a dog in the spray of an open "johnny pump," the New York City nickname for a fire hydrant, indicated by the patches of red and light blue on the right next to the boy. Playing in the street—such as in the fountain of refreshingly cold water from a hydrant—is a recurrent theme in Jean-Michel Basquiat's early work. A further example is the skelly court, a board drawn on the sidewalk for a game of skill popular among New York children. Basquiat himself was a New Yorker through and through. Apart from an eighteen-month stay with his family in Puerto Rico, he spent his childhood and youth in Brooklyn—up to the age of eighteen, when he moved out of his father's house—and then lived mainly in Manhattan until his death, in 1988. Scenes of children playing, as in *Boy and Dog in a Johnnypump*, are generally taken to be inspired by memories of his own childhood.

Impressions from early life are themes of many of Basquiat's drawings and paintings. Cartoon figures from books and comics, as well as athletes familiar from televised sporting events **(fig. 1)**, make frequent appearances in his work, as does the memory of being struck by a car and seriously injured at the age of seven. The hairstyle and skin color suggest that the figure in *Boy and Dog in a Johnnypump* could be a self-portrait. Short, thick dreadlocks are one of Basquiat's trademarks, appearing in the works that he himself identified as self-portraits. The accurate rendering of facial features

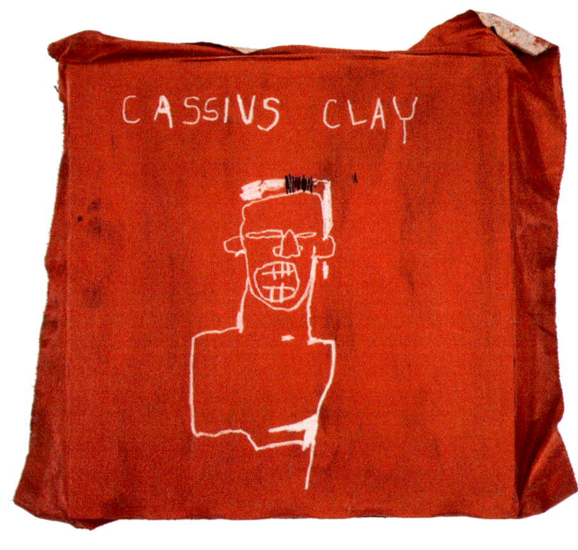

Fig. 1
Cassius Clay, 1982, acrylic and oil stick on canvas, 106.6 × 104 cm, Bischofberger Collection, Männedorf-Zurich, Switzerland

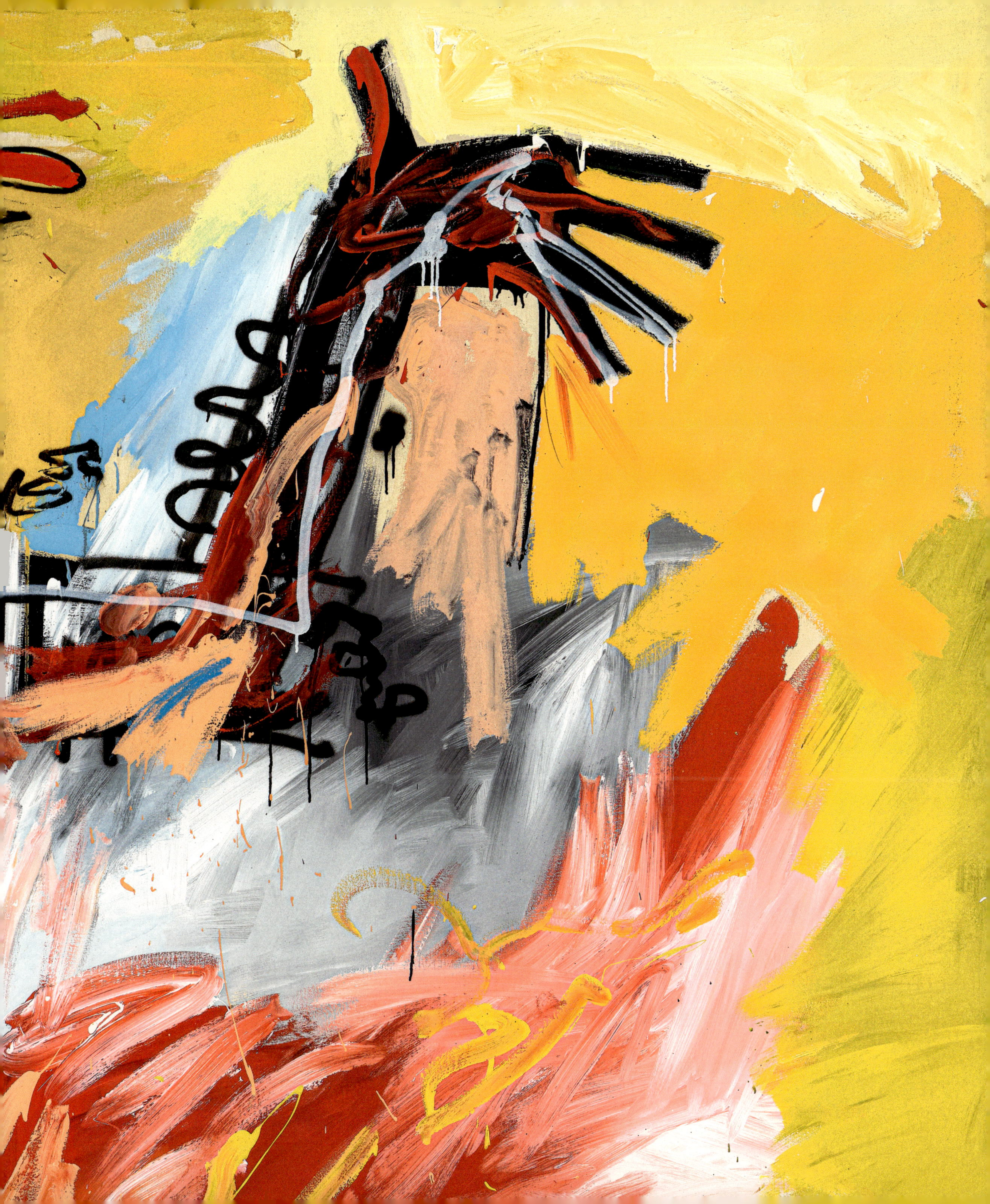

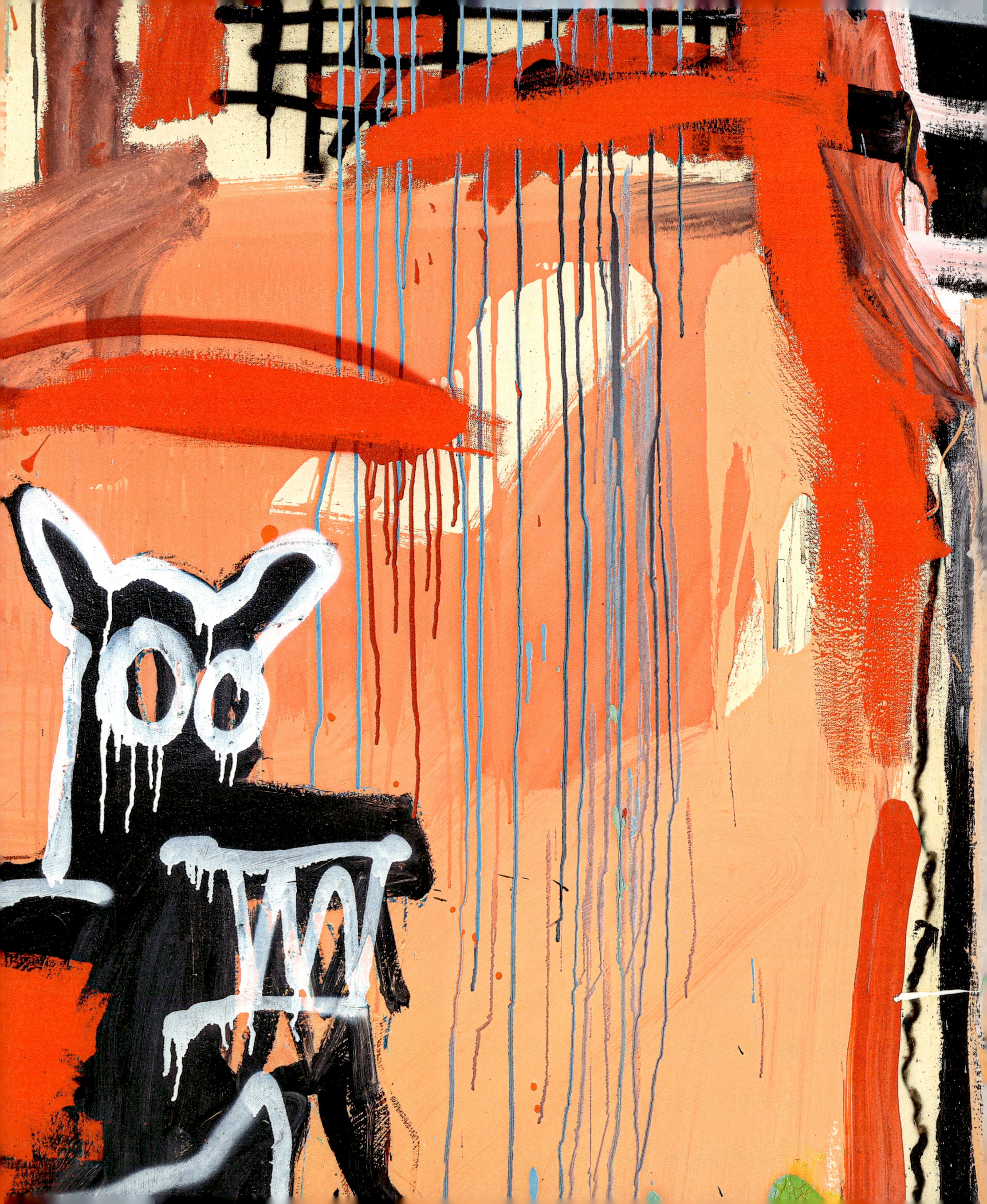

1) Jean-Michel Basquiat, "Jean-Michel Basquiat," interview by Démosthènes Davvetas, *New Art International*, no. 3 (October-November 1988), pp. 10-15; reprinted in Jordana Moore Saggese, ed., *The Jean-Michel Basquiat Reader: Writings, Interviews, and Critical Responses* (Oakland, 2021), pp. 61-62, here p. 62.

has no place in these pictures: instead, we repeatedly encounter artificial, grinning masks with elliptical or almond-shaped eyes and teeth clamped in a grid-like expression.

The figure of the Black man has a central place in Basquiat's work. His own experiences with racism and its impact on society and art, as well as the history of colonialism and the slave trade were issues of central concern to him: "I'm an artist who has been influenced by his New York environment. But I have a cultural memory. I don't need to look for it; it exists. It's over there, in Africa."[1] As in three further pictures, also painted in Modena in 1982 (*Profit I, Untitled [Angel]*, and *Untitled [Devil]*), the pose of the black silhouette allows for differing interpretations. What is the symbolic significance of the raised hands? Do they stand for joy, strength, self-confidence, triumph, freedom? Do they suggest that the figure is threatening the viewer, or that he is willing to surrender without a struggle? Is the boy a victim of oppression or a rebel against injustice? Are his teeth bared in a grin or enclosed by a muzzle that prevents the freedom of expression of opinion? Or is the set of teeth, like the visible skeleton, a symbol of death?

In *Boy and Dog in a Johnnypump*, as in many further works, Basquiat combines three painting media: conventional acrylic paint, oil stick—often used in his drawings—and the spray paint typically found in graffiti. Oil stick and spray paint serve to accentuate the contours of the figures or to highlight their bone structure: a technique that characterizes nearly all the Modena paintings from 1982. At the time, the use of spray paint for pictures on canvas was unusual, but Basquiat was familiar with the medium. From 1977 to 1979, the short texts that he and a school friend sprayed on walls under the pseudonym "SAMO" had attracted a great deal of attention.

MICHIKO KONO

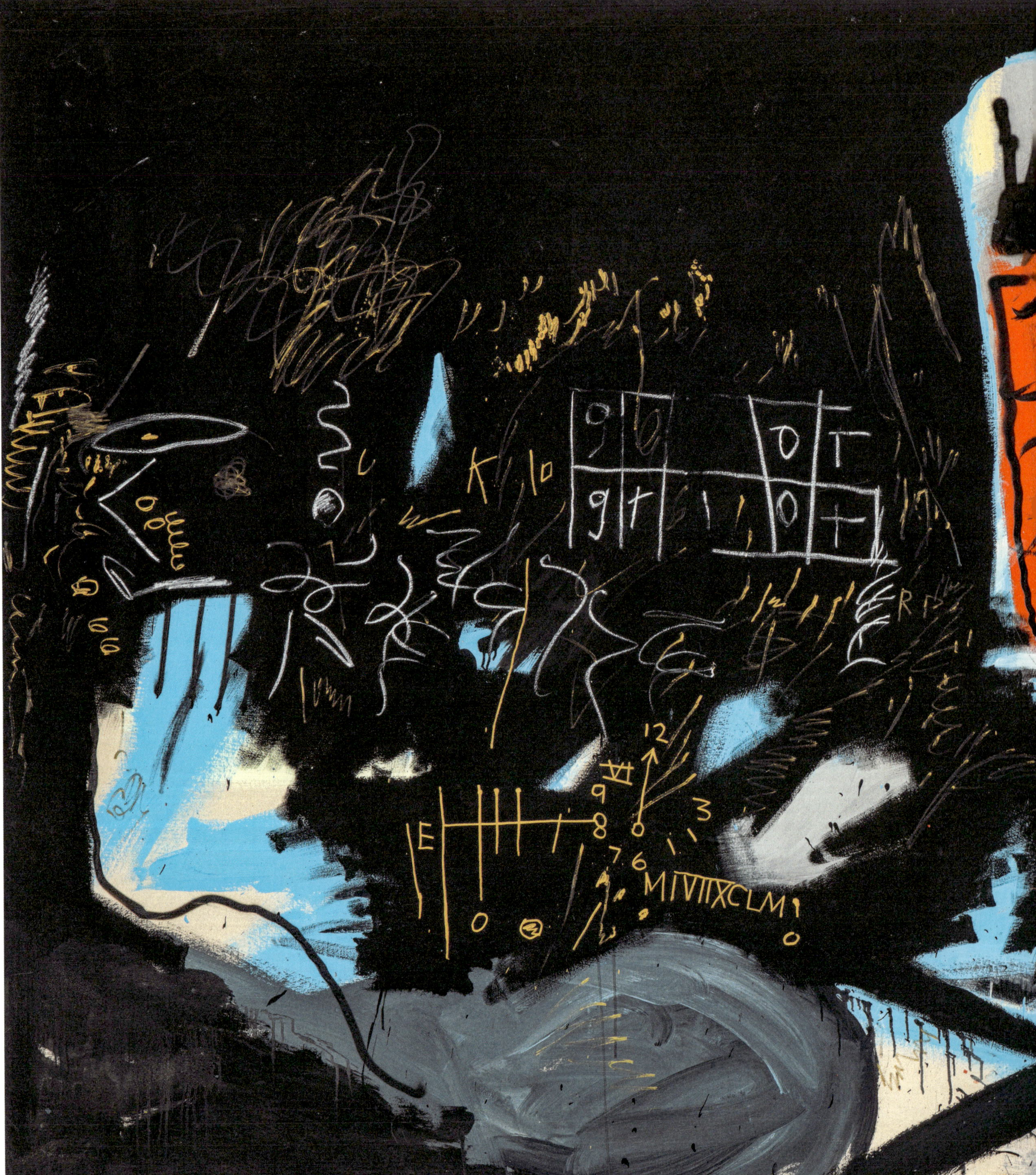

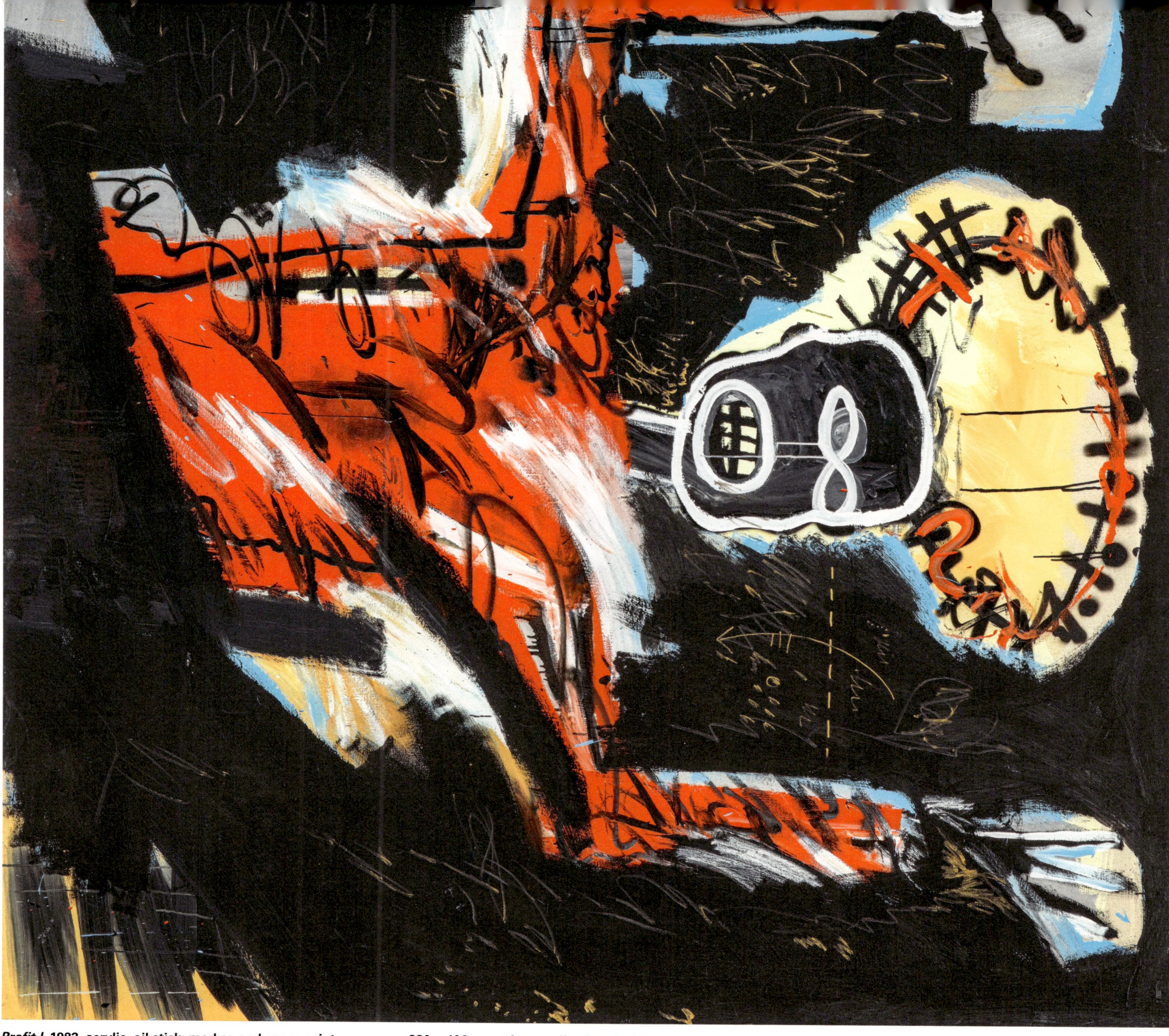

Profit I, 1982, acrylic, oil stick, marker, and spray paint on canvas, 220 × 400 cm, private collection, Switzerland

Profit I

A powerful half-length figure with raised arms looms out from
the largely black background. Its red body and mask-like face,
framed with white spray paint and what appears like an auratically
illuminated, crown-of-thorns halo, allude to the martyrdom and
apotheosis of Christ and at the same time suggest the fury of a
secular hero. The impressive visual impact and the complexity
of the depiction make this work one of the most significant in
Jean-Michel Basquiat's oeuvre.

The composition, however, exhibits a dichotomy between the
anonymized figure in the right half of the monumental canvas and
the background, scattered with numbers, letters, and graphic marks.
The figure's hands are raised, as in many of Basquiat's other
works. But in contrast to the depictions in paintings such as
Untitled **(fig. 1)**, showing anonymous gloved Black boxers in victory
poses as they celebrate their triumph over the White man,[1] the
position of the arms in *Profit I* is ambivalent. Instead of being
encased in boxing gloves, the hands—that on the viewer's left
rendered with spray paint, the right one painted with a brush—show
the fingers outstretched. Rather than a gesture of victory, the
right-angle created
by the lower and upper
arm bent at the elbow
suggest the reaction,
under duress, of a
police suspect told to
put his hands up. Here,
then, Basquiat trans-
forms the victory
pose of his warriors,
prepared to fight with
swords, arrows, lances,
and bare fists, into a
gesture of power-
lessness, signified by
the demonstratively
empty raised hands. He
presents the African
American man as humil-
iated and abused,
through exclusion,

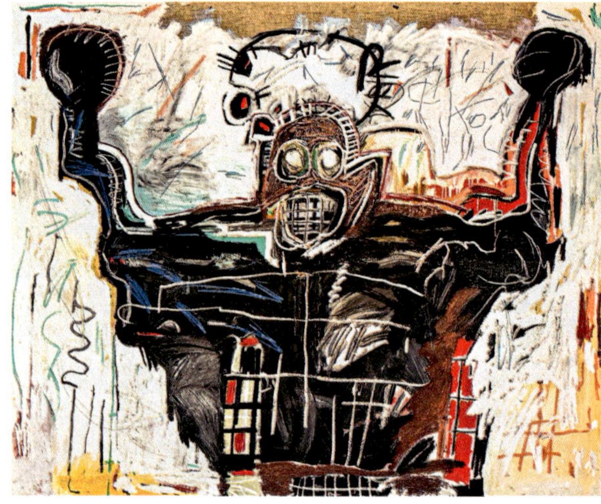

Fig. 1
Untitled, 1982,
acrylic and oil
stick on linen,
193 × 239 cm,
private
collection

1) In the early
twentieth century,
contests between
Black and White
boxers became a
surrogate for
"race struggle."
At a time when a
Black person could
still be lynched
for attacking a
White man, the
physical victory
of a Black boxer
over a White
opponent was a
source of pride to
Black Americans.
For Basquiat,
boxing was an
emblem of the
struggle against
oppression and
racism. The figure
of the boxer came
to epitomize Black
empowerment.

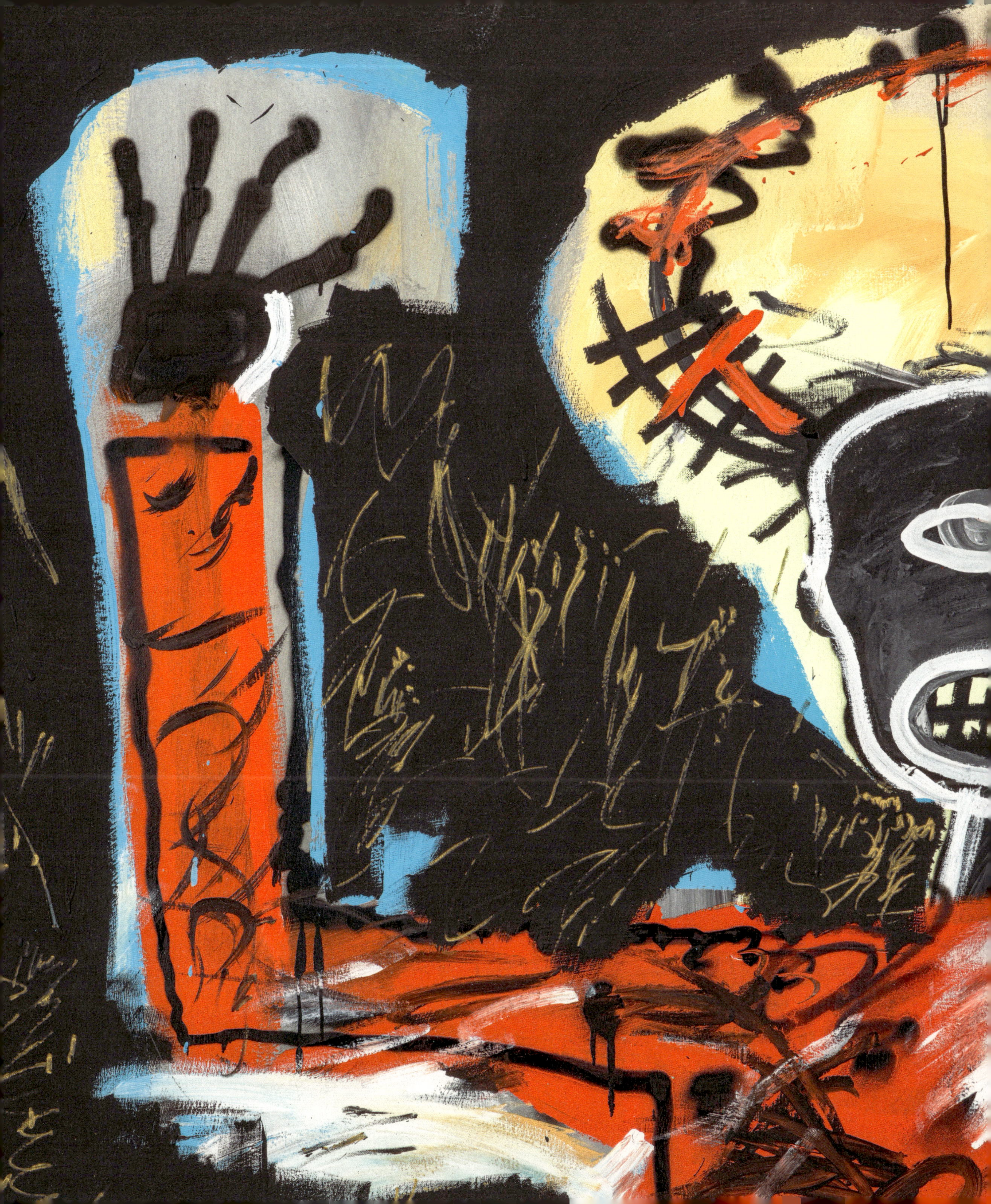

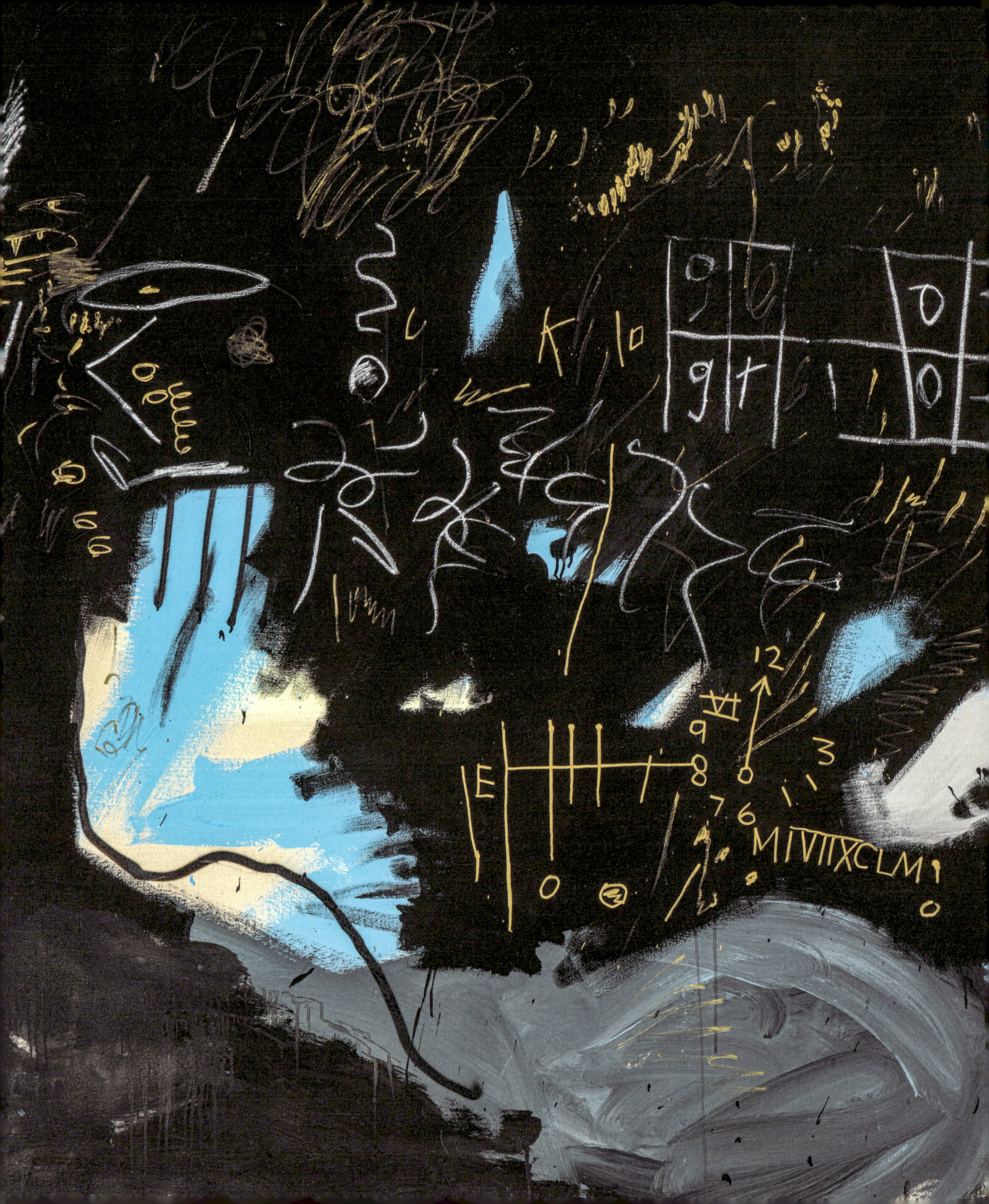

2) "Profit," here, is defined as "the excess of returns over expenditure in a transaction or series of transactions, *especially*: the excess of the selling price of goods over their cost"; *Merriam Webster Dictionary*.

3) Glenn O'Brien, "Basquiat and the New York Scene 1978-82," in *Basquiat*, ed. Dieter Buchhart and Sam Keller, exh. cat. Fondation Beyeler, Riehen/ Basel (Ostfildern, 2010), pp. V-VIII, here p. VIII.

exploitation, racial profiling, and police violence. Radical passivity and the role of the helpless victim in the face of arbitrary police violence and hate crime are contrasted with empowerment. Nevertheless, the yellowish halo and the inner crown of thorns hold a message of hope, which is reinforced by the brushwork in the painting of the right hand. The gestural brushstrokes endow the figure with life and energy, almost in the manner of an apotheosis, elevating a human being to a god-like figure. This all takes place against a black background, like a school blackboard, with sprinklings of blue, yellowish, and grayish color, to which Basquiat adds scribbles, numbers, signs, and marks in white oil stick and gold marker. Nothing is concrete but always merely hinted at, as in the representation of an abstract system. The title, *Profit I*, referring to the relationship of revenue to net proceeds,[2] is associated with the capitalist economic system, based on both exploitation and the promise of a positive return. The portentous, yet meaningless numbers, signs, and marks can be read as flaws in the system of financial capitalism. The number 9 in the clockface, for example, is followed by the Roman "VI," and the number MIVIIXCLM is just as meaningless as the letter "E" in the graph with the implausible zero point. Basquiat breaks open the matrix and creates a grid of banal signs, devoid of meaning, that seeks to challenge our economic system instead of affirming it. Thus, his inimitable line, combat-ready and wielded with razor sharpness, a line that is both damaged and damaging, also becomes the existential divide between powerlessness and self-empowerment, between human existence and the insistent, stifling forces of everyday and institutional racism, of oppression, violence, and death—experiences that Basquiat personally had to contend with. The journalist Glenn O'Brien bears witness to this: "Once, the car I was driving, with Jean-Michel as a passenger, was stopped by the police, and we had legitimate reasons to worry about being searched. I said, 'They can't search us legally. They don't have probable cause.' To which Jean replied, 'They can do anything they want.'"[3]

DIETER BUCHHART

Untitled (Woman with Roman Torso [Venus])

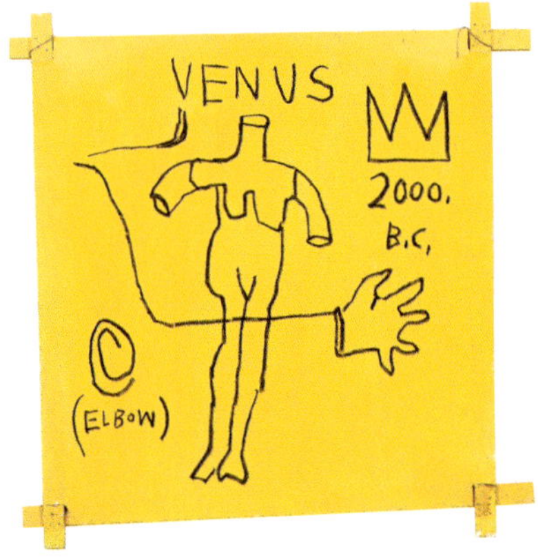

Untitled (Venus 2000 B.C.), 1982, acrylic and oil stick on canvas on tied wood supports, 153 × 150.5 cm, private collection

A standing nude figure, with bare breasts and without either head or arms, is a motif that repeats across several canvases that Jean-Michel Basquiat produced in 1982. In *Untitled (Woman with Roman Torso [Venus])* it appears on the right side of the composition, rendered in black acrylic paint on a yellow ground. The figure also comes into view as the central element on the spare yellow ground of his painting *Untitled (Venus 2000 B.C.)* **(fig. 1)**. This time, however, it is rendered more simply in oil stick, without the striations modeling the torso and abdomen or the shading that we find in the Modena painting. Variations of this motif also abound in other works, such as the Xerox and acrylic collage *Venus*, in which Basquiat has modified the figure to give us only a partial view of it. In all, we can identify some version of this figure in eight of the artist's works from 1982 alone. The subtitle "Woman with Roman Torso (Venus)" given to this originally untitled work suggests a connection between this painting, which Basquiat completed while in residence in Modena, and others that depict the figure with the label "Venus."

Like Basquiat's obsession with Leonardo da Vinci's *Mona Lisa* (ca. 1503-06) or Édouard Manet's *Olympia* (1863)—two other famous female figures in the history of art—his inclusion of Venus in several compositions does not preclude his interrogation of the motif. In other words, although this Venus may be a figure that bears a resemblance to other iterations of the motif in the artist's oeuvre, in this instance it reveals a unique juxtaposition of the artist's personal life and his attempts to establish his own legacy.

Classical art, particularly sculpture, was certainly a recurring subject for the artist, who encountered such works in museums, via songs by mid-twentieth century musicians (e.g., Nat King Cole's "Mona Lisa," of 1950, or Miles Davis's "Venus de Milo," from 1957), and in the many textbooks and art catalogues in his personal library. In fact, the combination of this assigned name and the figure's appearance—bare torso, amputated arms—reminds us of the ancient Greek sculpture known as the *Venus de Milo* **(fig. 2)** attributed to Alexandros de Antioch, which depicts the Greek goddess of love and beauty Aphrodite, whose Roman counterpart was Venus.

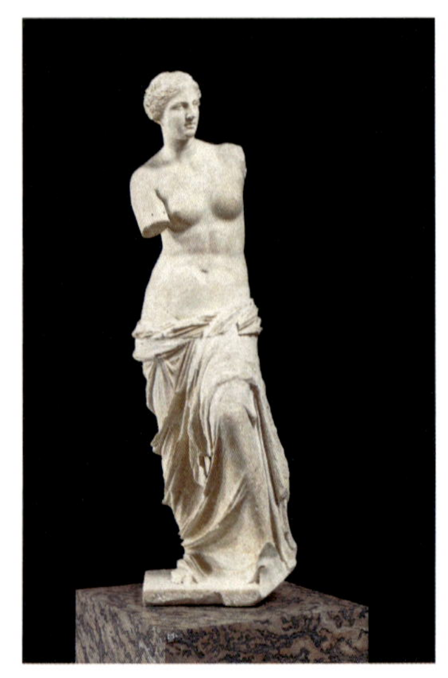

Statue of Aphrodite (known as *Venus de Milo*), 150-125 BCE, marble, height 204 cm, Musée du Louvre, Paris

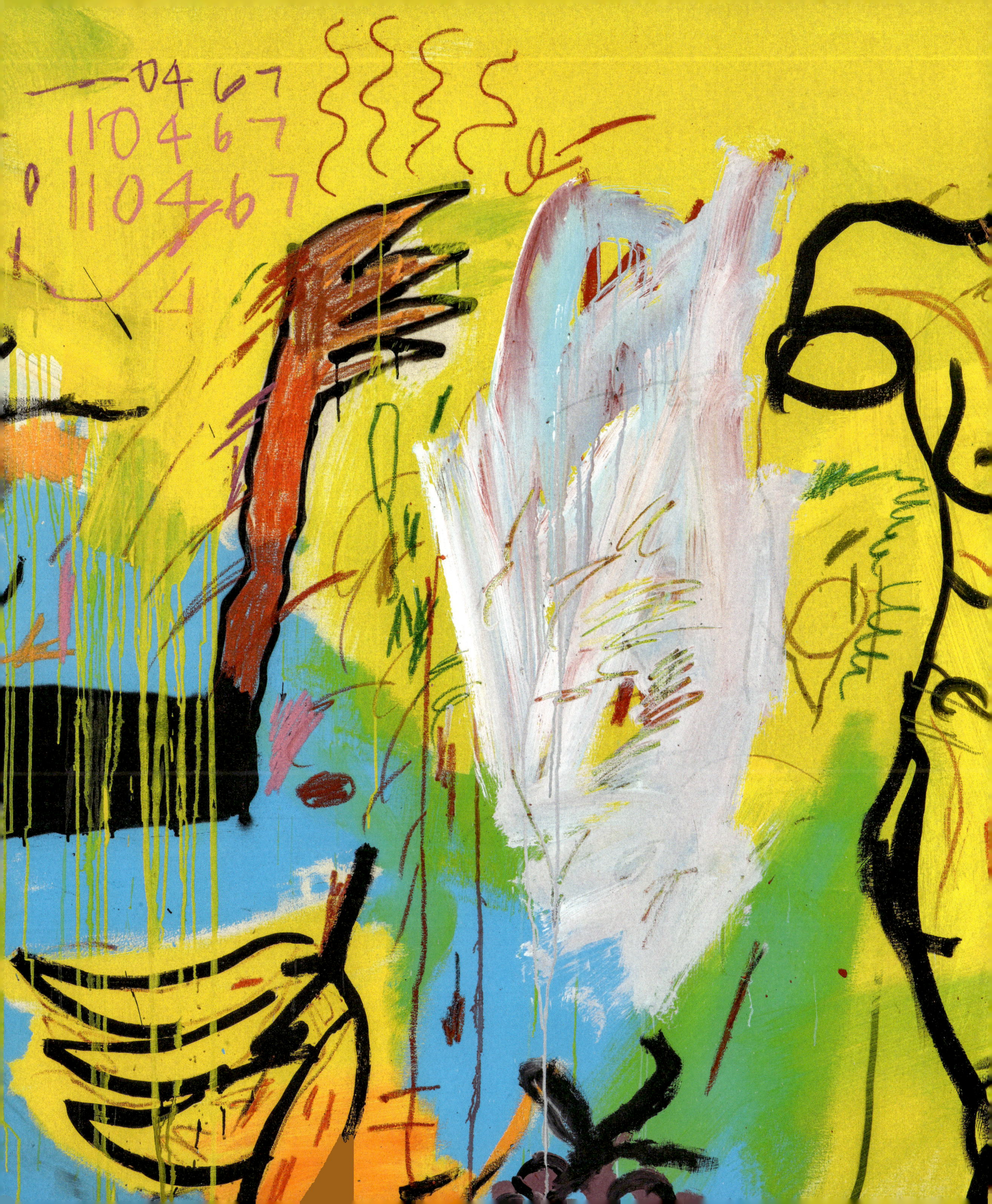

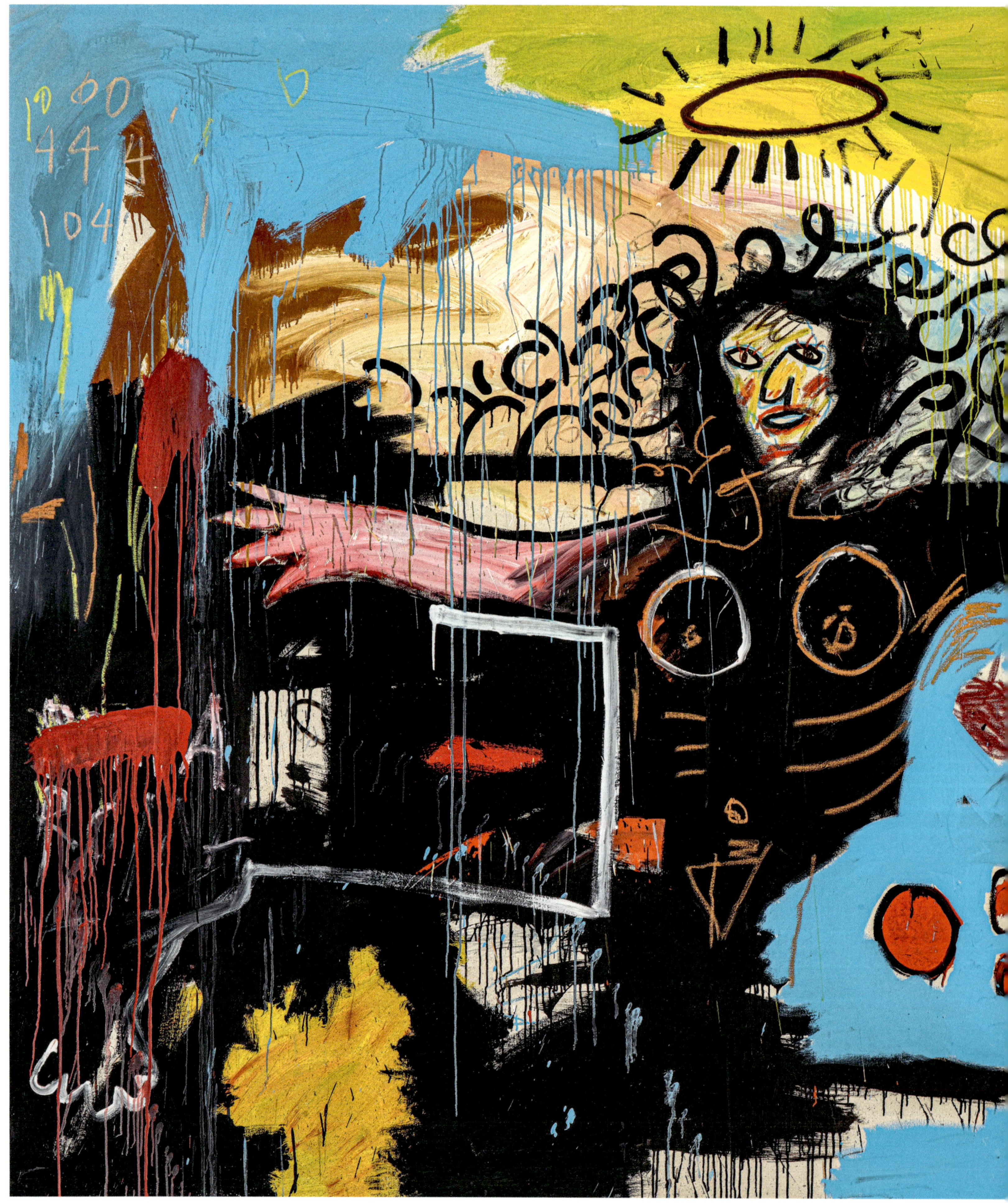

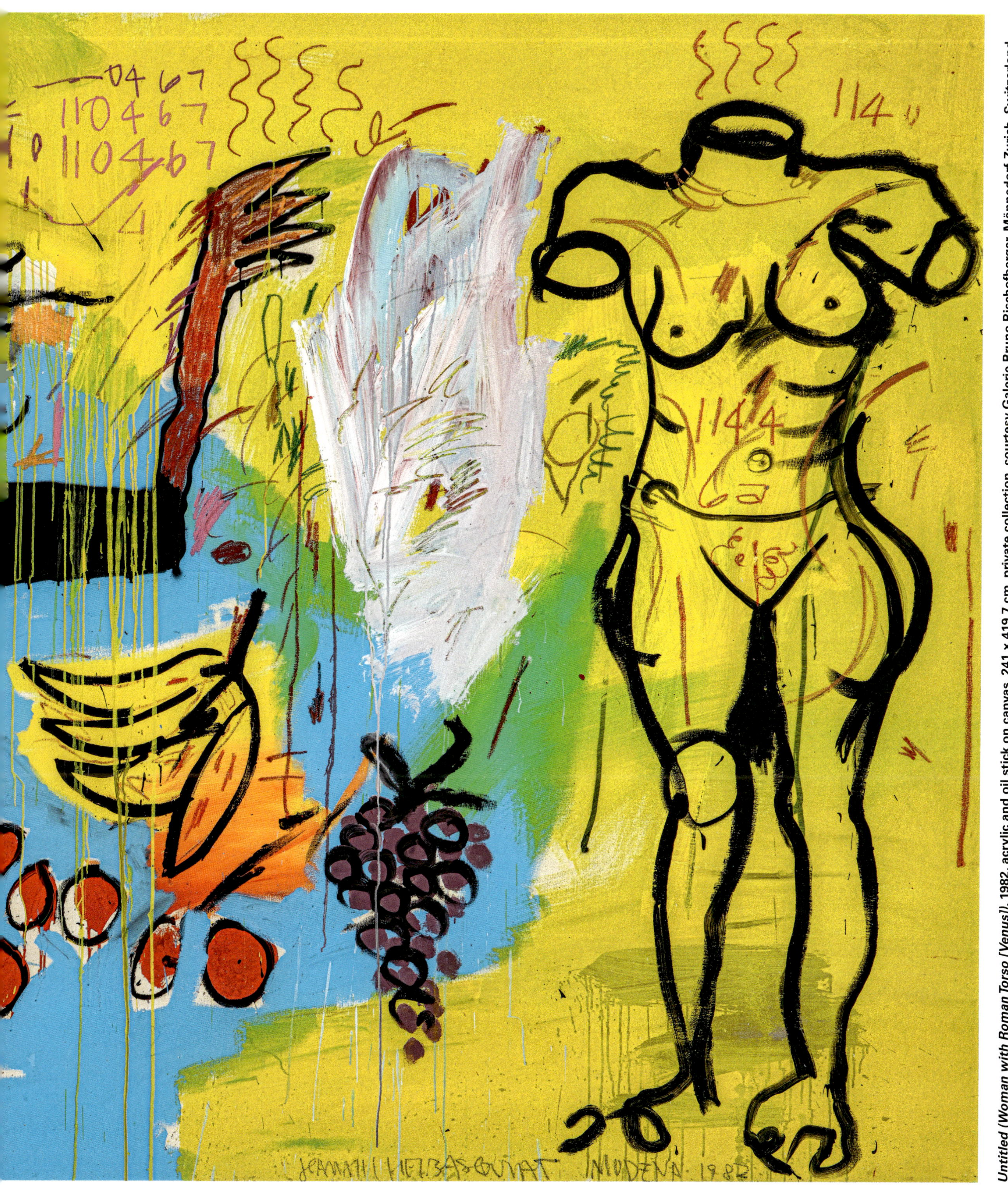

Untitled (Woman with Roman Torso [Venus]), 1982, acrylic and oil stick on canvas, 241 x 419.7 cm, private collection, courtesy Galerie Bruno Bischofberger, Männedorf-Zurich, Switzerland

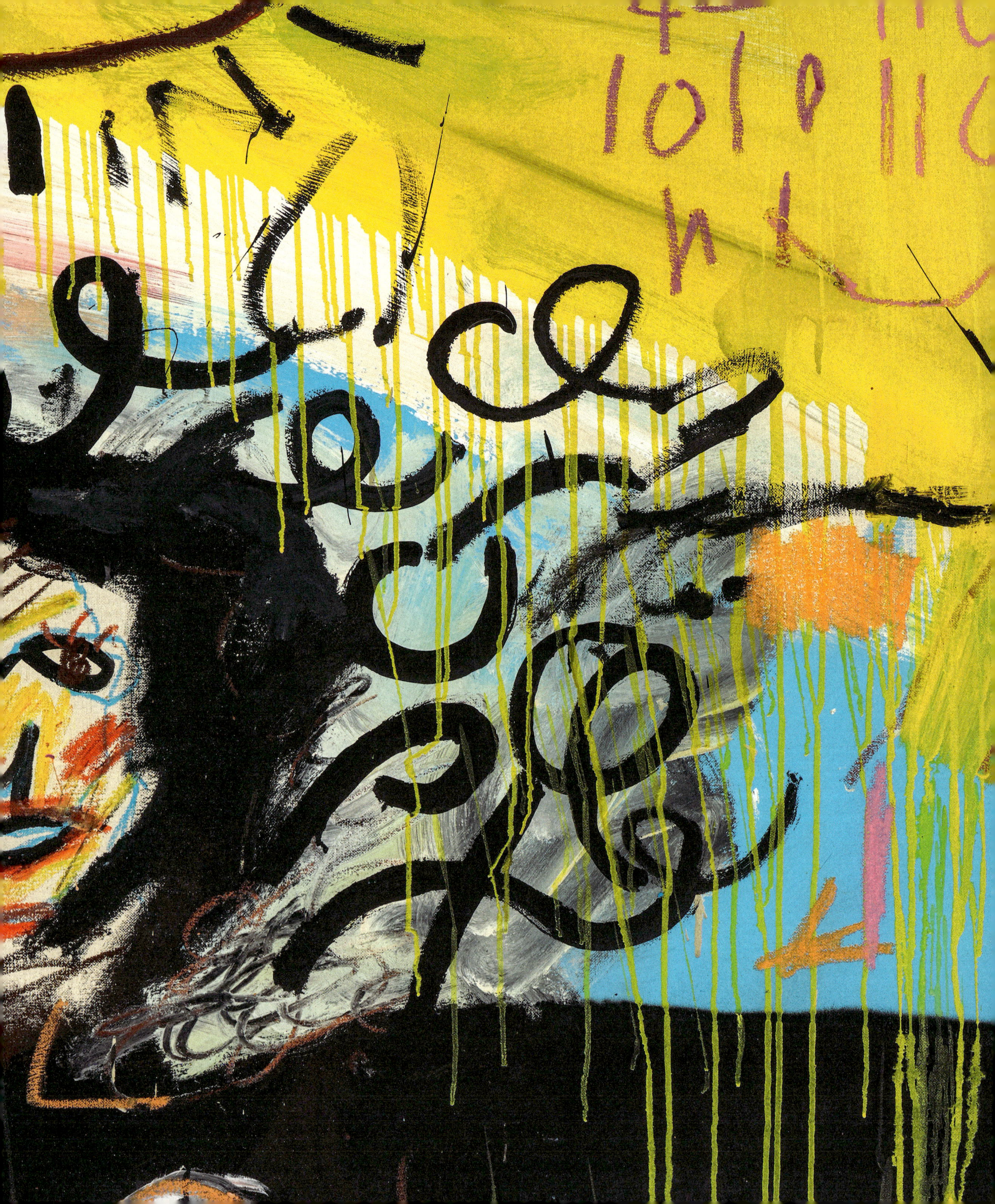

In a departure from the Greek example, we see that Basquiat's
Venus lacks a head and does not bear the drapery rendered in the
original sculpture, leaving her lower extremities exposed to the
viewer. This decapitation may signal a conflation of the *Venus
de Milo* with another, dynamic, Hellenistic sculpture housed in the
Louvre, *The Winged Victory of Samothrace* (200-175 BCE), which
itself lacks a head. On the left of Basquiat's composition, we
see a female figure that evokes yet another character from Greek
mythology. All around its head, the artist has included a mass of
curled, black lines reminiscent of the hair of Medusa, rendered in
the form of snakes. While we might first think of Medusa in her
monstrous form, some more recent reclamations of the myth by
feminist scholars affirm her status as a great beauty. It was only
after Medusa's affairs with Neptune that her hair was transformed
into snakes. We must also consider the power of the juxtaposition
at play here—that is, a classically White Venus versus a Black
Medusa. By combining references to famous works of art, Basquiat
can signal both his admiration for and awareness of a Eurocentric
history of art as well as its entanglement with ideas of race. This
is particularly important at this early stage of the artist's
career, considering Basquiat's status as a self-taught artist who
was forced to continually prove his knowledge to critics that cast
him as an ignorant naïf or street urchin suddenly launched to art
superstardom at the behest of an adoring all-White audience.
Considering the range of Basquiat's own sources, it is also quite
possible that the link between Medusa on the left of the composition and the headless figure on the right lies in the work of the
psychoanalyst Sigmund Freud. In his short text "Das Medusenhaupt"
(Medusa's Head), written in 1922, Freud argues for a connection
between "the terror of Medusa" and "the fear of castration"—that
is, decapitation equals castration.[1]

But there is a deeply personal element to Basquiat's Venus
figure as well. During the time he was in Modena, Basquiat was
accompanied by his friend Kai Eric as well as his girlfriend
Suzanne Mallouk. According to Mallouk, Jean-Michel began calling
her "Venus" from their very first encounter. As reported in
Jennifer Clement's memoir *Widow Basquiat*: "Jean-Michel comes
into the bar every day. He reads Suzanne his poems from his 'Black
and White Notebooks.' He calls her 'Venus.'"[2] Basquiat's nickname
for Mallouk adds yet another, more intimate, layer of meaning to
the work.

When we see the nude figure drawn in outline—with neither
arms nor head—we think not only of Basquiat's citation of classical
art examples or his emphatic declaration of his place as a serious
artist. These works also evoke the personal experience of Basquiat,
and perhaps even his attempt to introduce Mallouk into that pantheon
of legendary women.

JORDANA MOORE SAGGESE

1) Sigmund Freud,
"Medusa's Head
(1940 [1922]),"
in *Freud on Women:
A Reader*, ed.
and with an
introduction by
Elisabeth Young-
Bruehl (New York
and London, 1992),
pp. 272-73, here
p. 272.

2) Jennifer
Clement, *Widow
Basquiat: A Love
Story* (Edinburgh,
2000; 1st American
ed. New York,
2014), p. 29.

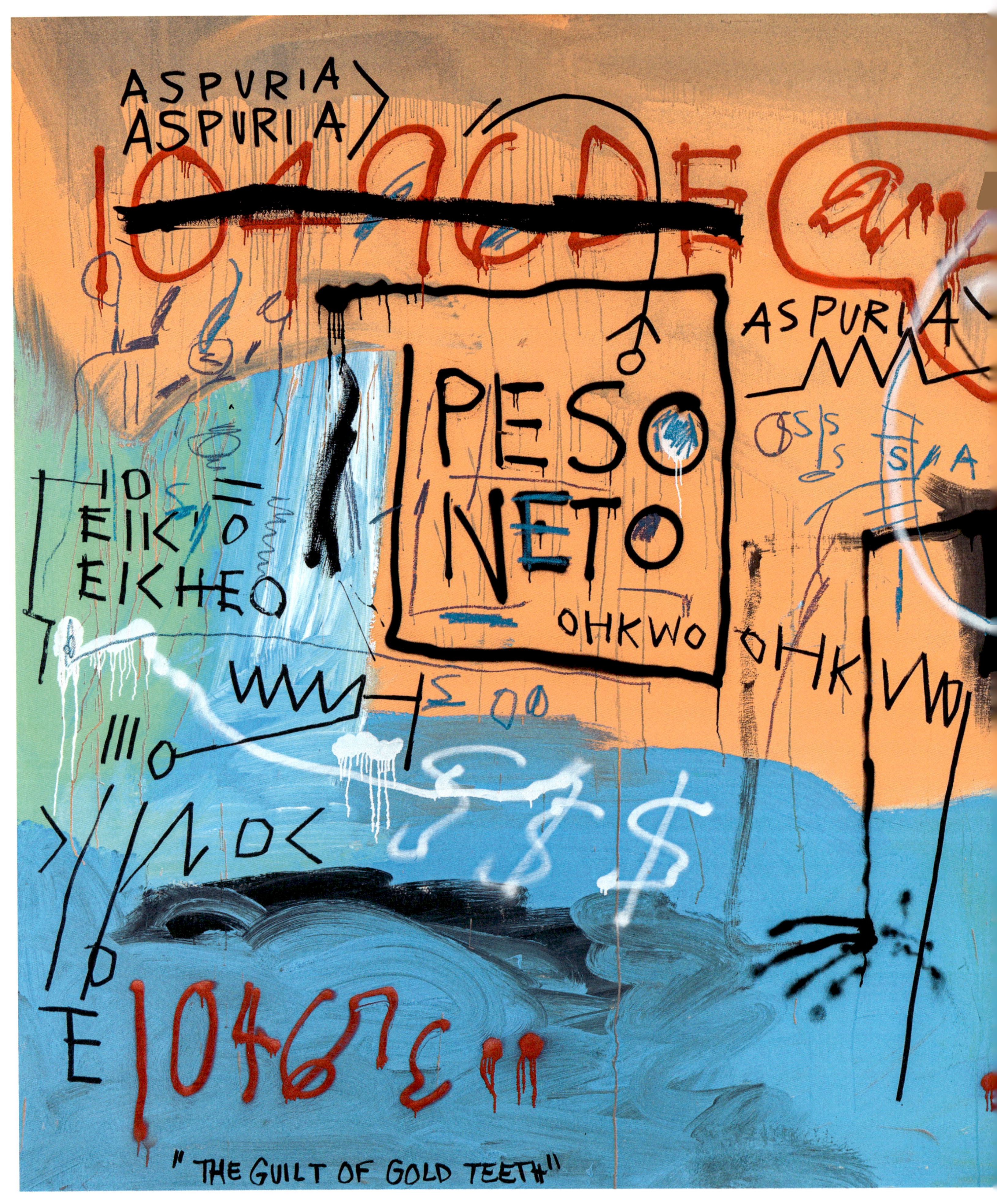

ASPURIA
ASPURIA
ASPURIA
PESO
NETO
OHKWO
OHK
EICHO
"THE GUILT OF GOLD TEETH"

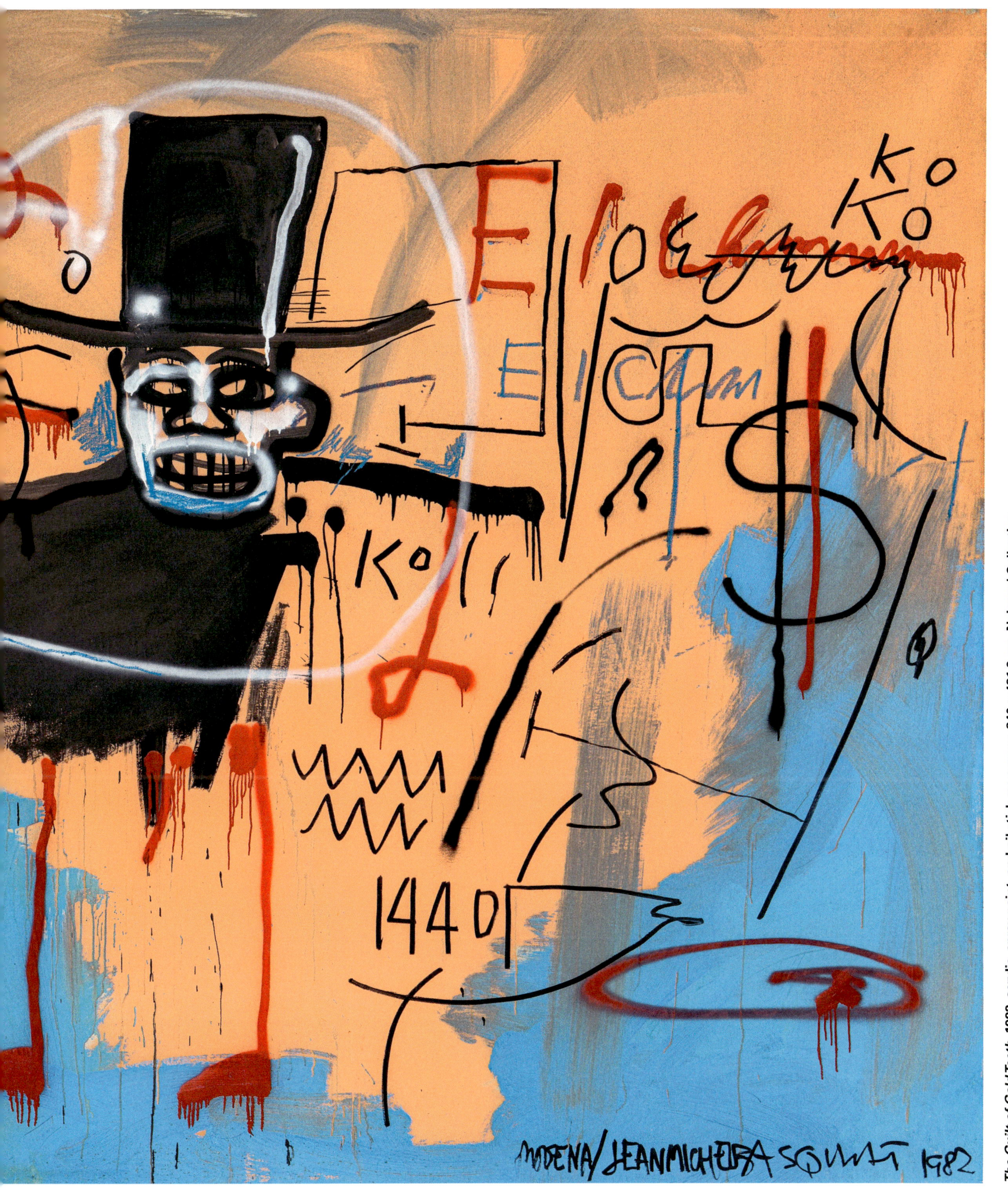

The Guilt of Gold Teeth, 1982, acrylic, spray paint, and oil stick on canvas, 240 x 421.3 cm, Nahmad Collection

The Guilt of Gold Teeth

A brightly colored and dynamic work, Jean-Michel Basquiat's 1982 painting *The Guilt of Gold Teeth* is distinguished by the dominant male figure near the center of the composition extending vertically across its surface on an over-life-size scale. The skeletal appearance of the figure's arms, hands, and legs are matched by the bright white skull that appears under a black stovepipe hat. With gnashed teeth and arms outstretched, the figure gazes directly out at us. A black cape drapes over his shoulders, while the lower half of the figure's body remains unclothed. Here, we see not just a generic figure, but a manifestation of the Vodou loa, or spirit, Baron Samedi, also known as Bawon Samedi in the West African context or Papa Gede in the Americas.

Vodou emerged from the syncretion, or strategic blending, of the West African religious practice of *Vodoun* with Catholicism. Although known by the more sensationalized and derogatory term "voodoo" in the United States, and often confused with mythologies of zombies and voodoo dolls, the practice of Vodou is instead a method of honoring ancestors. Vodou practitioners speak of "serving the spirits" and invoke the loa—intermediary figures between God and man—for protection, healing, and guidance. A loa of the dead, Baron Samedi is a guardian of the past, history, and heritage.

While much has been written about the work of Jean-Michel Basquiat, and particularly his use of skulls and black figures, the clear fascination he had with the history, politics, and culture of Haiti—the birthplace of his father, Gerard Basquiat—remains an under-explored element of his artistic practice. We find references throughout Basquiat's oeuvre to the history of the island via depictions of figures like the revolutionary hero François-Dominique Toussaint Louverture (1743-1803) **(fig. 1)** and the ruthless

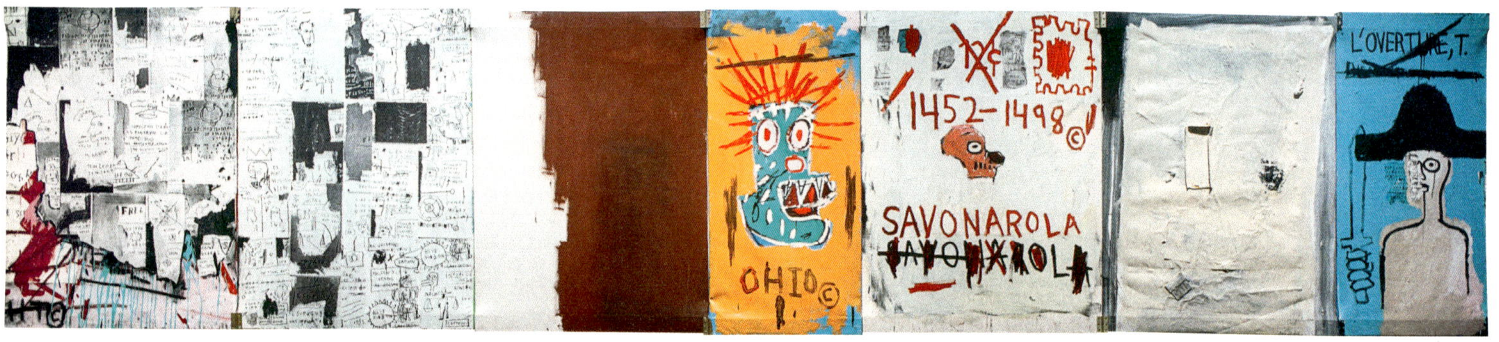

dictator François Duvalier (1907-1971), who served as the country's president from 1957 until his death. In *The Guilt of Gold Teeth*, Basquiat demonstrates his awareness of not only Haitian religion but its confluence with politics as well. We might, in fact, read the figure of Baron Samedi as simultaneously representing someone else. During his violent reign over Haiti, Duvalier declared himself a Vodou priest and adopted the dress (dark sunglasses, dark suits)

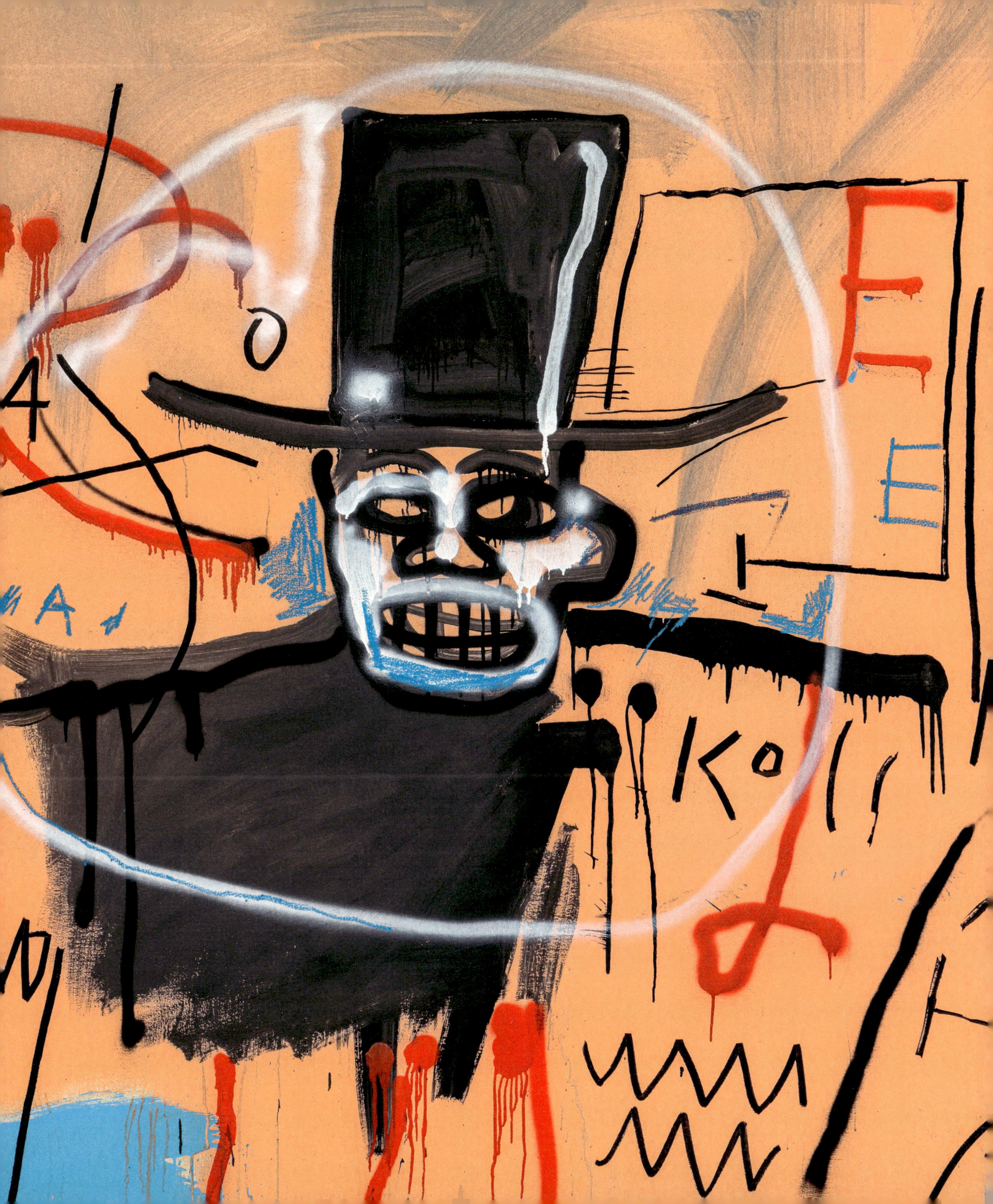

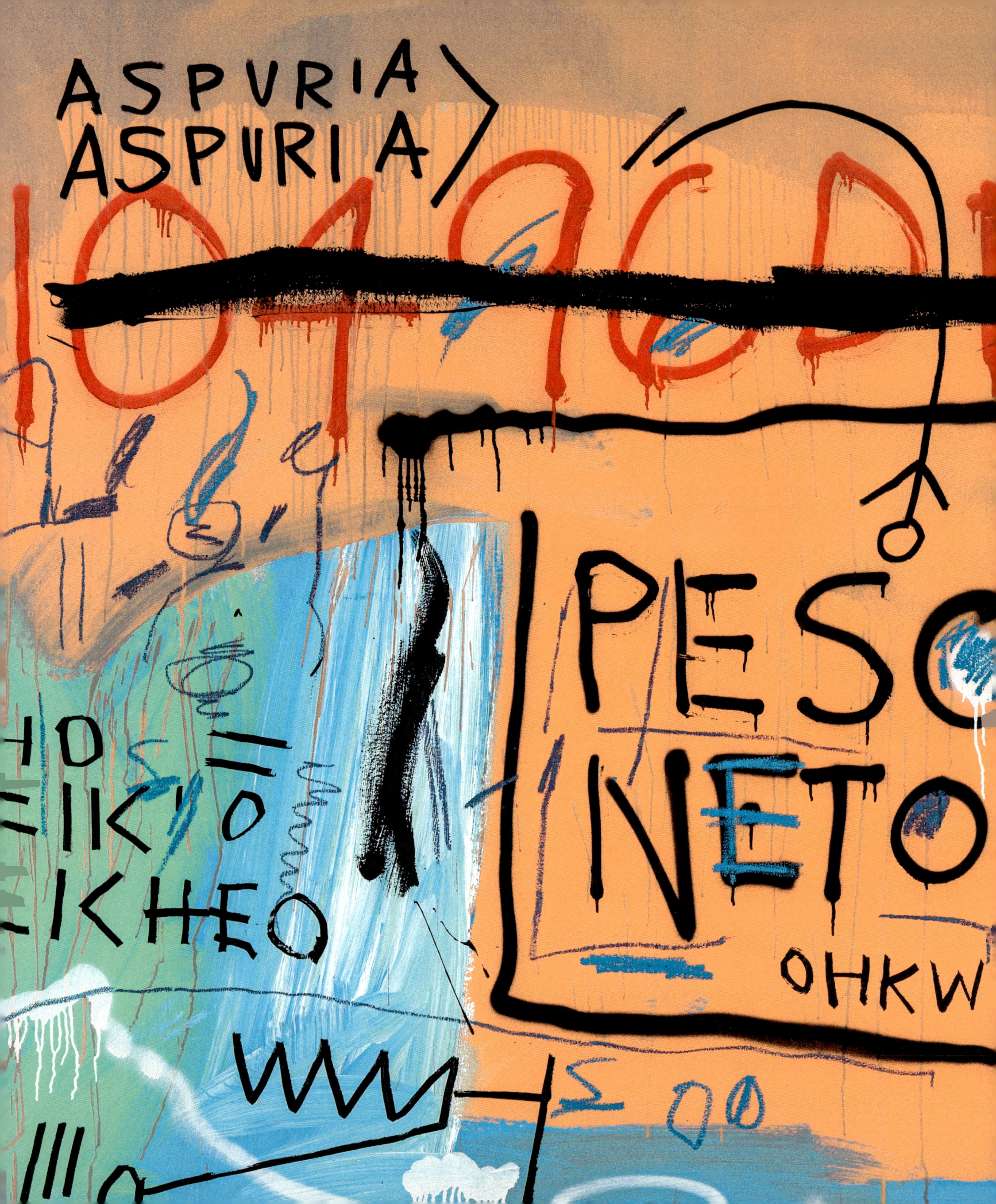

ASPURIA
ASPURIA
PESO
NETO
OHKW
ICHEO

and mannerisms (deep, gravelly voice) of Baron Samedi. In a conscious and dark entanglement of politics with religion, the evocation of Papa Gede led Duvalier to emerge a quasi-deity: Papa Doc—a conflation of his identification with Papa Gede and his profession as a physician. In *The Guilt of Gold Teeth*, this black-hatted figure calls to mind at once both Papa Doc and Papa Gede.

The ambiguous nature of signification—in this case, the slippery relationship between an image and its meaning—extends to language as well. We can see scattered across the surface of this painting words, numbers, and phrases that the artist has written (in oil stick and in spray paint) over the colored ground, some of which have been crossed out in the artist's trademark style. With many of these words, Basquiat challenges the straight line we often assume between a word and its meaning. The "guilt" of the work's title, for example, demonstrates Basquiat's tendency to play with language. As we read, we are stuck between the noun "guilt" and its homophone—the adjective "gilt," meaning covered in gold.

Given that Basquiat was a child of a first-generation Puerto Rican American mother, we often detect elements of Spanish in the artist's paintings as well. One of the most readily recognizable of Basquiat's phrases, "peso neto"—a Spanish term that translates to "net weight"—appears, outlined in a black box, just to the left of the central figure. The juxtaposition of Spanish words and a Haitian figure places these two diasporas, Puerto Rico and Haiti, neighbors in the Caribbean Sea, in close visual proximity to one another. In other words, these two places are brought together not only through the artist's biography but through explicit references to their languages and cultures. These diasporic communities are connected via New York—the center of Basquiat's short life. As we look more closely at the background of the painting, we might notice that the peachy-orange color occupying the top two-thirds of the composition suggests a land mass (an island perhaps?), whose aquatic border in pale blue makes up the lower third of the painting. New York, like Haiti and Puerto Rico, is an island.[1]

In *The Guilt of Gold Teeth* we see Jean-Michel Basquiat's sophisticated manipulation of language alongside his masterful handling of paint. The point here is not to argue for one inter-pretation over another, but to recognize that in this painting the artist asks us to consider the complexity of meaning and of Blackness—an identity that connects people on a global scale and exceeds geographic, religious, political, chronological, or even linguistic boundaries.

JORDANA MOORE SAGGESE

1) The specificity of the colors here—orange, blue, and pale green—also call to mind the precise colors of the New York City subway map that was first developed in 1979, in response to pressure to replace the 1972 diagram-matic representation of New York with a geographical one. Cf. Alice Rawsthorn, "The Subway Map That Rattled New Yorkers," *The New York Times*, August 5, 2012, https://www.nytimes.com/2012/08/06/arts/design/the-subway-map-that-rattled-new-yorkers.html (accessed January 24, 2023).

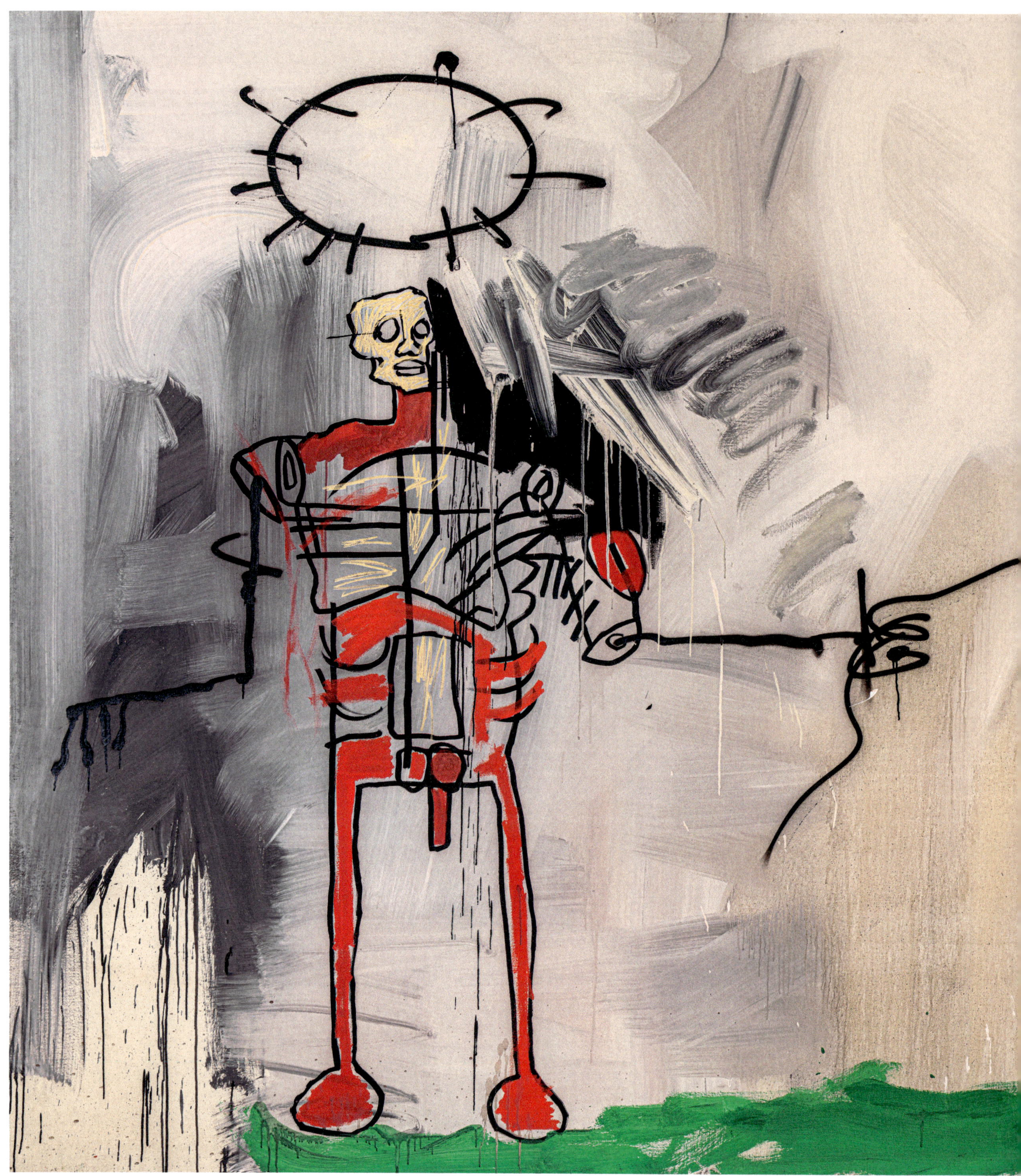

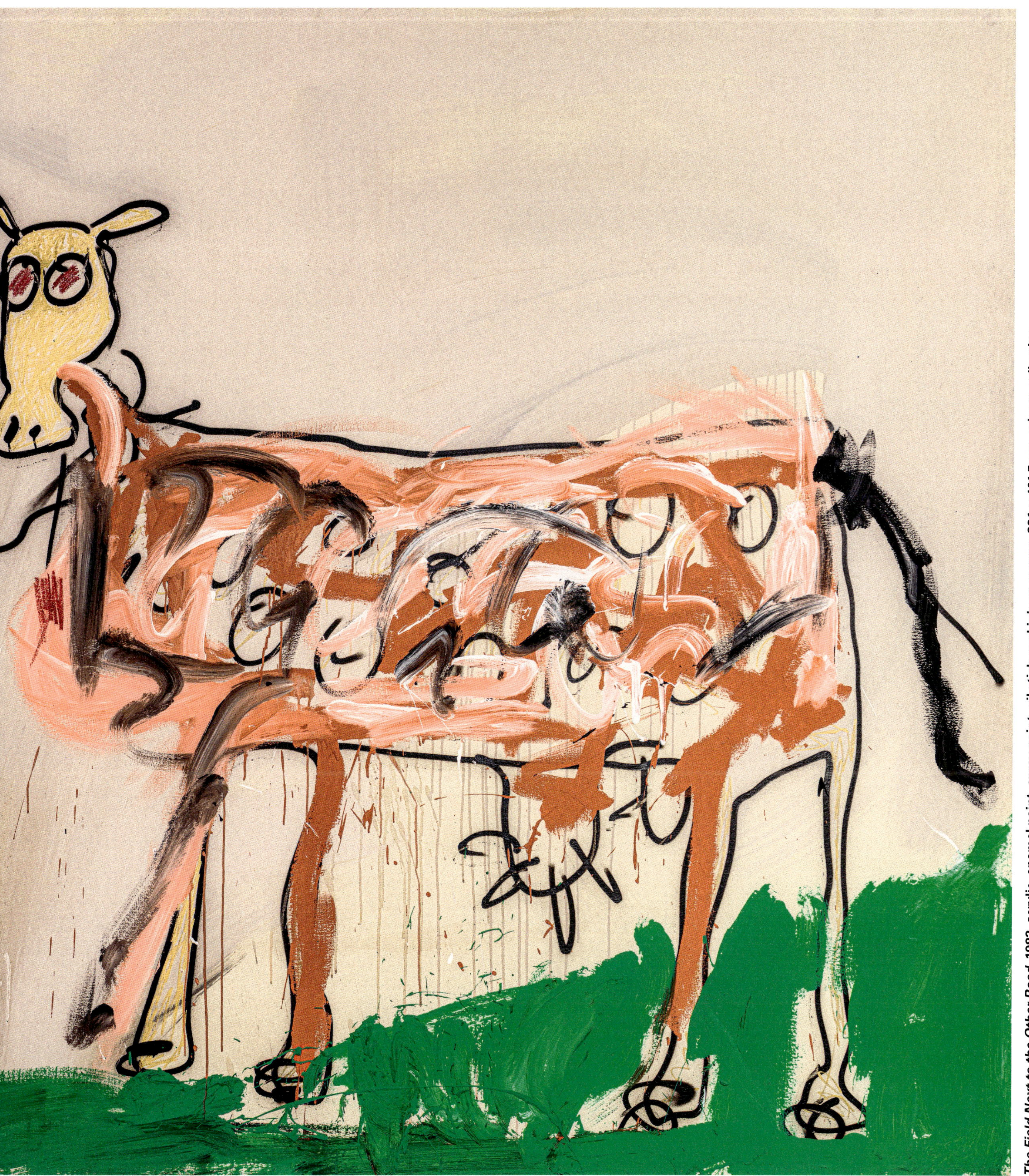

The Field Next to the Other Road, 1982, acrylic, enamel paint, spray paint, oil stick, and ink on canvas, 221 x 401.5 cm, private collection

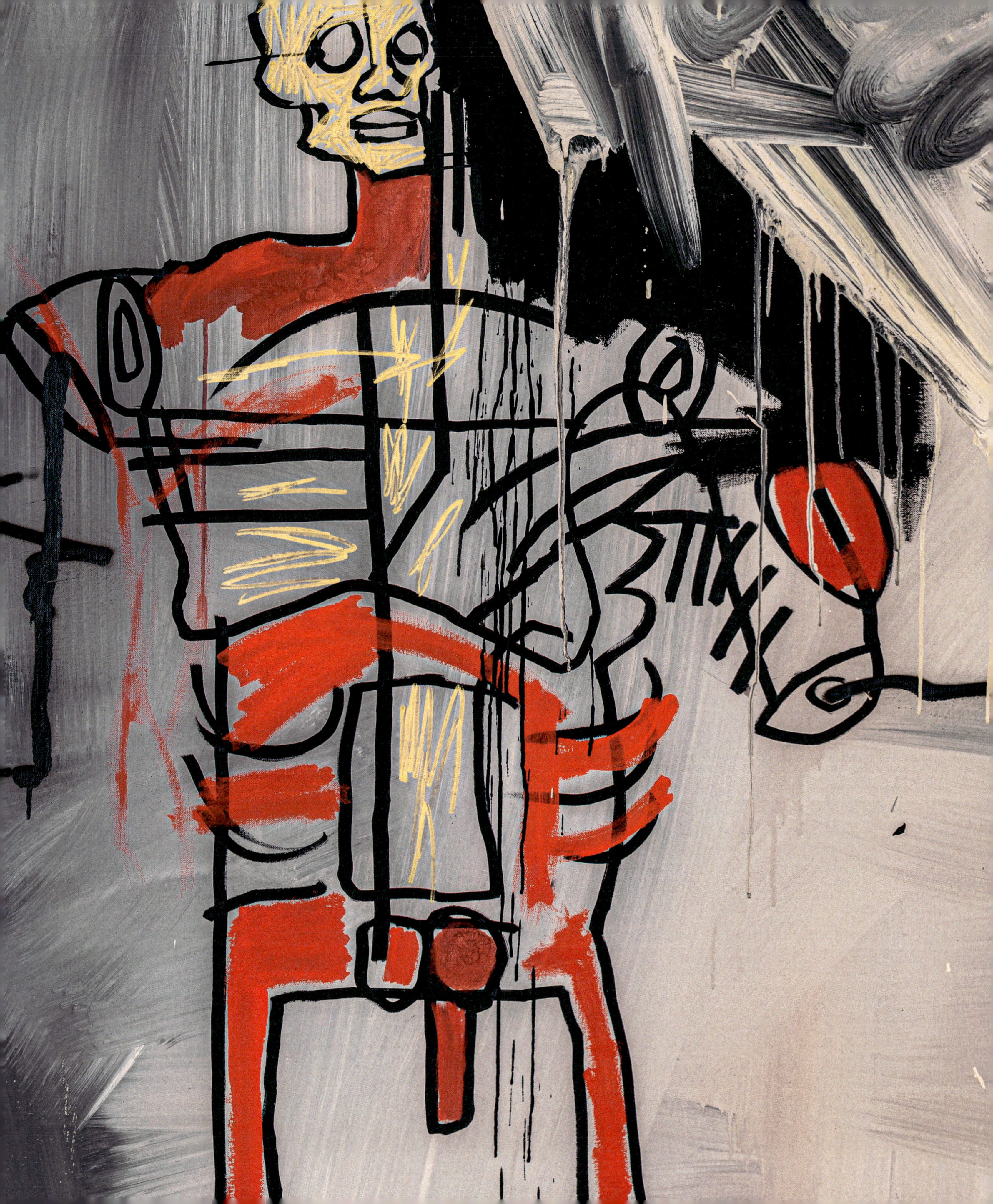

The Field Next to the Other Road

In *The Field Next to the Other Road*, a skeletal male figure, topped with a circular halo, is shown with a cow on a tether. Is the animal following the human figure or shrinking away from it? Who is leading whom? The depiction of the cow's legs, with the duplication of its limbs recalling the motion lines seen in comics, permits either conclusion: the animal could be either meekly submissive or stubbornly pulling back against the tether, grasped by the human figure, that prevents it from escaping. Jean-Michel Basquiat draws the silhouettes of the human and the cow with spray paint and acrylic before filling in the bodies, likewise with acrylic, roughly applied with accents of red, or brown and beige with gray. The sparse lines and reduced palette create an impression of hasty, impetuous execution. Apart from the triangular strip of green at the lower edge of the picture, which can be interpreted as a meadow, there is no spatial elaboration of the scene. Despite the dynamism of the composition, the motifs on the large canvas, roughly 400 centimeters wide and more than 200 centimeters high, appear to be effortlessly captured.

Basquiat painted *The Field Next to the Other Road* at a turning point in his spectacular career, when his work, already noted and admired by art institutions, began to command the attention of influential galleries. The painting seems to visualize this situation, on the verge of a breakthrough. Motifs from earlier works reappear but are accompanied by new features that will characterize the artist's future work. His raw, spontaneous style of painting would continue to evolve, with the emergence of the halo, as a recurrent motif—attributable to Basquiat's cultural, spiritual, and religious socialization—that subsequently assumes the shape of a crown as his career progresses. The skeleton, too, with the outstretched arms of the Messiah (*Untitled [Angel]*, 1982), or with the appearance of a boxer (*Untitled*, 1982, Museum Bojimans van Beuningen, Rotterdam), is a motif that runs through Basquiat's entire oeuvre. The skull and the cow establish associations with Pablo Picasso and Jean Dubuffet, artistic exemplars who made a lasting impression on Basquiat. One thinks, in particular, of Picasso's bulls' heads, with their huge gaping eye sockets, as

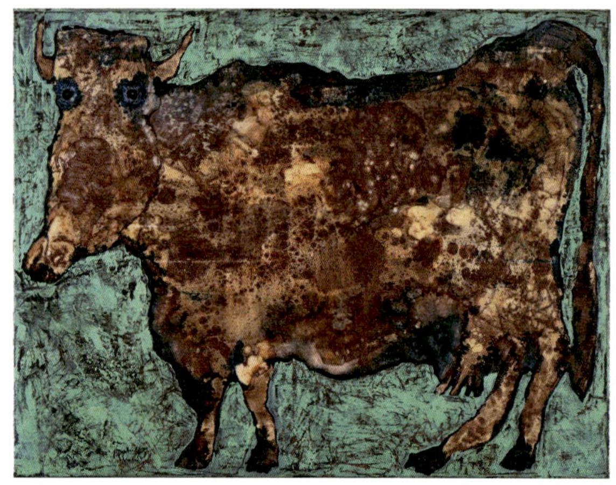

Jean Dubuffet,
*Vache au nez
subtil*, 1954,
oil and
enamel paint
on canvas,
88.9 × 116.1 cm,
The Museum of
Modern Art,
New York

in *Nature morte au crâne de taureau* (1939)
and *Tête de taureau sur une table* (1942),
or of Dubuffet's *Vache au nez subtil* **(fig. 1)**.

An important source of inspiration for
Basquiat was the medical reference work
Gray's Anatomy. His mother gave him a copy
of the book when he was recovering in the
hospital after being hit by a car at the
age of seven. The frequent depictions of
skeletons and skulls in his work are evidence
of his enduring fascination with the textbook
and its illustrations.

A striking feature of *The Field Next
to the Other Road* is that the picture
dispenses entirely with the mixture of
letters, words, and signs that is otherwise
so characteristic of Basquiat's work. The
emphasis, instead, is firmly on the painterly
gesture, as indicated by the outsize propor-
tions of the canvas and also by the approach to line and color.
The application of the spray paint is deliberate and targeted, in
lines that have a graphic quality, while the planes are dominated
by bold brushstrokes with acrylic paint. As in the Modena cycle
as a whole, Basquiat focuses on the search for a new formal
language, combining the lines of the hastily executed drawing
with painterly elaboration.

FIONA HESSE

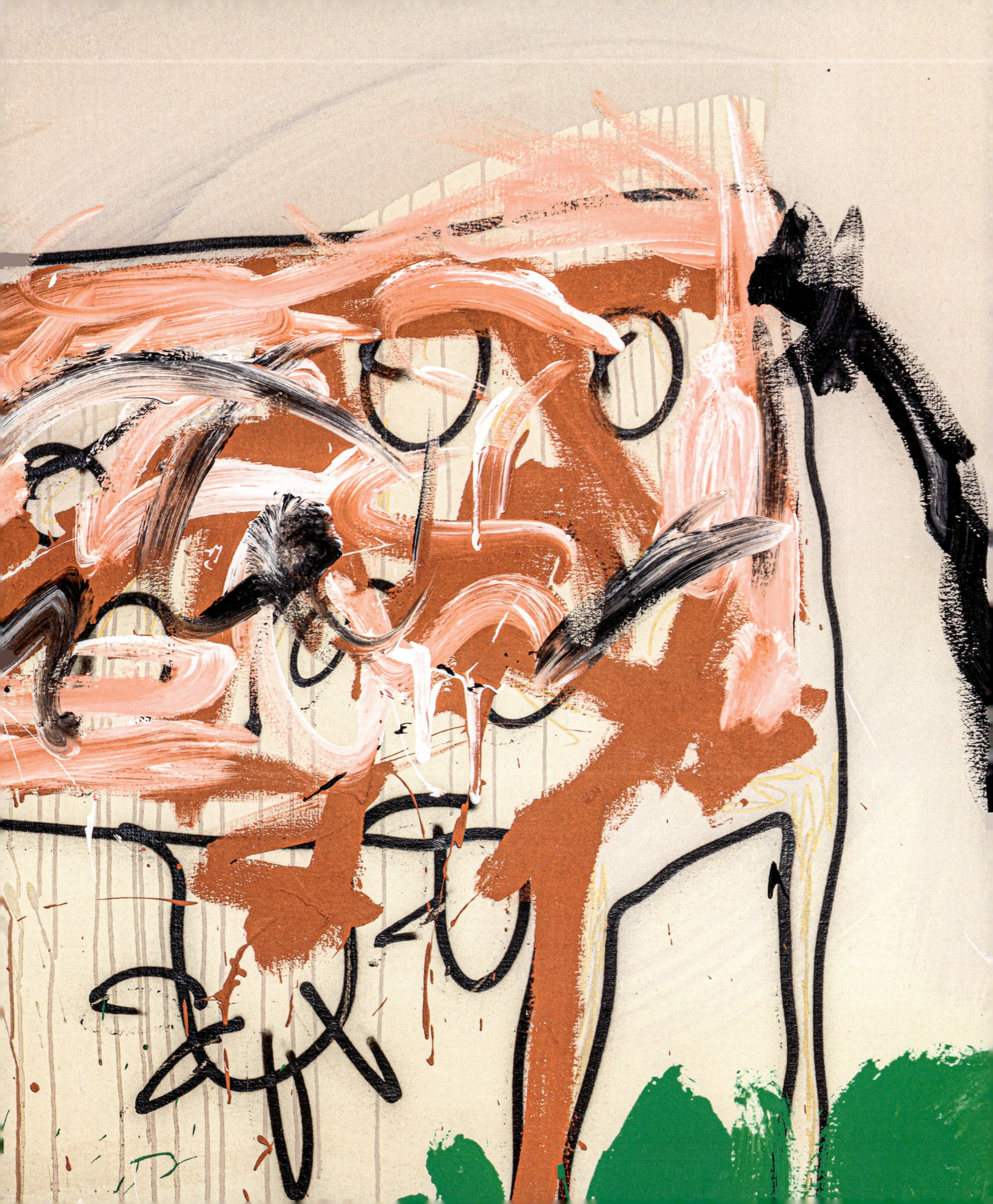

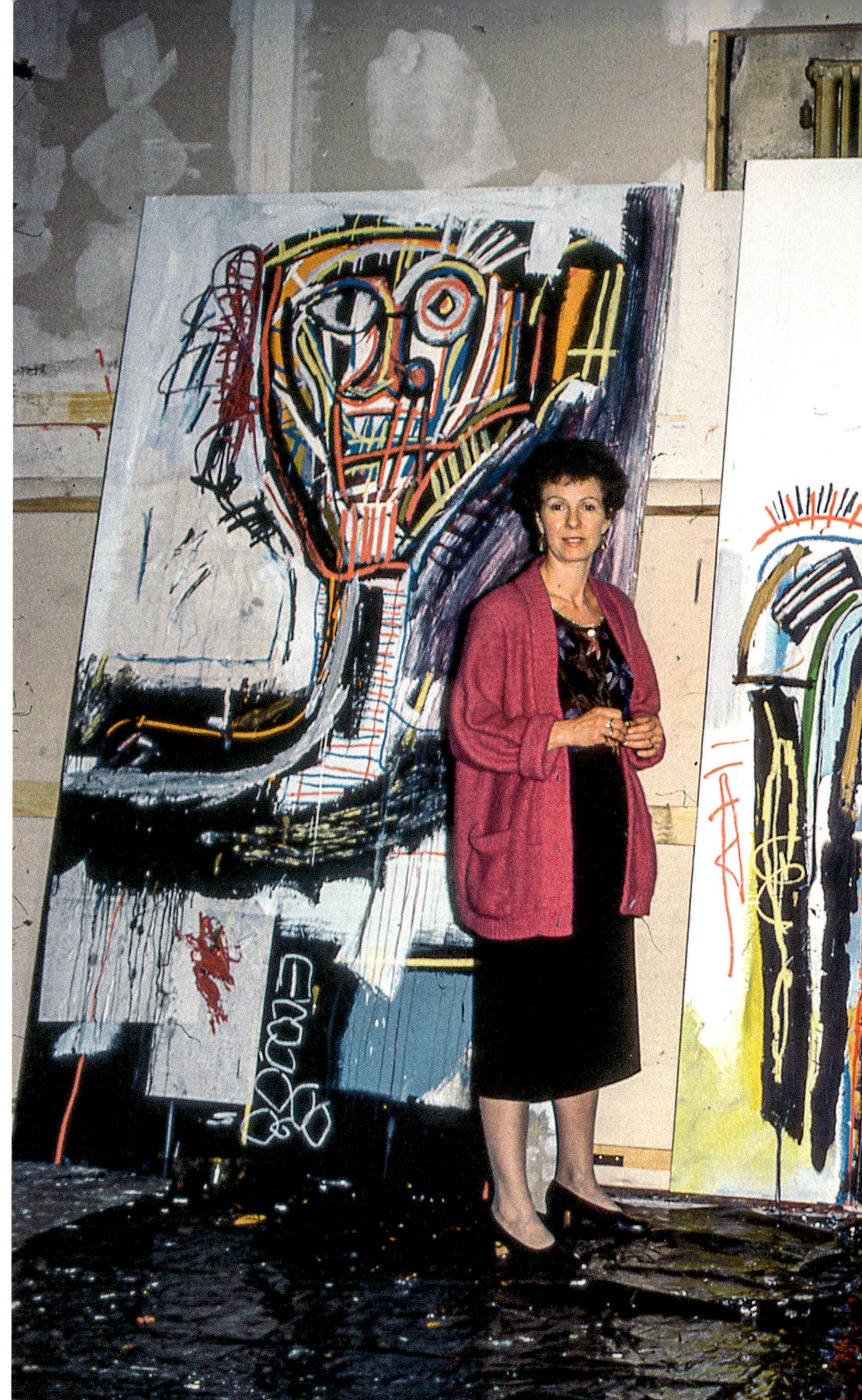

Annina Nosei and Jean-Michel Basquiat in front of paintings from the series *Prophets* in his studio at the Annina Nosei Gallery, New York, 1982, photographed by Naoki Okamoto

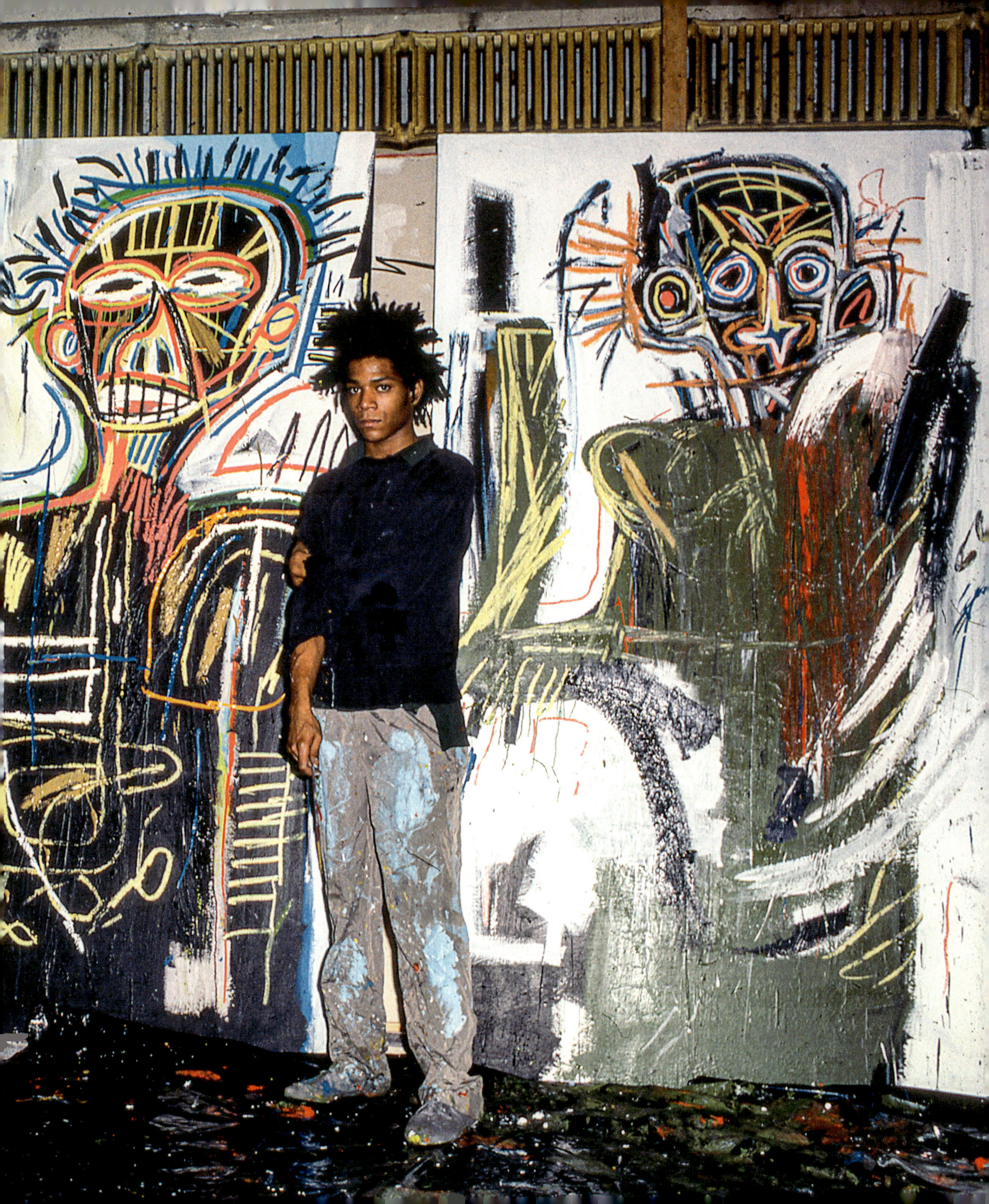

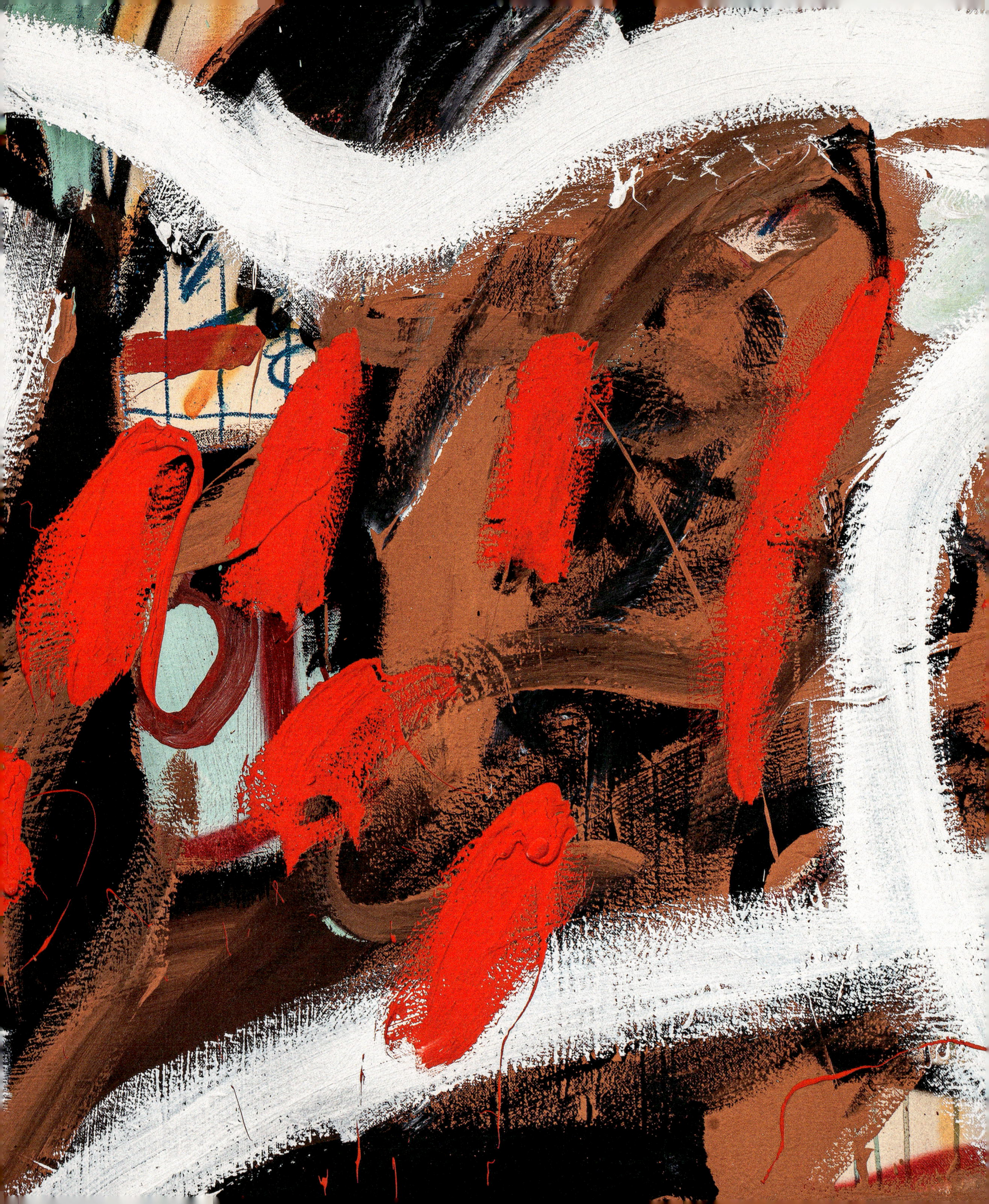

Basquiat, Cy Twombly, and the Transavanguardia

In May 1981 Jean-Michel Basquiat, then twenty years old, had his first solo exhibition at the Galleria d'Arte Emilio Mazzoli in Modena. Just over a year later, in June 1982, the New York artist returned to Modena to produce paintings on-site for a second—planned but never mounted—solo exhibition at the Mazzoli gallery. At the time, the new tendency in Italian art known as Transavanguardia had gained a significant international reputation and the Mazzoli gallery was a leading address for those in Italy who welcomed the return to figurative art and the move away from Conceptual Art and Arte Povera.

For his first solo show in Modena, when Basquiat was still signing his works "SAMO©"—with the exception of several works on paper and probably four canvases he painted on-site—the artist selected pieces he had produced in New York.[1] For the show in early summer 1982, however, the gallery asked him to create all of the works to be shown in Modena in a nearby warehouse, half of which was set up as a restoration studio, the other half for artists. The restorer working there collaborated with the gallery, constructing supports or mounting works on paper onto canvas. Basquiat was provided with canvases—originally prepared for Mario Schifano but never used—that varied in width from 4 to 5 meters. Basquiat also found canvases in the studio that Schifano had completed shortly before his arrival.

In 1981 Basquiat had already painted works with his characteristic content and style, but he had never had to deal with canvases of the size proposed by the Mazzoli gallery. Although he was accustomed to working on the sides of buildings, tackling such a large empty canvas was quite another matter. In Modena, moreover, Basquiat had to paint in a space that lacked the "visual noise" of the streets of New

Demetrio Paparoni

York and was instead surrounded by unfamiliar works by other artists. Schifano's canvases, the same size as those he was about to start painting on, must have been an intrusive presence. While Basquiat was not unduly influenced by them, they were doubtless hard to ignore. This is suggested in *Profit I* **(cat. pp. 54–55)**, in which the image emerges from a black background that seems to echo Schifano's large canvas *Acquario* (1982). *Profit I*'s yellows and reds also seem to reflect the presence of *Acquario* in the studio. It is furthermore possible to see similarities between the thickly layered paint in Schifano's seven-meter-wide untitled landscape[2] and the use of impasto in Basquiat's *Untitled (Devil)* and *Boy and Dog in a Johnnypump* **(cat. pp. 30–31 and 48–49)**. Schifano's painting *Figura* **(fig. 1)** was likewise in the building. Here, too, we see similarities in Basquiat's brushstrokes in the graffiti-free backgrounds of *Untitled (Angel)* **(cat. pp. 38–39)** and *Boy and Dog in a Johnnypump*.

Born in 1934 in Khoms, Libya—then an Italian colony—Schifano moved to Rome while he was still young. From 1960 to 1962 he produced monochrome works influenced by Minimalism but later shifted toward Pop Art, using flat colors and incorporating writings and the logos of major American companies. The images he produced in the 1960s made him the most important representative of Italian Pop Art. In 1977-79 he then took up a more gestural style in his figurative works.

Mario Schifano, *Figura*, 1982, oil and enamel paint on canvas with painted wooden frame, 280 × 462 cm, courtesy Emilio Mazzoli

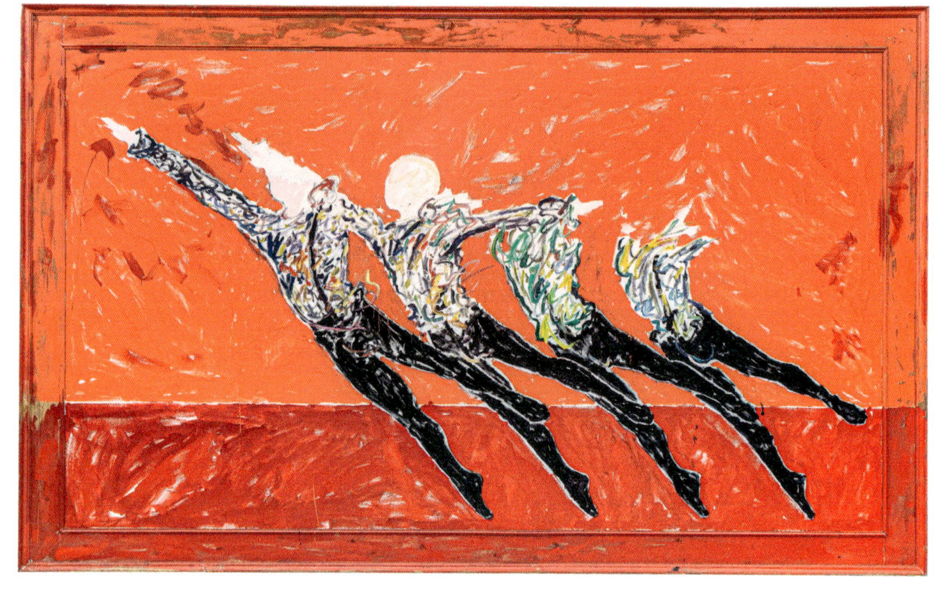

Incorporating techniques such as stencils and spray paint, these new paintings had much in common with street art.

In 1979 the Italian critic Achille Bonito Oliva coined the name "Transavanguardia italiana" to group together the work of Enzo Cucchi, Sandro Chia, Francesco Clemente, Nicola De Maria, and Mimmo Paladino.[3] These five artists, whose work was starting to gain international attention, saw themselves as an Italian version of postmodernism in the visual arts. In outlining the features of this new movement, Bonito Oliva cited the return to subjectivity, nomadism, and the influence of the genius loci as its fundamental elements.[4] These characteristics presuppose not so much the idea of going beyond the concept of the avant-garde as a tendency to situate oneself "at an oblique angle," indeed, at any subjective angle, to it. Nomadism is intended to describe an artist's interest in experimenting with different artistic styles, while with genius loci, Bonito Oliva was referring to an artist's impulse to establish their roots in their birthplace. By this he meant not only their circumscribed regional area but also their country—without necessarily excluding references to earlier twentieth-century European artistic avant-gardes. For his part, Clemente, who was interested in the art and culture of East and South Asia, particularly India, and found that his work did not fit in with the genius loci concept, distanced himself from the group almost immediately. He nevertheless agreed to participate in a number of exhibitions with the other four.

At the time, Basquiat had already encountered the Transavanguardia and was familiar with Clemente's and Chia's work—indeed, Chia was the person who had suggested that Emilio Mazzoli put on a solo exhibition of Basquiat's work.[5] Clemente and Chia had become familiar names in New York's artistic circles in 1980. Cucchi, too, was already known in the United States since, like Chia and

Clemente, his work had been shown at the Sperone West-
water gallery, beginning in 1980. It was also in 1980
that Paladino had two solo exhibitions in New York,
at the gallery of Basquiat's first art dealer, Annina
Nosei, and at the Marian Goodman Gallery. In 1984, two
years after his planned second exhibition at the Mazzoli
gallery, Basquiat was asked to name the contemporary
Italian artists he liked; he answered: Clemente and
Cucchi.[6] In fact, of these artists, the only one with
whom Basquiat had had a meaning-
ful friendship and intellectual
rapport was Clemente, whose
portrait he painted in 1985 **(fig. 2)**.
A couple years later, it was
Clemente's turn to make a
portrait of Basquiat **(fig. 3)**. When
Basquiat came to Modena for the
second time, the two men were
already good friends, whose
relationship led to a series of
collaborations, some of them
involving Andy Warhol.

While he was in Modena in
1982, though, Basquiat didn't
meet any other artists. The
only Italian presence with which
he could exchange ideas was
that represented by Schifano's
paintings stored in the warehouse
where he was working. Schifano
had already had exhibitions in
the Mazzoli gallery before the
advent of the Transavanguardia—
and Bonito Oliva was a friend of
his. Although, like Cucchi, Chia,
and Clemente, Schifano lived in
Rome, it was in Modena that he

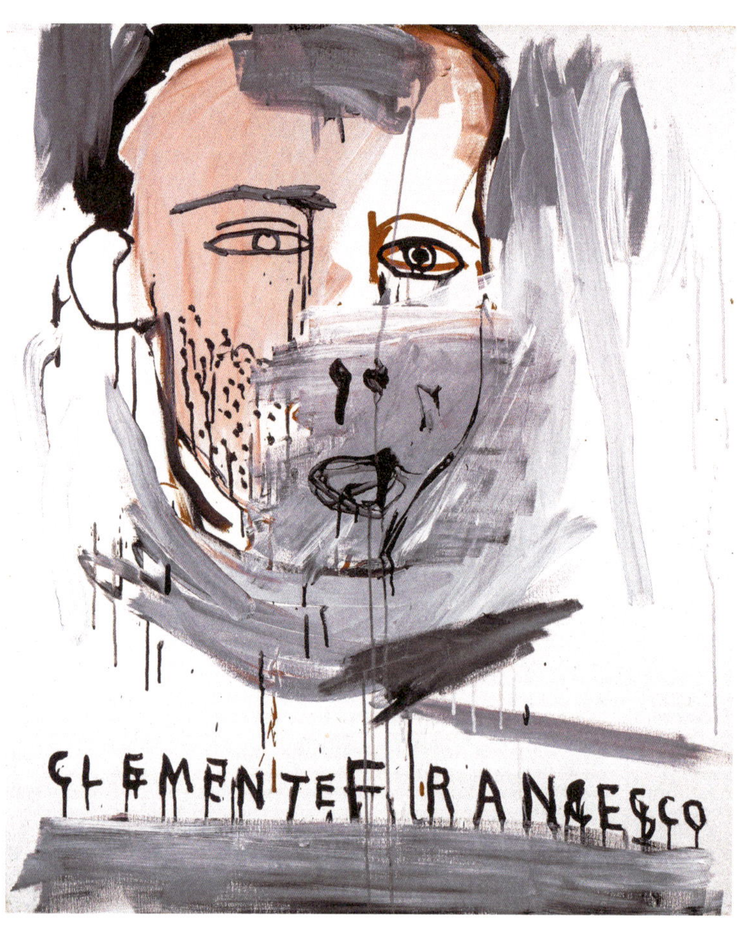

Fig. 2
*Francesco
Clemente*, 1985,
acrylic on
canvas,
106.5 × 91.5 cm,
collection
of Alba and
Francesco
Clemente

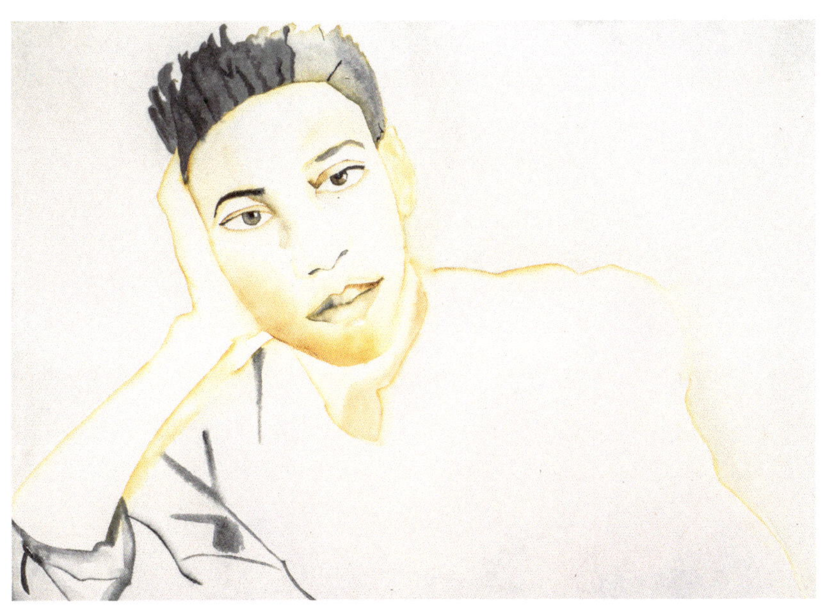

Fig. 3
Francesco Clemente, *Jean-Michel Basquiat*, 1982–87, watercolor on paper, 35.6 × 50.8 cm, collection of Alba and Francesco Clemente

had the opportunity to see the work of the five young artists exhibiting at the same gallery as him. The influence it had on him was significant enough to lead him, in the early 1980s, to produce a series of paintings of fish, horses, human figures, fruit, landscapes, and houses, characterized by the use of gestural brushstrokes. As a result of these new works, Schifano began to be regarded as one of the leading exponents of the return to figurative art.

In 1979 Clemente showed a series of sixteen drawings at the Mazzoli gallery titled *Proverbi* **(fig. 4)**, which feature a recurring image of a man simultaneously vomiting, urinating, and defecating under a banner presenting well-known proverbs turned into their opposite, such as "Two birds in the hand are worth one in the bush," "Half a loaf is worse than none," and "All that glitters is gold." In another drawing, he depicts a samurai cutting off his own head (*Untitled [Self-Decapitating Man]*, 1971, Kunstmuseum Basel). As in some of Clemente's earlier works, these present a combination of image and text that would, to a much greater extent, become a distinctive characteristic in Basquiat's work.

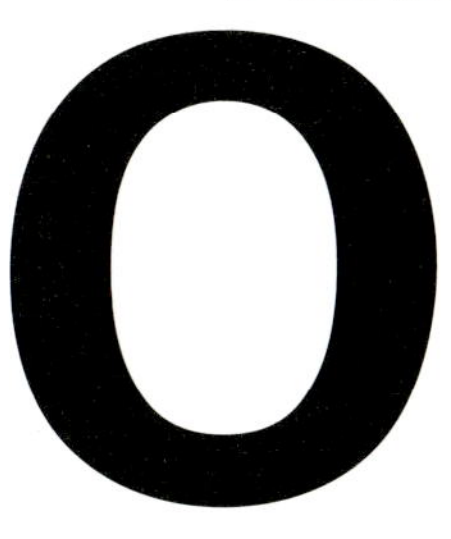Of the five artists of the Transavanguardia, it was Paladino who most strongly favored forms of archaism, handling them with control and elegance. What chiefly distinguished his work from Basquiat's was that Paladino rejected a symbolic and narrative interpretation of his paintings, whereas Basquiat, like Clemente, had no inhibitions about the achievements of modern

Francesco Clemente, *Proverbi*, 1976, India ink on paper, 16 pieces, 33 × 22 cm each, collection of Alba and Francesco Clemente

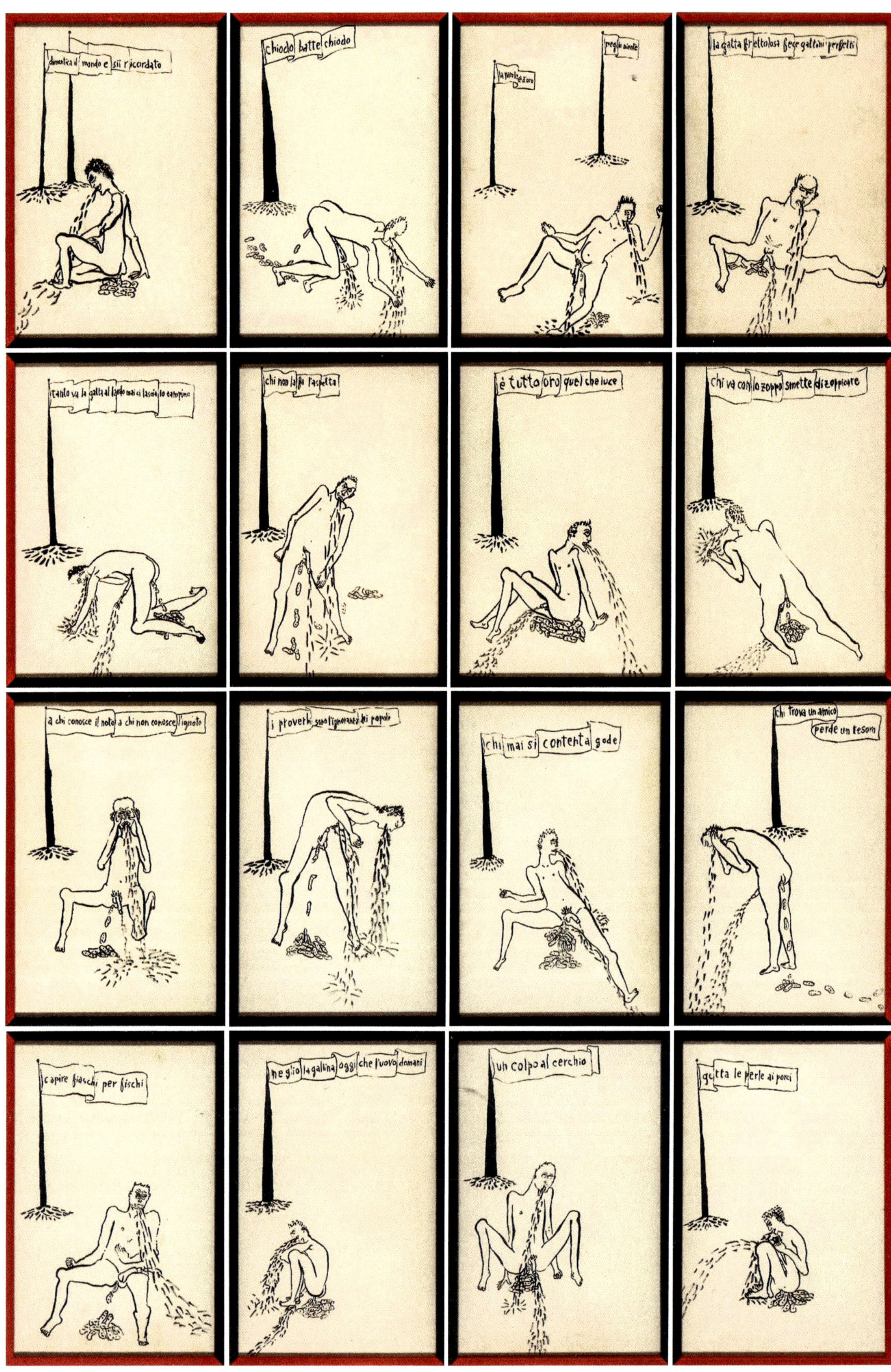

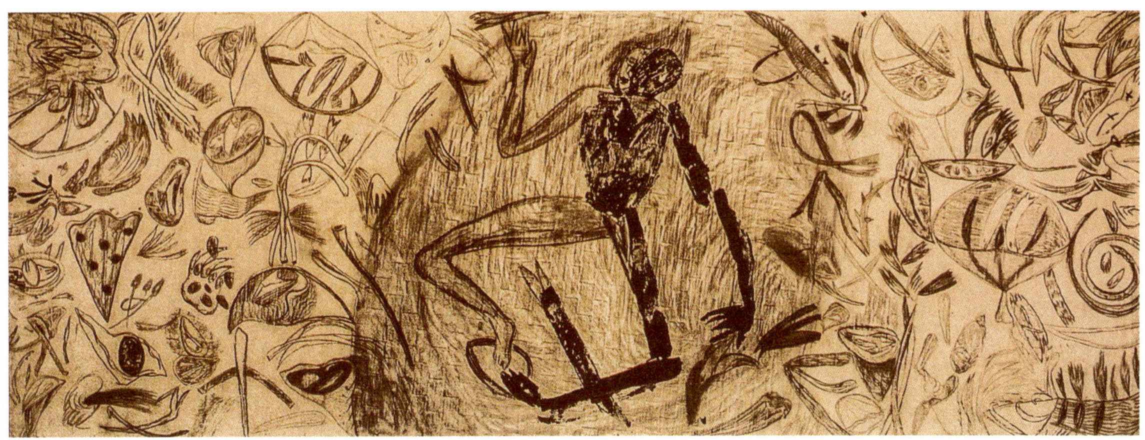

art and didn't hesitate to make use of syncretic
symbols and narrative. There is nothing in Paladino's
work of the period that recalls Basquiat's style and
constructive dynamism. Yet, the contemporary artistic
climate was clearly one in which painters with
dissimilar characteristics were moved to pursue a path
leading in the same direction. Some of Paladino's works,
such as *Con due dita* (1980) or *Re uccisi al decadere
della forza* **(fig. 5)**, however distant from Basquiat's, are
evidence of the degree to which the spirit of the times
resulted in interconnecting themes.

The works Basquiat produced in Modena in 1982
reveal the extent to which the artist's imagination was
stimulated by his surroundings. *Untitled (Woman with
Roman Torso [Venus])* **(cat. pp. 62–63)** draws on a multitude of
genres—from portraiture to still life and from the nude
to an anatomical study. Viewing the painting, we get the
impression that the artist wanted, as was his practice,
to record the visual experiences he encountered on his
sojourn in Italy. In addition to his stay in Rome, he
made excursions from Modena to Venice, Florence, and
Bologna, where he also visited museums. During these
trips, Basquiat made numerous drawings that suggest a
kind of visual travel diary. One of them shows his girlfriend Leslie Winer. She is depicted wearing glasses,
smoking, and reading in bed. On the lower left edge of
the image, Basquiat wrote "For Fred Flintstone" and
"Leslie ©" **(fig. 6)**. He drew a crown over Leslie's name
and, on the right, recorded the place and date: "Hotel
Inglettera [*sic*], Rome #138, 1982." Two other drawings,
False and *Bishop*, have the same format as the portrait

Fig. 5
Mimmo Paladino,
*Re uccisi al
decadere della
forza*, 1981,
oil, pastel, and
pencil on paper,
277 × 750 cm,
Terrae Motus
Collection,
Reggia di Caserta,
Caserta

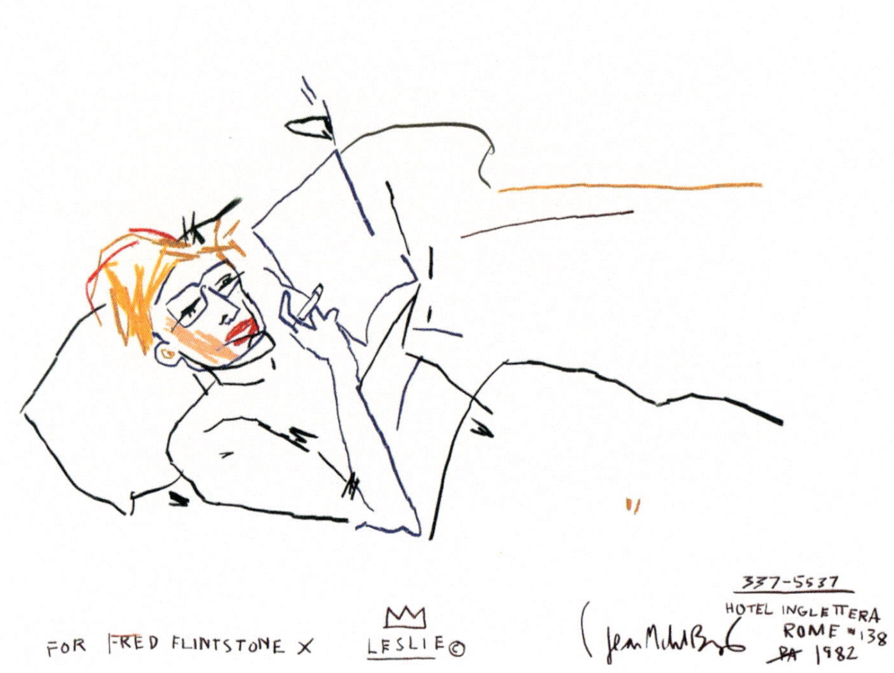

Leslie, 1982,
oil stick
on paper,
56 × 76 cm,
private
collection

of Leslie. The drawings are not signed or dated but nevertheless clearly products of the time the artist visited Rome in 1982. On these sheets, Basquiat sketched figures, names, and dates that reference ancient history and Greco-Roman and Christian culture, up to the barbarian invasions.

One of the drawings, titled *False* **(fig. 7)**, depicts the she-wolf suckling Romulus, the initials "SPQR" for "Senatus Populusque Romanus" associated with the Roman politician Brutus, and the words "Brutus as 1st consul." The sheet also contains sketches of classical sculptures depicting a bust of Pericles, a statue of Aphrodite, a column, an image of St. Paul, Alexander the Great on horseback, and a Greek soldier. Beneath a stylized figure with wide-open eyes and the title "barbarian invader" we see the words: "sees Rome for the first time." These and other images together with explanatory labels fill the surface with names—Plato, Homer, Socrates—and dates. Some of the dates correspond to important events, such as the destruction of Carthage in 146 BCE, while others don't seem to have any special meaning. At the top, next to the words "true" and "false," appear two little boxes, both containing an "X." Basquiat has drawn a line

"That [material in my pictures] was from going to Italy, and copying names out of tour books, and condensed histories."

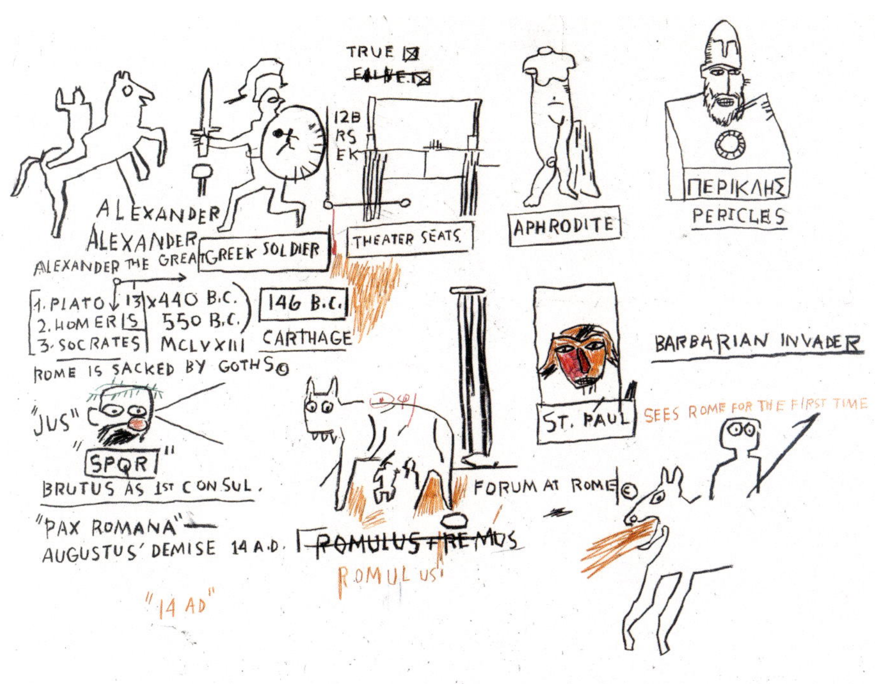

Fig. 7

False, 1982 (?), acrylic, oil stick, charcoal, graphite, and colored pencil on paper, 56 × 76.5 cm, private collection

through "false," not to cancel it out but, as the artist himself explained, to make it retreat to the background or, alternatively, as he said on other occasions, to draw attention to it.[7] By directing our attention to the word "false," Basquiat emphasizes the notion that the narrative that we call "history" is a mixture of truth and legend. The drawing *Bishop* refers to the history of the Holy Roman Empire, concentrating on the figure and events of Charlemagne, crowned emperor by Pope Leo III. The writing includes lettering in English and a Latin phrase from Catholic liturgy.

These drawings, like the subjects in *Untitled (Woman with Torso [Venus])*—the yellow figure's torso recalling a Greek statue alongside a half-figure with a yellow-and-white face and a black body and a halo reminiscent of the iconography of the Greek black-figure vases so often found in Italian museums—are a record of aspects of past art history that made an impression on Basquiat during his stay in Italy. He himself emphasized the attention he paid to the traces of ancient history still present in the country. When the curator and critic Henry Geldzahler asked him a year later what had prompted him to include the names of pre-Socratic philosophers in his works, Basquiat replied as if he attached no particular importance to his selection, saying: "That was from going to Italy, and copying names out of tour books, and condensed histories."[8] As always, Basquiat's work reflects his experiences in the moment, in the "here and now."

The presence of architectural details or pre-Christian classical sculptures in his work is not due to their aesthetic qualities but to the significance they had for him as signs of history. In rendering them on the canvas, Basquiat uses a childish comic-book drawing style. His attraction to Greco-Roman culture comes principally from ideas he took from the work of Cy Twombly, another artist who had chosen to make his home in Rome, in 1957. In the same 1983 conversation with Geldzahler, Basquiat remarked: "My favorite Twombly is *Apollo and the Artist*, with the big 'Apollo' written across it" **(fig. 8)**.[9] The sojourn in Rome in summer 1982 represented for Basquiat a way of entering into contact with the historic-poetic world evoked by Twombly when he wrote on his paintings the names of ancient gods, poets, philosophers, and Roman historians—such as Diana, Venus, Apollo, Lucullus, Virgil, and Horace—along with dates, text fragments, notes, sketches, and "scribbles." After arriving in Modena, Basquiat went on to include the Venus motif in his latest work. Later, back in New York, he would also discuss it with his friend Francesco Clemente and say that it was a reference to Twombly.[10]

In 1982, before Basquiat went to Modena to paint the large canvases for the intended second exhibition, two of his works painted for the previous solo show (*Untitled [Red Man]* and *Untitled*, both from 1981) were included in *Transavanguardia: Italia/America*, an exhibition curated by Achille Bonito Oliva **(figs. pp. 21 and 99)**. The show opened in March in a large hall at Modena's Galleria Civica, featuring, in addition to paintings by the Italian artists Cucchi, Chia, Clemente, De Maria, and Paladino, works by Basquiat, David Deutsch, David Salle, Julian Schnabel, and Robert Zakanitch. With the exception of the pieces by the

"My favorite Twombly is *Apollo and the Artist,* with the big 'Apollo' written across it."

latter three, lent by the Galerie Bruno Bischofberger in Zurich, all the others came from the Mazzoli gallery.[11]

Transavanguardia: Italia/America realized Bonito Oliva's desire to position the phenomenon of the return to subjectivity in painting and its new relationship with the past as the basis of what he would describe as the last great Italian art movement of the twentieth century, deserving of the same international recognition as Futurism, Pittura Metafisica, and Arte Povera. Combining images and words was an approach found in many of the works by the artists in the exhibition, but Basquiat's paintings stand out for the way the surface of the canvas is scattered with drawings recalling those of children, the world of the comic strip, or the patterns drawn in chalk or paint by children playing in the street. These seemingly more instinctive elements would go on to become one of the cornerstones of Basquiat's signature style.

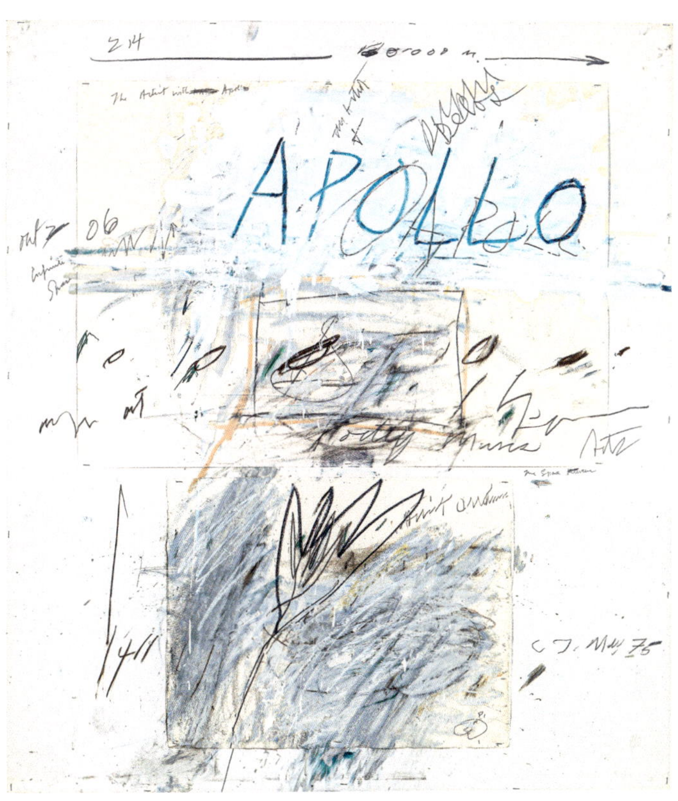

Fig. 8
Cy Twombly, *Apollo and the Artist*, 1975, oil, wax crayon, and pencil with drawing paper, cardboard, and staples on paper, 141.9 × 127.5 cm, private collection

1)	The main body of the exhibition that opened on May 25, 1981, centered around some ten canvases. Unfortunately, the photographs of the show's installation have been lost. Emilio Mazzoli, in conversation with the author, Modena, December 12, 2022.

2)	*Untitled*, 1982, oil and enamel paint on canvas, 265 x 700 cm, collection of Emilio Mazzoli, Modena.

3)	In 1978 the Mazzoli gallery mounted an exhibition curated by Achille Bonito Oliva titled *Tre o quattro artisti secchi*. It featured works by the artists Sandro Chia and Enzo Cucchi. The third of the "three artists" mentioned in the title was Bonito Oliva, as he saw himself as an artist (and, in fact, in the second half of the 1960s, the critic had been one of the artists of the artistic and literary group Poesia Visiva). But the title's "three or four artists" was meant to indicate that an artistic movement was emerging to which further names would be added. Although the term "Transavanguardia" does not appear in the exhibition catalogue, both Bonito Oliva and Mazzoli saw the movement as having been launched by this show. The gallery subsequently mounted solo shows of work by Francesco Clemente, Mimmo Paladino, and Nicola De Maria. The movement was officially presented in 1979 at the exhibition *La Transavanguardia Italiana* in Acireale in Sicily, featuring the work of all five artists.

4)	On nomadism, see Achille Bonito Oliva, *The Italian Trans-avantgarde / La Transavanguardia Italiana* (Milan, 1980), pp. 13-14.

5)	See Phoebe Hoban, *Basquiat: A Quick Killing in Art* (London, 1998), p. 75.

6)	Jean-Michel Basquiat, "The House of Jean-Michel," interview by Lisa Licitra Ponti, *Domus*, no. 646 (January 1984), pp. 66-68; reprinted in Jordana Moore Saggese, ed., *The Jean-Michel Basquiat Reader: Writings, Interviews, and Critical Responses* (Oakland, 2021), pp. 39-40, here p. 39. Four years later, asked in an interview by Démosthènes Davvetas which European artists he liked best, Basquiat mentioned A. R. Penck as well as Clemente and Cucchi. Jean-Michel Basquiat, "Jean-Michel Basquiat," interview by Démosthènes Davvetas, *New Art International*, no. 3 (October-November 1988), pp. 10-15; reprinted in Saggese 2021, pp. 61-62, here p. 62.

7)	"I cross out the words to move them into the background a bit. I like the copyrights because they look good." Jean-Michel Basquiat, "Warten auf Basquiat," interview by Isabelle Graw, *Wolkenkratzer Art Journal*, no. 1 (January-February 1987), pp. 44-51, here p. 51; published in English as "Interview by Isabelle Graw: Frankfurt, 1986," in Saggese 2021 (see note 6), pp. 63-64, here p. 63.

8)	Jean-Michel Basquiat, "Art: From Subways to Soho: Jean-Michel Basquiat," interview by Henry Geldzahler, *Interview* 13, no. 1 (January 1983), pp. 44-46, here p. 46; reprinted in Saggese 2021 (see note 6), pp. 32-38, here p. 35.

9)	Geldzahler 1983 (see note 8), p. 46; Saggese 2021 (see note 8), p. 36.

10)	Francesco Clemente, in conversation with the author, January 11, 2022.

11)	*Transavanguardia: Italia/America*, ed. Achille Bonito Oliva, exh. cat. Galleria Civica del Comune di Modena (Modena, 1982), p. 142.

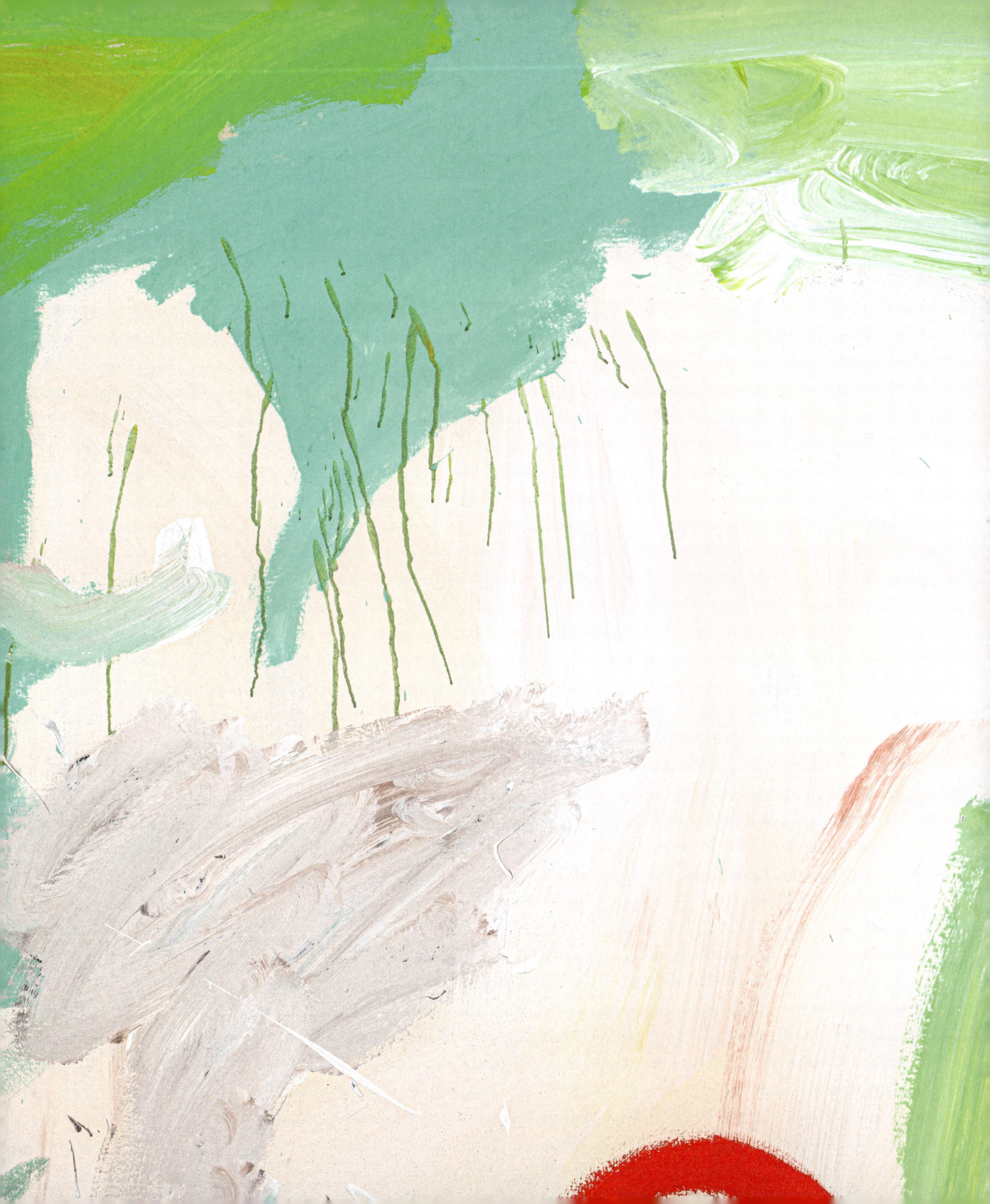

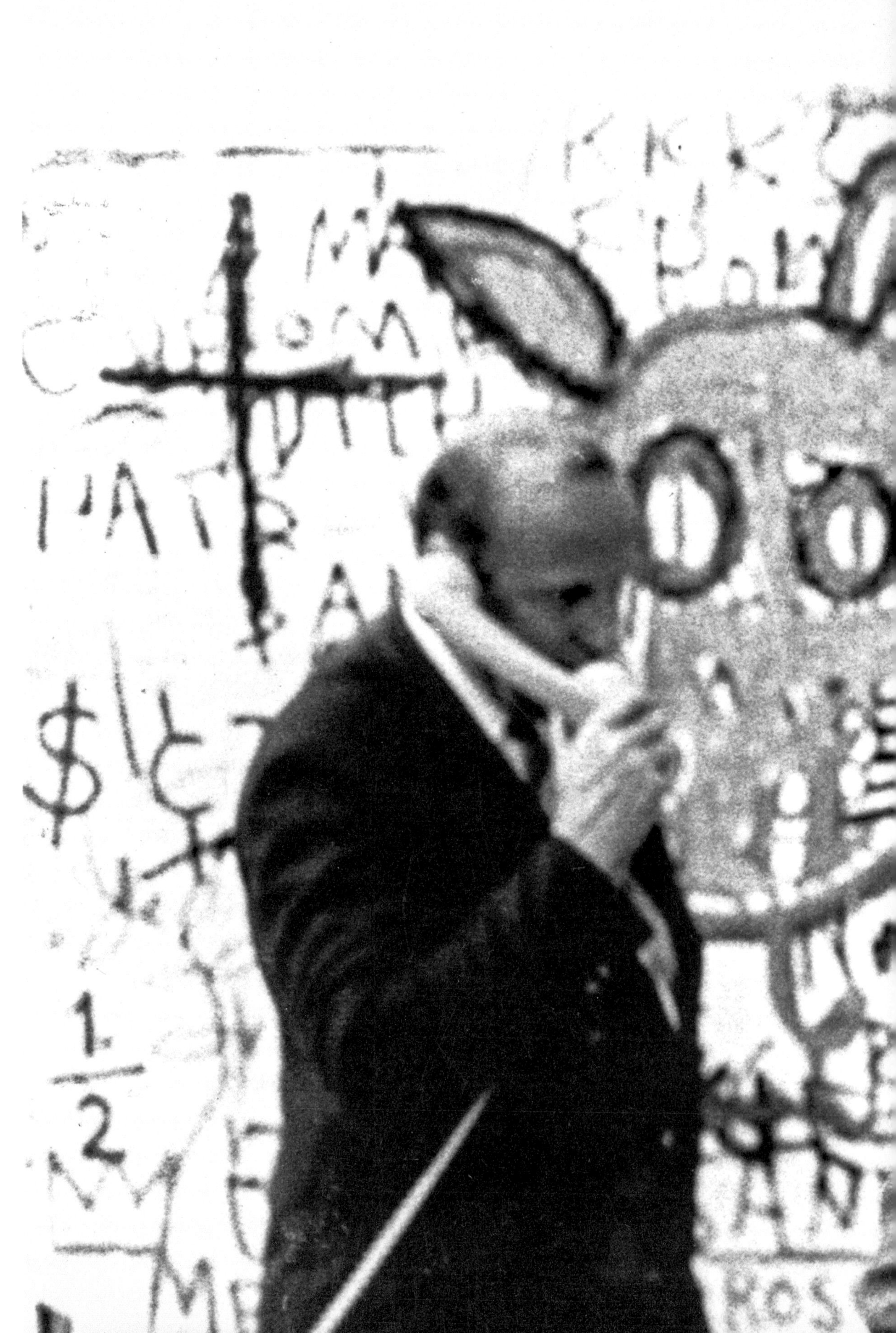

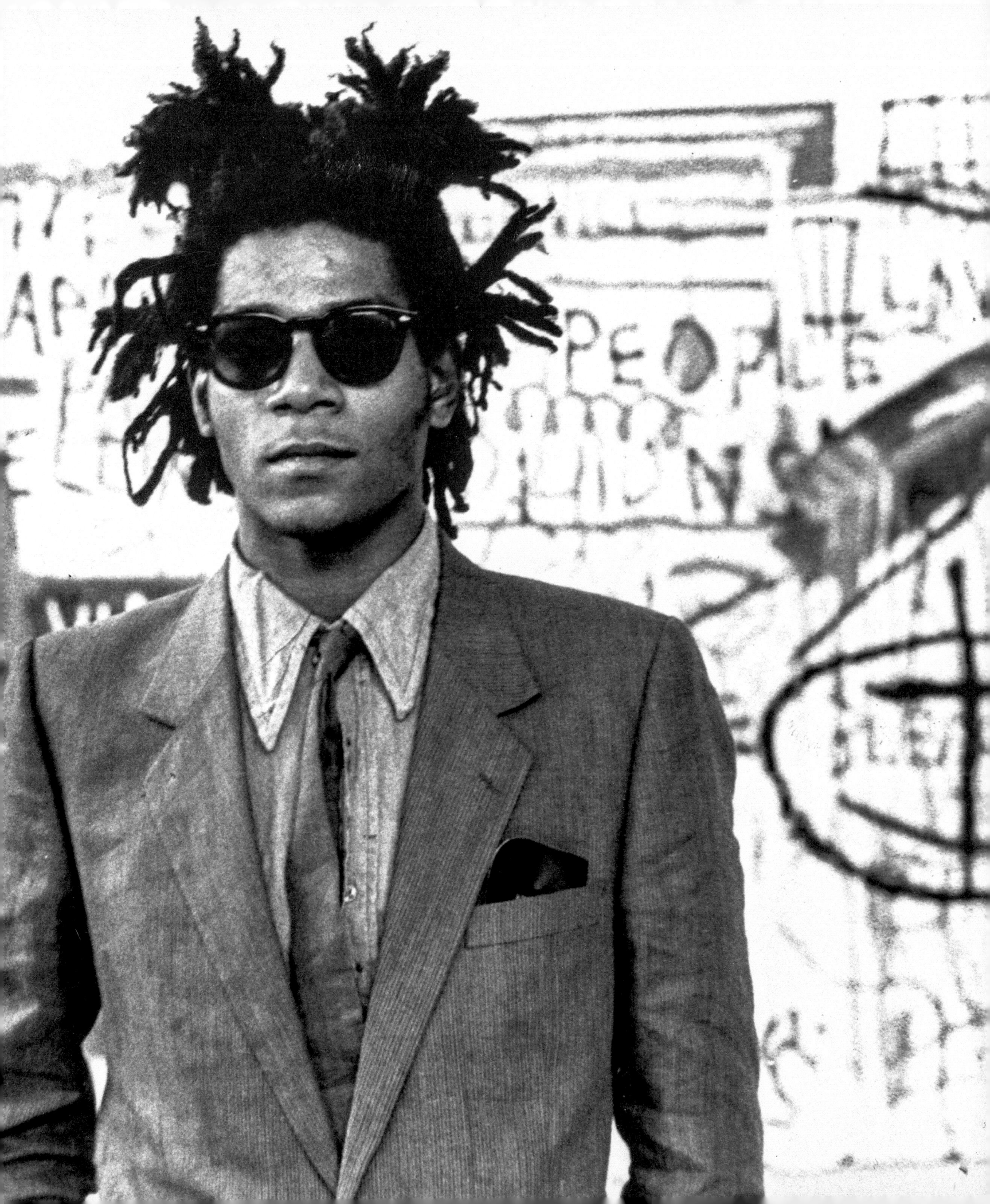

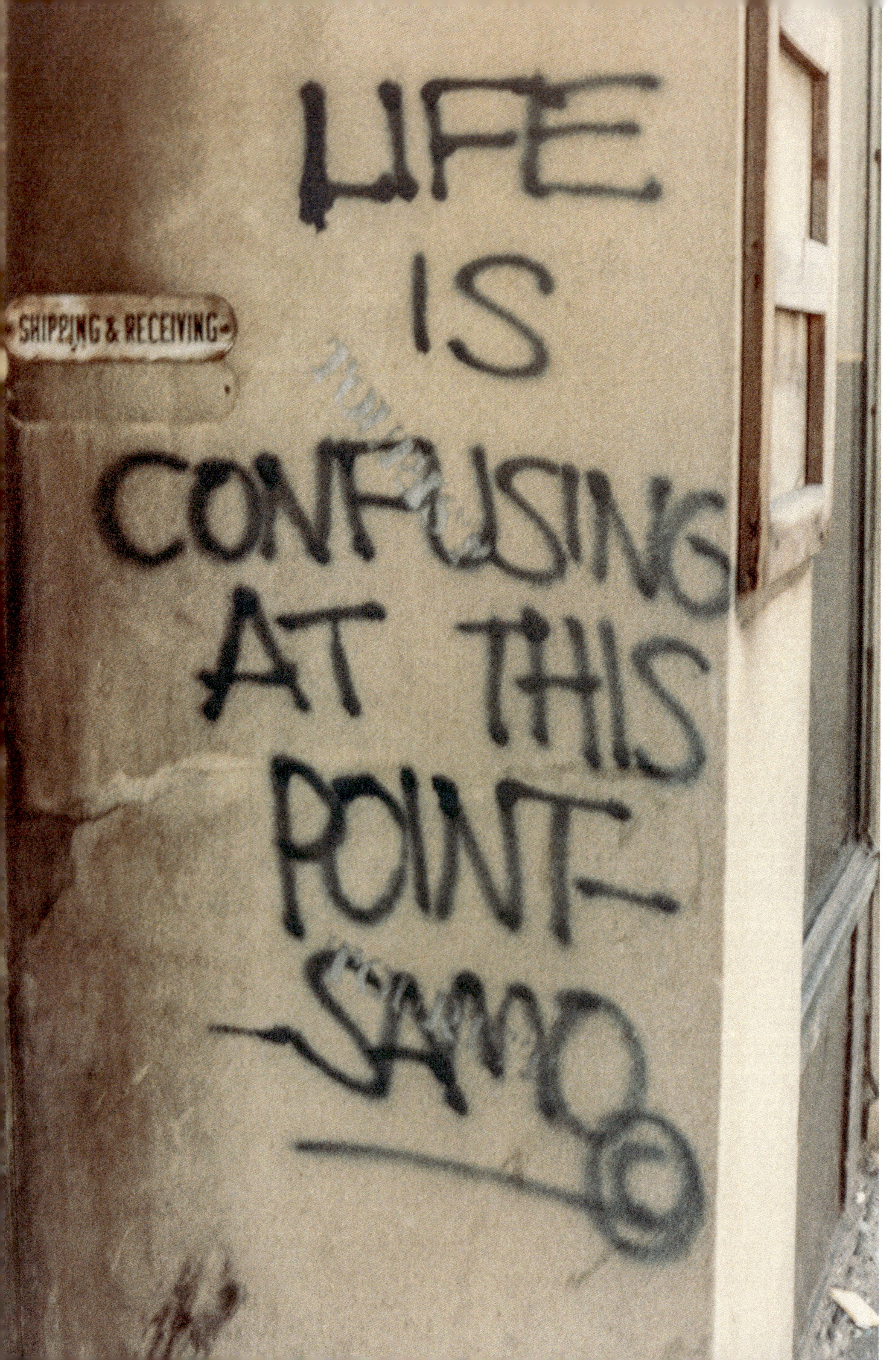

SAMO©,
Life Is Confusing at This Point, photographed by Vijya Kern, New York, 1980

Chronology: Basquiat in Modena

Compiled
by Iris Hasler

Jean-Michel Basquiat is born on December 22, 1960, in Brooklyn, New York City, as the first of three children, to Gerard Basquiat, a native of Haiti, and Matilde Andrades, whose parents had immigrated to New York from Puerto Rico. As a child and teenager, he began to paint and draw prolifically, with comics and cartoons inspiring him to incorporate words and short sentences into his pictures. In 1977, together with his friend Al Diaz, a graffiti artist, he forms a duo known as SAMO (an abbreviation for "same old shit"), writing short, poetic statements, often with a humorous twist, on subway trains and the walls of buildings near the gallery district in Lower Manhattan. The pair sign their work with the tag "SAMO©" **(fig. 1)**. They initially use Magic Marker, but then switch to spray paint, until early 1979, when their tag "SAMO© IS DEAD" appears, signaling the end of their collaboration.

1981

February-April

Basquiat attracts the attention of the institutional art world through the group exhibition *New York/New Wave* (February 15–April 5) at P.S. 1 Contemporary Art Center—now known as MoMA PS1—in the Long Island City neighborhood of Queens. The show is organized by Diego Cortez, the co-founder of the Mudd Club in Lower Manhattan, which is frequented by young artists and musicians. Cortez becomes Basquiat's principal supporter. The exhibition features works by 119 artists, including Nan Goldin, Keith Haring, Robert Mapplethorpe, Kenny Scharf, and Andy Warhol.

Basquiat is allotted an entire wall for the show, which he fills with twenty-three paintings and drawings of varying sizes on canvas, paper, wood, metal, and even rubber **(fig. p. 20)**. The works attract the attention of the dealers Bruno Bischofberger (Zurich), Emilio Mazzoli (Modena), and Annina Nosei (New York), in response to an invitation from Sandro Chia to attend the opening. The programs of the three galleries overlap, through co-representing artists such as Chia, along with Francesco Clemente, Enzo Cucchi, and Mimmo Paladino. Cortez tours the dealers through the exhibition, and all three of them buy works by Basquiat. Mazzoli invites the young painter, then just twenty years old, to hold a one-man show at his gallery.

May   Basquiat travels to Europe for the first time, for his first solo exhibition at the Galleria d'Arte Emilio Mazzoli in Modena, Italy **(fig. 2)**, which runs from May 23 to June 20. The show takes its title, *SAMO*, from the pseu-

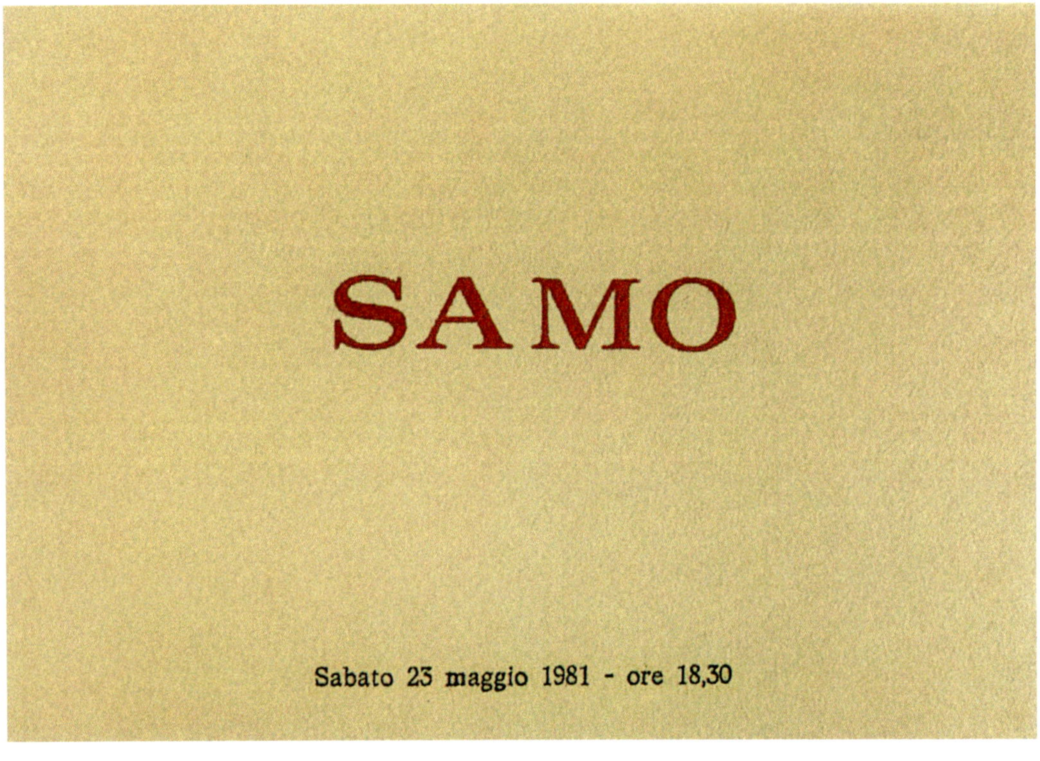

Fig. 2
Invitation to the exhibition *SAMO* at the Galleria d'Arte Emilio Mazzoli in Modena, 1981

donym that Basquiat has already abandoned. Cortez accompanies the artist, bringing with him the works Mazzoli had bought in New York. Basquiat is also provided with materials to create new paintings and stays in Modena for two weeks. The works from this period include *Untitled (Red Man)* **(fig. p. 21)** and *Untitled* **(fig. 3)**. The exhibition is a disappointment. Attendance at the opening is sparse, and only a few works are purchased, by friends of Mazzoli as a personal favor. The dealer reimburses Basquiat for the unsold pictures.

September-November

In New York, Basquiat persuades Annina Nosei to include him in the group show at her gallery *Public Address* (October 31-November 19), which deals with themes of social and political importance. Bill Beckley, Mike Glier, Keith Haring, Jenny Holzer, Barbara Kruger, and Peter Nadin are also among the participants. The rear section of the gallery is reserved for Basquiat's paintings, depicting police officers, rabbis, Native Americans, and other figures.

Following the exhibition, Nosei becomes Basquiat's dealer. Since he doesn't have a studio of his own, she provides him with a space in the basement of her gallery at 100 Prince Street.

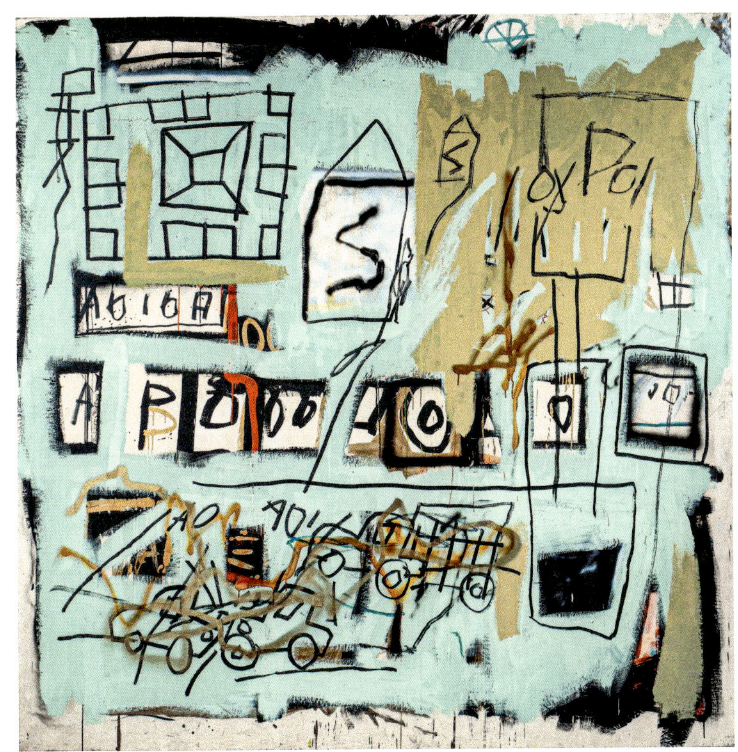

Fig. 3
Untitled,
1981, acrylic
and spray paint
on canvas,
203 × 203 cm,
The Schorr
Family
Collection,
on loan to
the Princeton
University
Art Museum,
New Jersey

<u>1982</u>   Basquiat's art is featured in ever more exhibitions. He works feverishly to meet the demand for new pictures.

March   *Jean-Michel Basquiat* at the Annina Nosei Gallery (March 6–April 1) is the artist's first exhibition under his real name. Among the works on view are *Arroz con Pollo, Untitled (Per Capita)*, and *Crowns (Peso Neto)*. The exhibition is a resounding success. As one art critic comments, "Basquiat's greatest strength is his ability to merge his absorption of imagery from the streets, the newspapers, and TV with the spiritualism of his Haitian heritage, injecting both into a marvelously intuitive understanding of the language of modern painting."[1]

That same month, two paintings by Basquiat are featured in the group show *Transavanguardia: Italia/ America* (March 21–May 2), curated by Achille Bonito Oliva, at the Galleria Civica del Comune in Modena. Devoted to a new generation of figurative artists in Italy and New York, the exhibition includes works by Sandro Chia, Francesco Clemente, Enzo Cucchi, David Salle, and Julian Schnabel, together with the two pictures by Basquiat, which he had painted in Modena in 1981.

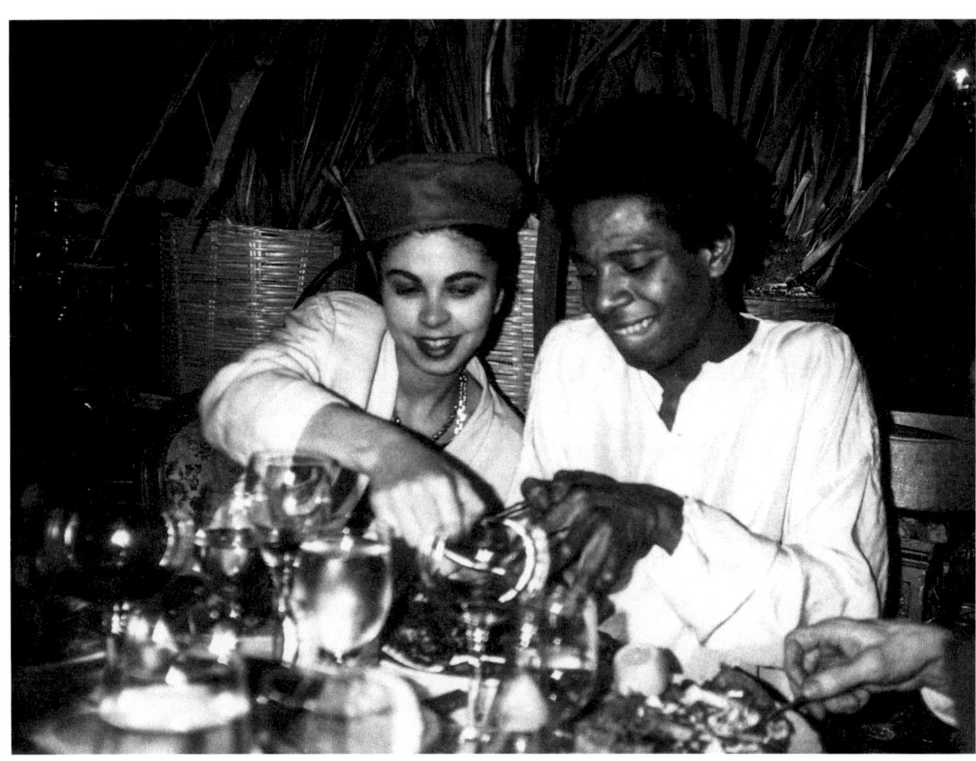

Fig. 4
Suzanne Mallouk and Jean-Michel Basquiat at a restaurant, New York, 1981

April   Basquiat travels to Los Angeles for his exhibition at
         Larry Gagosian's gallery, *Jean-Michel Basquiat: Paintings*
         (April 8–May 8) **(fig. 5)**, organized at the instigation of
         Annina Nosei. All of the exhibited works are sold,
         including *Six Crimee, Untitled (L.A. Painting),* and
         Untitled (Yellow Tar and Feathers), all from 1982.

May   Basquiat plans to leave the Annina Nosei Gallery. In a
         subsequent interview, he states his reason for the
         separation, claiming, "she sold paintings that weren't
         finished. She said someone was interested in the painting
         and sold it despite my protests."[2]
             Nevertheless, Basquiat continues to use the studio
         in Nosei's gallery, at least until August 1982, when he
         destroys a number of his canvases there. The professional
         arrangement is terminated in November 1982, when Basquiat,
         disregarding Nosei's advice, accepts a proposal for a solo
         exhibition at the Fun Gallery in Manhattan's East Village.
         In the meantime, Bruno Bischofberger hears that Basquiat
         is seeking a new gallery. The artist agrees to make the
         Galerie Bruno Bischofberger in Zurich his exclusive inter-
         national representative, an agreement that lasts until
         Basquiat's death.

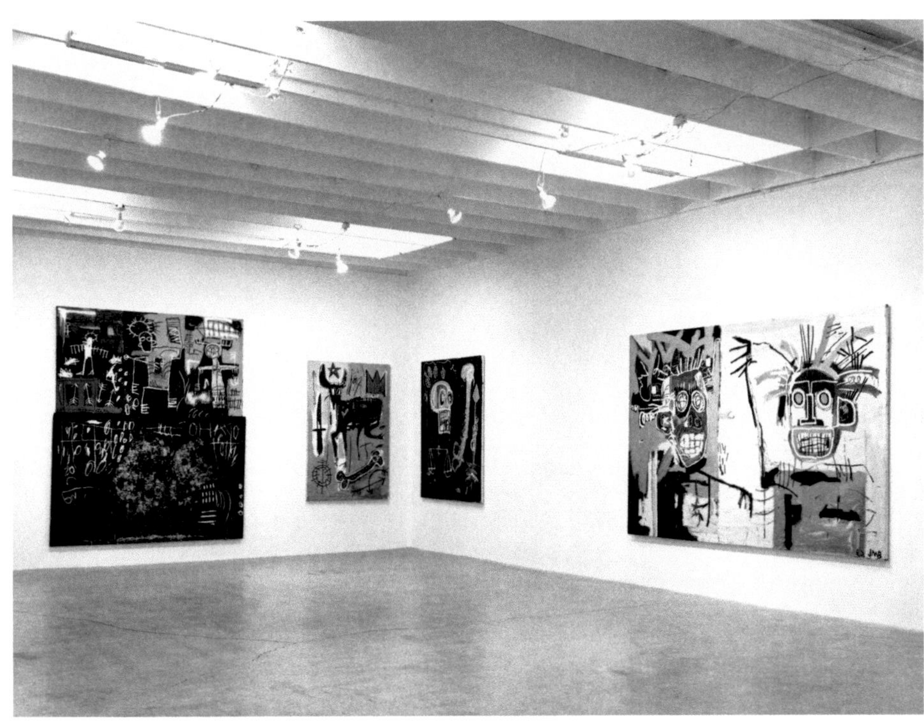

Fig. 5
Installation
view of the
exhibition
*Jean-Michel
Basquiat:
Paintings*
at Larry
Gagosian's
gallery,
Los Angeles,
1982

June   After a brief stay in Rome, Basquiat returns to Modena for a second exhibition at the Galleria d'Arte Emilio Mazzoli, again facilitated by Nosei. He is accompanied by his partner Suzanne Mallouk **(fig. 4)** and the couple's mutual friend Kai Eric.

Mazzoli provides Basquiat with space in a large warehouse and painting materials to create a suite of new works. Within a few days, the artist makes eight large-scale paintings, measuring at least 220 by 400 centimeters. The on-site production of new works for an immediately upcoming exhibition puts Basquiat under immense pressure.[3]

The plans for the exhibition are abandoned after disagreements arise between Annina Nosei, Emilio Mazzoli, and the artist. Mazzoli seeks to claim all the credit for organizing and financing the show and for the creation of the works. Nosei, as Basquiat's dealer, on the other hand, demands a share of the profits. Mazzoli pays Basquiat for the completed works before the artist returns to New York. Four of the eight paintings (*Profit I*, *Boy and Dog in a Johnnypump*, *Untitled [Woman with Roman Torso (Venus)]*, and *The Guilt of Gold Teeth*) are bought by Bruno Bischofberger through Annina Nosei. The remaining works find their way into various international collections.

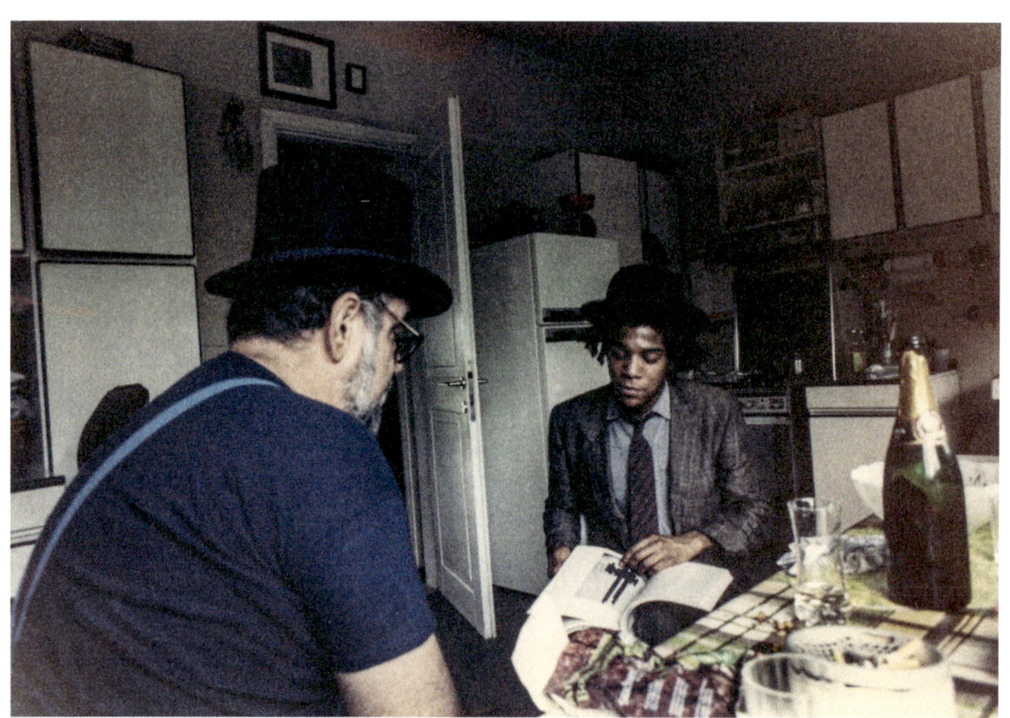

Fig. 6
Emilio Mazzoli and Jean-Michel Basquiat in Modena, 1982

In the same month, *Documenta 7* (June 19-September 28)
opens in Kassel, with two works by Basquiat: *Acque Peri-
colose (Poison Oasis)* (1981) and *Arroz con Pollo* (1981).
Basquiat is the youngest of the 182 artists in the show.

September   Basquiat travels to Zurich for his first solo exhibition
at the Galerie Bruno Bischofberger, titled *Jean-Michel
Basquiat* (September 11-October 9) **(fig. 7)**. Of the paintings
he made in Modena, only *Profit I* is shown **(cat. pp. 54–55)**.

October   The painting *The Field Next to the Other Road* **(cat. pp. 72–73)**,
created in Modena, is exhibited on its own at the Galleria
Mario Diacono in Rome.

In the following six years, Basquiat rapidly achieves
international recognition. He becomes friends with Andy
Warhol, and from 1984 on, the two artists—at times joined
by Francesco Clemente—work together on a series of
projects referred to as "collaborations." Basquiat travels
to Los Angeles, Paris, Milan, Madrid, and Zurich, and,
further afield, to Tokyo, Hawaii, Jamaica, and the Ivory
Coast.

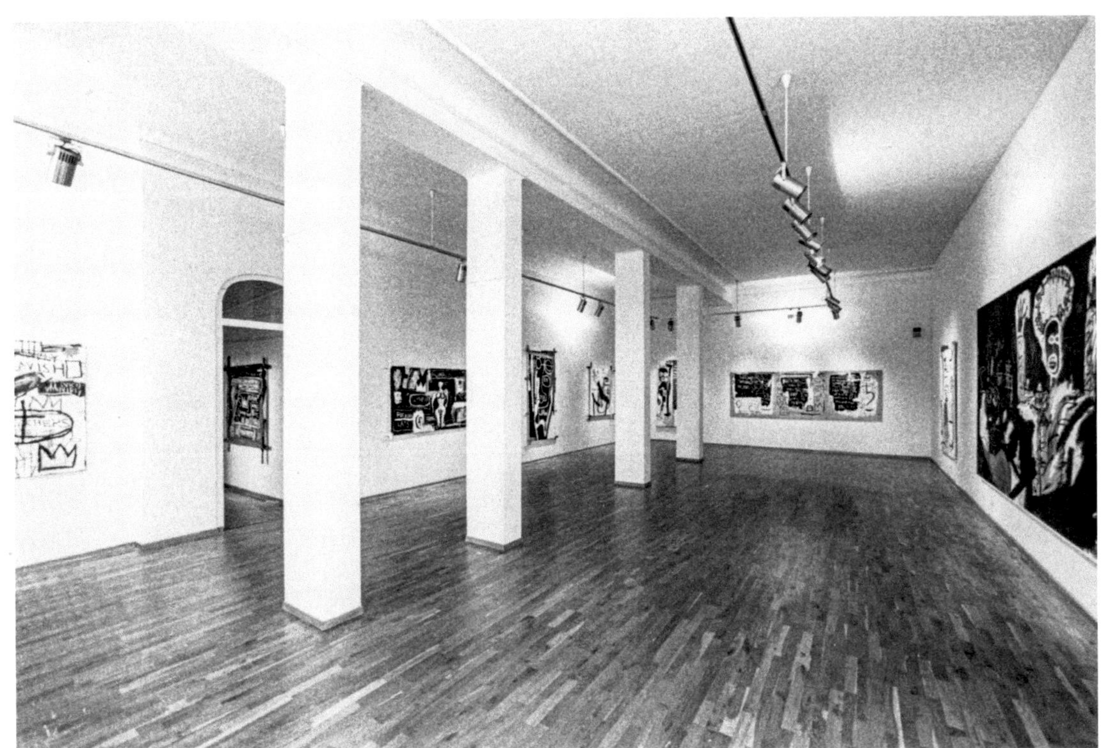

Fig. 7
Installation
view of the
exhibition
*Jean-Michel
Basquiat*
at the
Galerie Bruno
Bischofberger,
Zurich, 1982

On August 12, 1988, at the age of twenty-seven, Basquiat dies of a drug overdose in his New York apartment. In less than a decade, he created an extensive body of work, comprising over 1,000 paintings and objects as well as 3,000 works on paper, and established a new visual language combining figurative painting with densely packed elements of writing. Thematically, his art repeatedly reflects the oppression, marginalization, and exploitation of Black American people.

1) Jeffrey Deitch, "Jean-Michel Basquiat," *Flash Art International* 107, no. 16 (May 1982), pp. 49-50, here p. 50; reprinted in Jordana Moore Saggese, ed., *The Jean-Michel Basquiat Reader: Writings, Interviews, and Critical Responses* (Oakland, 2021), p. 110.

2) Jean-Michel Basquiat, "Warten auf Basquiat," interview by Isabelle Graw, *Wolkenkratzer Art Journal*, no. 1 (January-February 1987), pp. 44-51, here p. 51; published in English as "Interview by Isabelle Graw: Frankfurt, 1986," in Saggese 2021 (see note 1), pp. 63-64, here p. 64.

3) Cf. the essay by Iris Hasler in this catalogue, pp. 19-27, here p. 22.

Sources

Eric Fretz, *Jean-Michel Basquiat: A Biography* (Santa Barbara et al., 2010), esp. pp. 67-97.

Phoebe Hoban, *Basquiat: A Quick Killing in Art* (London, 1998), esp. pp. 68-120.

Tobias Müller, "Chronology," *Basquiat*, exh. cat. Museo Revoltella, Trieste (Milan, 1999), pp. 197-203, esp. pp. 199-200.

Michel Nuridsany, *Jean-Michel Basquiat* (Paris, 2015), esp. pp. 216-23.

M. Franklin Sirmans, "Chronology," in *Jean-Michel Basquiat*, ed. Richard Marshall, exh. cat. Whitney Museum of American Art, New York; The Menil Collection, Houston; Des Moines Art Center; Montgomery Museum of Fine Arts (New York, 1992), pp. 233-50, esp. pp. 238-41.

Jean-Michel Basquiat at the Galerie Bruno Bischofberger in Zurich, 1982, photographed by Beth Phillips

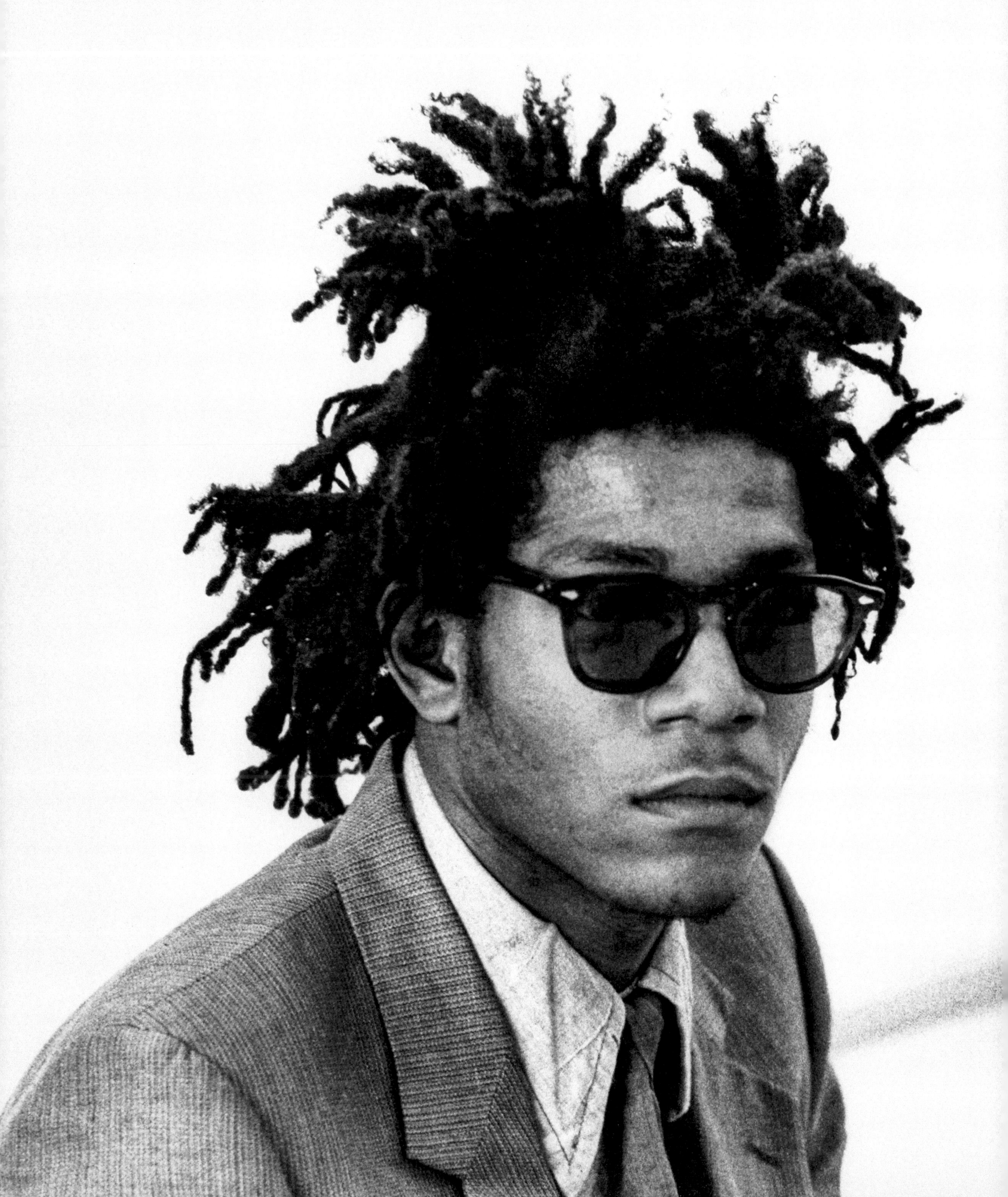

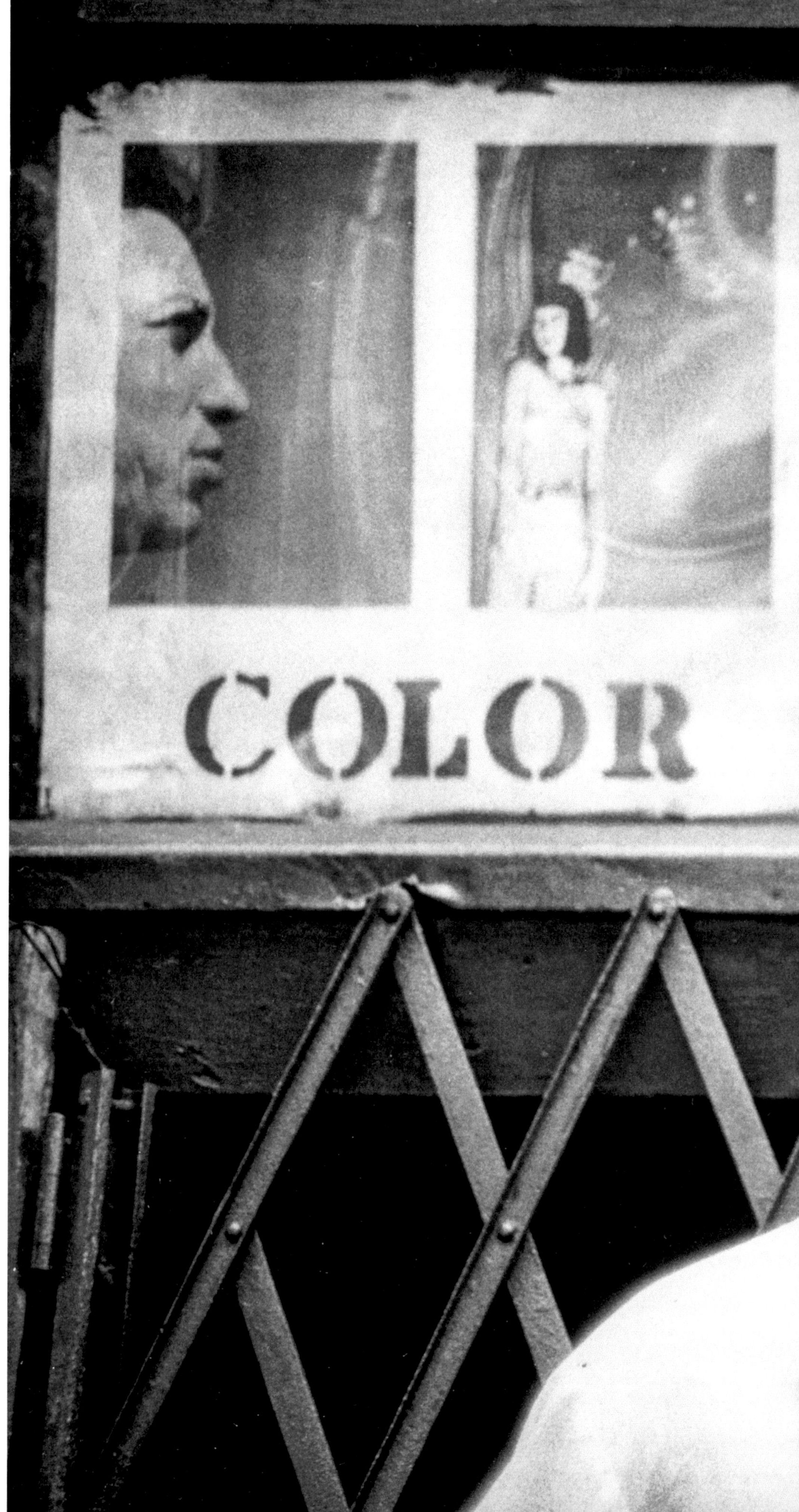

Jean-Michel Basquiat
in New York, 1980,
photographed by
Robert Carrithers

35 MM
SLIDES
XEROX

Untitled (Devil)

1982

Acrylic and spray paint on canvas, 238.7 × 500.4 cm
On the reverse: "JEAN MICHEL BASQUIAT 1982 MODENA"
Private collection

pp. 30–35

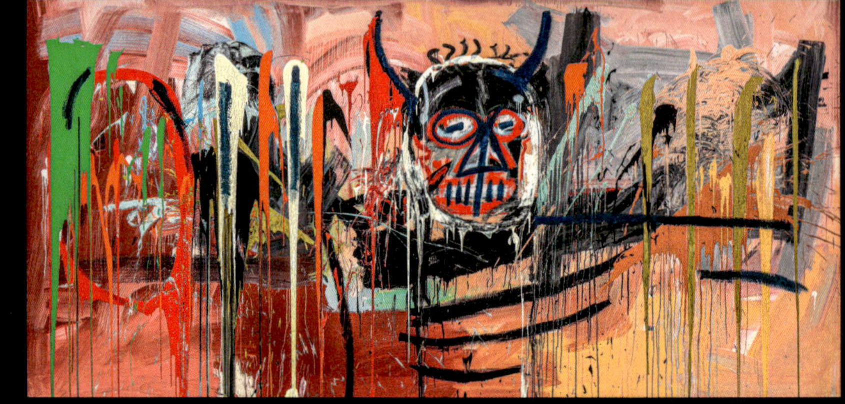

Boy and Dog in a Johnnypump

1982

Acrylic, oil stick, and spray paint on canvas, 240 × 420.4 cm
Lower right: "BASQUIAT 1982 MODENA"; on the reverse: "JEAN MICHEL BASQUIAT MODENA 1982"
Private collection

pp. 48–53

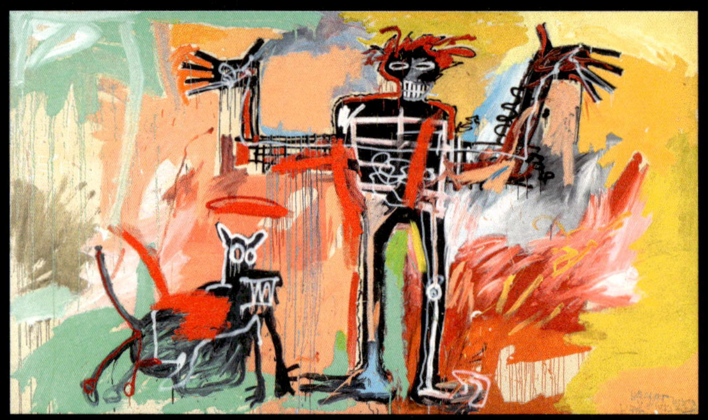

Profit I

1982

Acrylic, oil stick, marker, and spray paint on canvas, 220 × 400 cm
On the reverse: "Jean-Michel Basquiat MODENA 1982"
Private collection, Switzerland

pp. 54–59

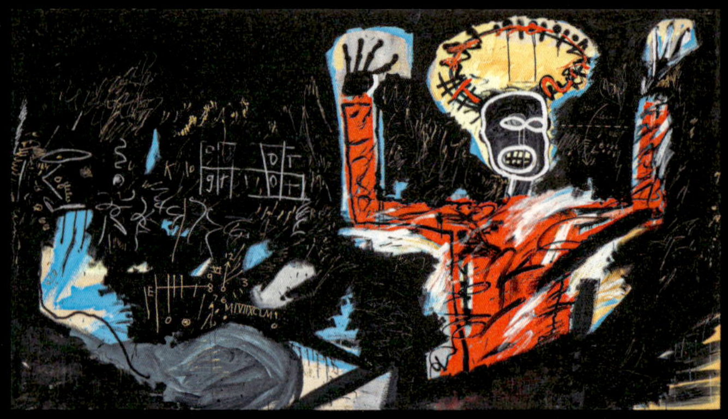

The Guilt of Gold Teeth

1982

Acrylic, spray paint, and oil stick on canvas, 240 × 421.3 cm
Lower left: "THE GUILT OF GOLD TEETH"; lower right: "MODENA / JEAN MICHEL BASQUIAT 1982"; on the reverse: "THE GUILT OF GOLD TEETH Jean-Michel Basquiat 1982 MODENA"
Nahmad Collection

pp. 66–71

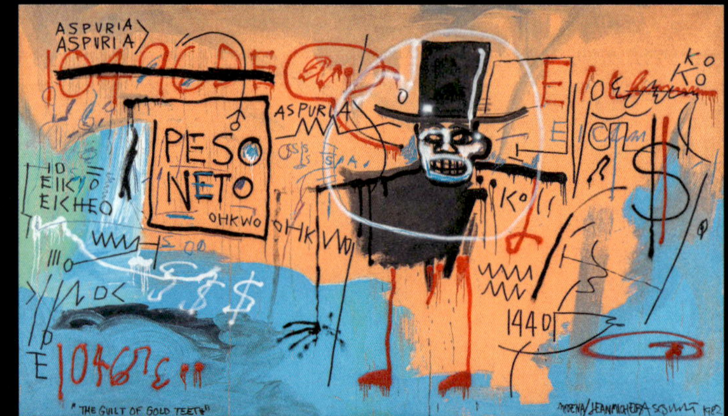

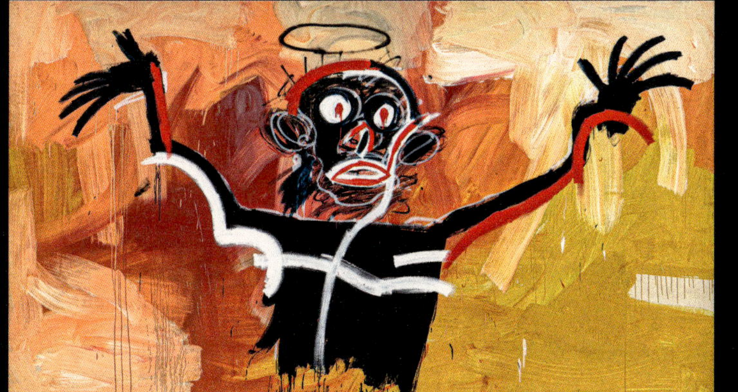

Acrylic and spray paint
on canvas, 244 × 429 cm
On the reverse:
"JEAN MICHEL BASQUIAT
1982 MODENA"
Private collection

pp. 36-41

*Untitled
(Angel)*

1982

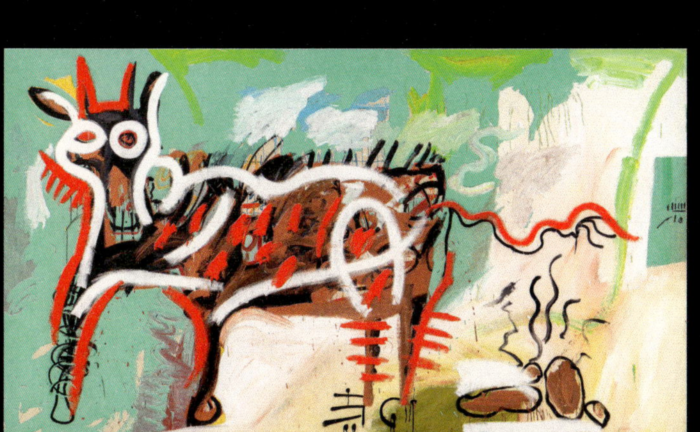

Acrylic, spray paint,
and oil stick on canvas,
239.4 × 420 cm
On the reverse: "JEAN
MICHEL BASQUIAT MODENA
1982"
Aby Rosen Collection,
New York

pp. 42-47

*Untitled
(Cowparts)*

1982

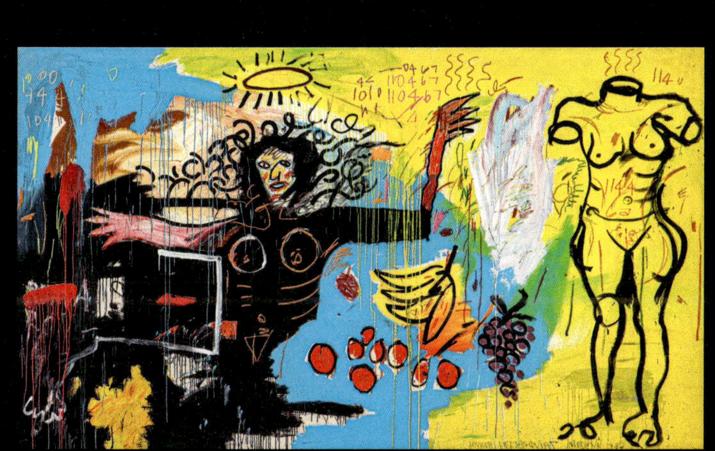

Acrylic and oil stick on
canvas, 241 × 419.7 cm
Lower right and reverse:
"JEAN MICHEL BASQUIAT
MODENA 1982"
Private collection,
courtesy Galerie Bruno
Bischofberger, Männedorf-
Zurich, Switzerland

pp. 60-65

*Untitled
(Woman with
Roman Torso
[Venus])*

1982

Acrylic, enamel paint,
spray paint, oil stick,
and ink on canvas,
221 × 401.5 cm
On the reverse: "JEAN
MICHEL BASQUIAT MODENA"
Private collection

pp. 72-77

*The Field
Next to the
Other Road*

1982

Selected

Jean-Michel Basquiat and Modena

Basquiat, Jean-Michel. "Art: From Subways to Soho: Jean-Michel Basquiat." Interview by
     Henry Geldzahler. *Interview* 13, no. 1 (January 1983), pp. 44-46.
Castle, Frederick Ted. "Saint Jean-Michel." *Arts Magazine* 63, no. 6 (February 1989),
     pp. 60-61.
Clement, Jennifer. *Widow Basquiat: A Love Story*. Edinburgh, 2000. 1st American ed.
     New York, 2014, pp. 91-92.
Diacono, Mario. *Jean-Michel Basquiat: Il campo vicino l'altra strada*, exh. broch.
     Galleria Mario Diacono. Rome, 1982. Reprinted in Mario Diacono. *Verso una nuova
     iconografia*. Reggio Emilia, 1984.
Fretz, Eric. *Jean-Michel Basquiat: A Biography*. Santa Barbara et al., 2010,
     esp. pp. 67-97.
Hoban, Phoebe. *Basquiat: A Quick Killing in Art*. London, 1998, esp. pp. 68-120.
McGuigan, Cathleen. "New Art, New Money: The Marketing of An American Artist."
     The New York Times Magazine (February 10, 1985), pp. 20-28, 32-35, 74.
Müller, Tobias. "Chronology." In *Basquiat*, exh. cat. Museo Revoltella, Trieste. Milan,
     1999, pp. 197-203, esp. pp. 199-200.
Nosei, Annina. "An Interview with Annina Nosei." By Jeffrey Deitch and Nicola Vassell.
     In *Jean-Michel Basquiat: 1981: The Studio of the Street*, publ. on the occasion
     of an exhibition at Deitch Projects, New York. Milan and New York, 2007,
     pp. 84-89.
Nuridsany, Michel. *Jean-Michel Basquiat*. Paris, 2015, esp. pp. 216-23.
Sirmans, M. Franklin. "Chronology." In *Jean-Michel Basquiat*, edited by Richard
     Marshall, exh. cat. Whitney Museum of American Art, New York; The Menil
     Collection, Houston; Des Moines Art Center; Montgomery Museum of Fine Arts.
     New York, 1992, pp. 233-50, esp. pp. 238-41.

Basquiat. Edited by Dieter Buchhart and Sam Keller. Exh. cat. Fondation Beyeler,
	Riehen/Basel. Ostfildern, 2010.
Basquiat. Edited by Marc Mayer. Exh. cat. Brooklyn Museum, New York; The Museum of
	Contemporary Art, Los Angeles; The Museum of Fine Arts, Houston. London, 2005.
Basquiat. Exh. cat. Museo Revoltella, Trieste. Milan, 1999.
Basquiat: Boom for Real. Edited by Dieter Buchhart and Eleanor Nairne with Lotte
	Johnson. Exh. cat. Barbican Art Gallery, London; Schirn Kunsthalle Frankfurt,
	Frankfurt am Main. Munich et al., 2017.
Basquiat, Jean-Michel. "The House of Jean-Michel." Interview by Lisa Licitra Ponti.
	Domus, no. 646 (January 1984), pp. 66–68.
——. "Jean-Michel Basquiat." Interview by Démosthènes Davvetas. *New Art International*,
	no. 3 (October–November 1988), pp. 10–15.
——. "Warten auf Basquiat." Interview by Isabelle Graw. *Wolkenkratzer Art Journal*,
	no. 1 (January–February 1987), pp. 44–51.
Bischofberger, Bruno. "Interview with Bruno Bischofberger." By Dieter Buchhart. In
	Basquiat by Himself, edited by Dieter Buchhart and Anna Karina Hofbauer. Munich,
	2019, pp. 90–93.
Galerie Enrico Navarra, ed. *Jean-Michel Basquiat.* 2 vols. Paris, 2000.
Holzwarth, Hans Werner, ed. *Jean-Michel Basquiat.* Cologne, 2020.
hooks, bell. "Altars of Sacrifice, Re-membering Basquiat." *Art in America* (June 1993),
	pp. 68–75.
Jean-Michel Basquiat. Edited by Dieter Buchhart in collaboration with Anna Karina
	Hofbauer. Exh. cat. Fondation Louis Vuitton. Paris, 2018.
Jean-Michel Basquiat. Edited by Richard Marshall. Exh. cat. Whitney Museum of American
	Art, New York; The Menil Collection, Houston; Des Moines Art Center; Montgomery
	Museum of Fine Arts. New York, 1992.
Jean-Michel Basquiat. Exh. cat. Serpentine Gallery. London, 1996.
Jean-Michel Basquiat: Of Symbols and Signs. Edited by Dieter Buchhart, Antonia
	Hoerschelmann, and Klaus Albrecht Schröder. Exh. cat. Albertina, Vienna. Munich
	et al., 2022.
Jean-Michel Basquiat: Une rétrospective. Exh. cat. Musée Cantini. Marseille, 1992.
Nosei, Annina. "Interview with Annina Nosei." By Dieter Buchhart. In *Basquiat: Pollo
	Frito: Street to Studio*, edited by Dieter Buchhart and Anna Karina Hofbauer.
	Munich, 2019, pp. 107–11, 146–47.
——. "Recollections." In *Basquiat's Defacement: The Untold Story*, edited by
	Chaédria LaBouvier, publ. on the occasion of an exhibition at the Solomon R.
	Guggenheim Museum. New York, 2019, p. 105.
Ricard, Rene. "The Radiant Child." *Artforum* 20, no. 4 (December 1981), pp. 35–43.
Saggese, Jordana Moore, ed. *The Jean-Michel Basquiat Reader: Writings, Interviews,
	and Critical Responses.* Oakland, 2021.
——. *Reading Basquiat: Exploring Ambivalence in American Art.* Berkeley et al., 2014.

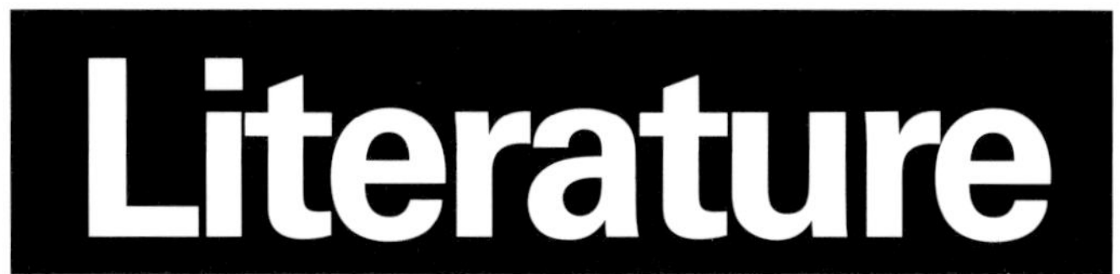

Exhibition

Basquiat: The Modena Paintings

Fondation Beyeler, Riehen/Basel
June 11–August 27, 2023

Fondation Beyeler

Director
Sam Keller

Managing director
Ulrike Erbslöh

Curators
Sam Keller and Iris Hasler

Registrars
Sarah Aubele, Noemi Monetti,
Tanja Narr, Nina Schmitz,
Sabina Schumpf, Steffen Zarutzki

Conservators
Hannah Backes, Markus Gross,
Eva Krug von Nidda, Aymeric Nager,
Friederike Steckling

Exhibition services
Ben Ludwig, David Vogt

Art education
Julia Beyer, Stefanie Bringezu,
Victoria Gellner, Meret Pardey,
Janine Schmutz

Communications, Public relations
Dorothee Dines, Jannik Hon,
Sandra Pfeiffer, Johanna Schedlbauer,
Clara Schuh-Reischl, Jan Sollberger,
Matthias Steck

Events, Fundraising
Susanne Battke, Chantal Blatzheim,
Angelika Bühler, Simone Füglistaller,
Shana Grüninger, Youlia Gueorguieva,
Lili von Habsburg, Nicola Hüll,
Anna Kargl, Martyna Smolinska

Controlling
Dorothea Merz

Further assistance
Raphaël Bouvier, Simon Crameri,
Helen Dienel, Ljiljana Jovic, Ulf Küster,
Claudia Lörracher, Lionel Schüpbach,
Olivia Sofia, Theodora Vischer,
Arnd Winter

Catalogue

Basquiat: The Modena Paintings

Also available in
a German edition.

Edited by
Sam Keller and Iris Hasler
for the Fondation Beyeler

**Catalogue management
and editing**
Franziska Stegmann
and Romina Del Principe,
Fondation Beyeler

Copyediting
Joann Skrypzak-
Davidsmeyer, Cologne

Translations
John Ormrod, Munich
(foreword, Buchhart,
Hasler, Hesse, Kono,
Moser)
Caroline Higgitt,
Edinburgh (Paparoni)

Graphic design
Christoph Steinegger,
Interkool

Project management
Richard Viktor Hagemann,
Hatje Cantz Verlag

Production
Christine Stäcker,
Stuttgart

Reproductions
Repromayer Medien-
produktionen GmbH,
Reutlingen

Printing
Offsetdruckerei Karl
Grammlich GmbH,
Pliezhausen

Paper
Profibulk 1.3 vol FSC,
150 g/m²
Invercote G FSC, 300 g/m²

Binding
Idupa Schübelin GmbH,
Owen

Copyright
© 2023 Beyeler Museum AG,
Riehen/Basel; Hatje Cantz Verlag
GmbH, Berlin; authors; and
translators

For the reproduced works by
Jean-Michel Basquiat: © The Estate
of Jean-Michel Basquiat. Licensed
by Artestar, New York

The Estate of Jean-Michel Basquiat
does not warrant or represent that
all of the works depicted in this
catalogue were created by Jean-
Michel Basquiat.

For the reproduced works by
Francesco Clemente: © Francesco
Clemente Studio; for Jean Dubuffet,
Mimmo Paladino, and Mario Schifano:
© 2023 VG Bild-Kunst, Bonn /
ProLitteris, Zurich; for Jackson
Pollock: © 2023 Pollock-Krasner
Foundation / VG Bild-Kunst, Bonn /
ProLitteris, Zurich; for Cy Twombly:
© Cy Twombly Foundation

A publication of the
Fondation Beyeler
Baselstrasse 101
4125 Riehen/Basel
Switzerland
Tel. +41 61 6459-700
www.fondationbeyeler.ch
info@fondationbeyeler.ch

ISBN 978-3-906053-74-5
(English museum edition)
ISBN 978-3-906053-73-8
(German museum edition)

German and English trade edition
Hatje Cantz Verlag GmbH
Mommsenstrasse 27
10629 Berlin
Germany
www.hatjecantz.com

A Ganske Publishing
Group company

ISBN 978-3-7757-5509-2
(English trade edition)
ISBN 978-3-7757-5508-5
(German trade edition)

Printed in Germany

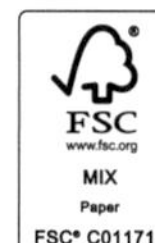

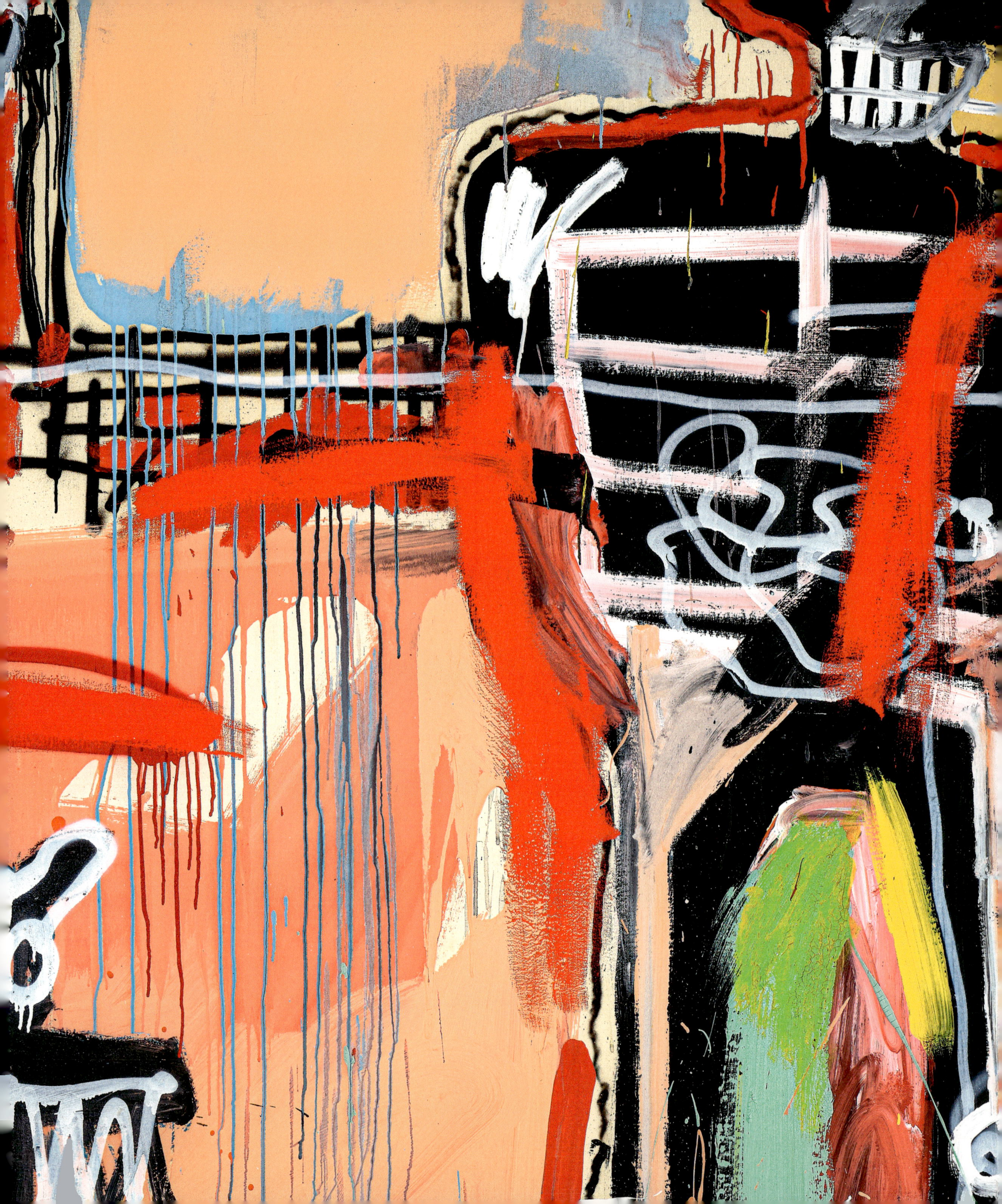

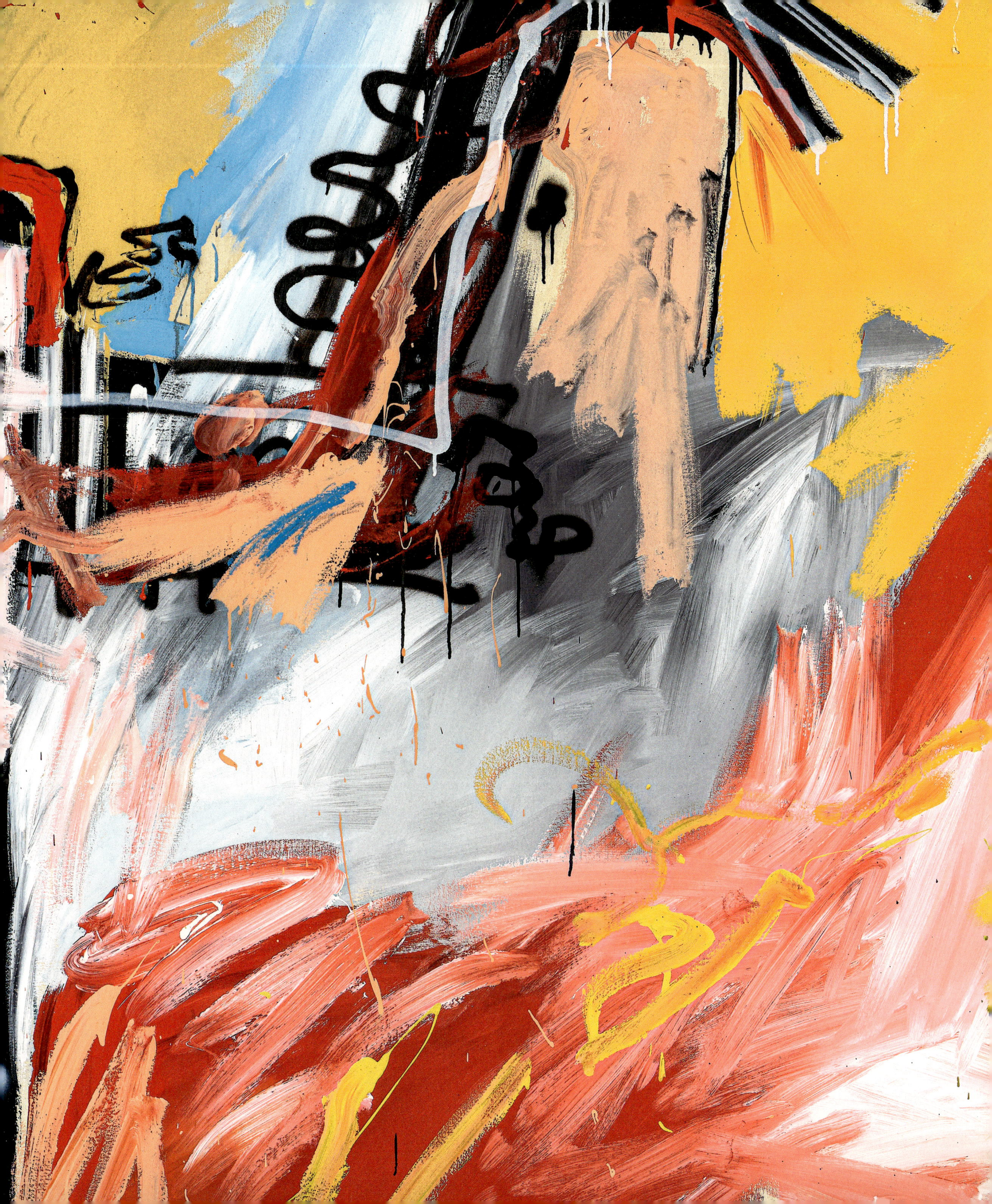

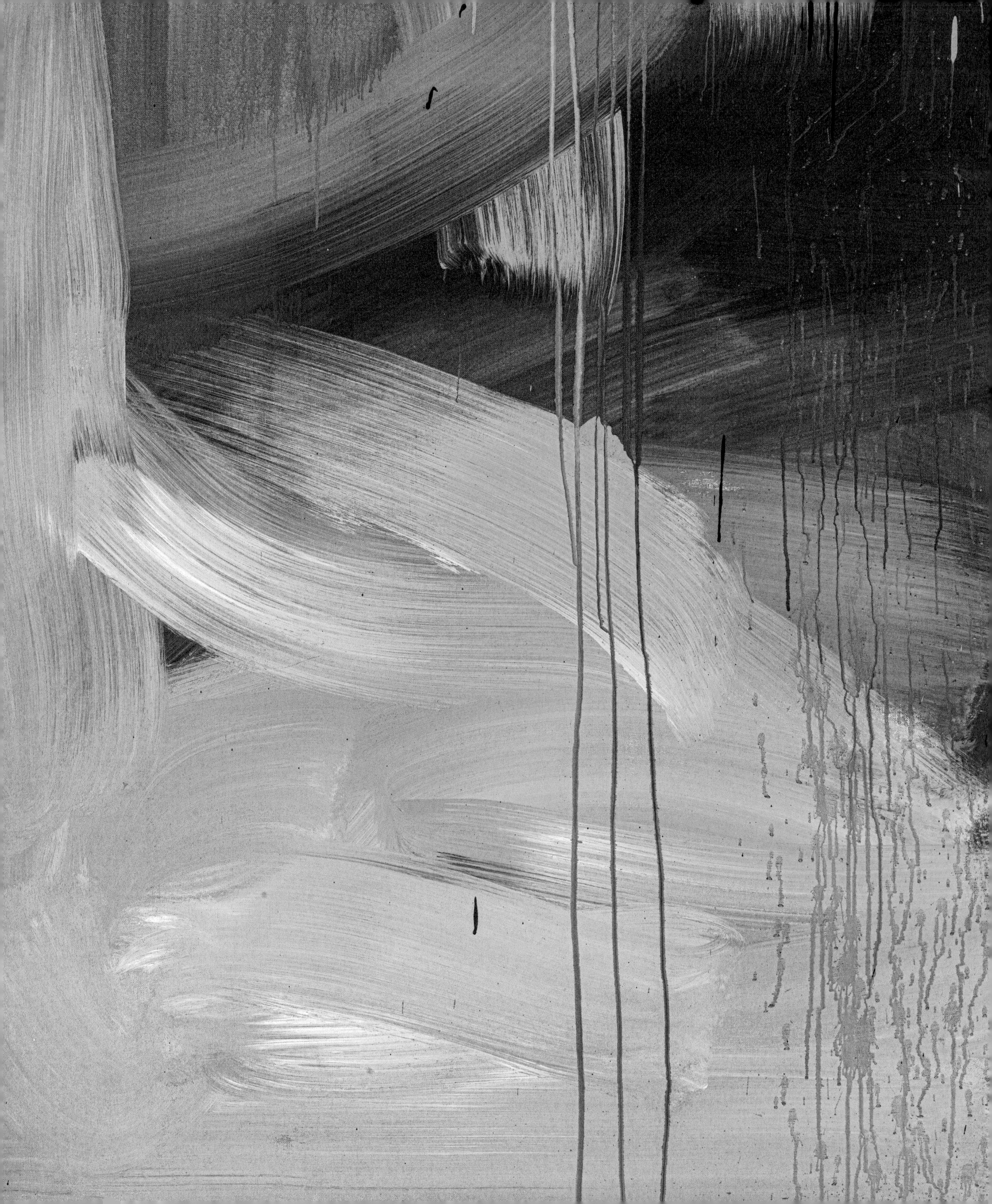

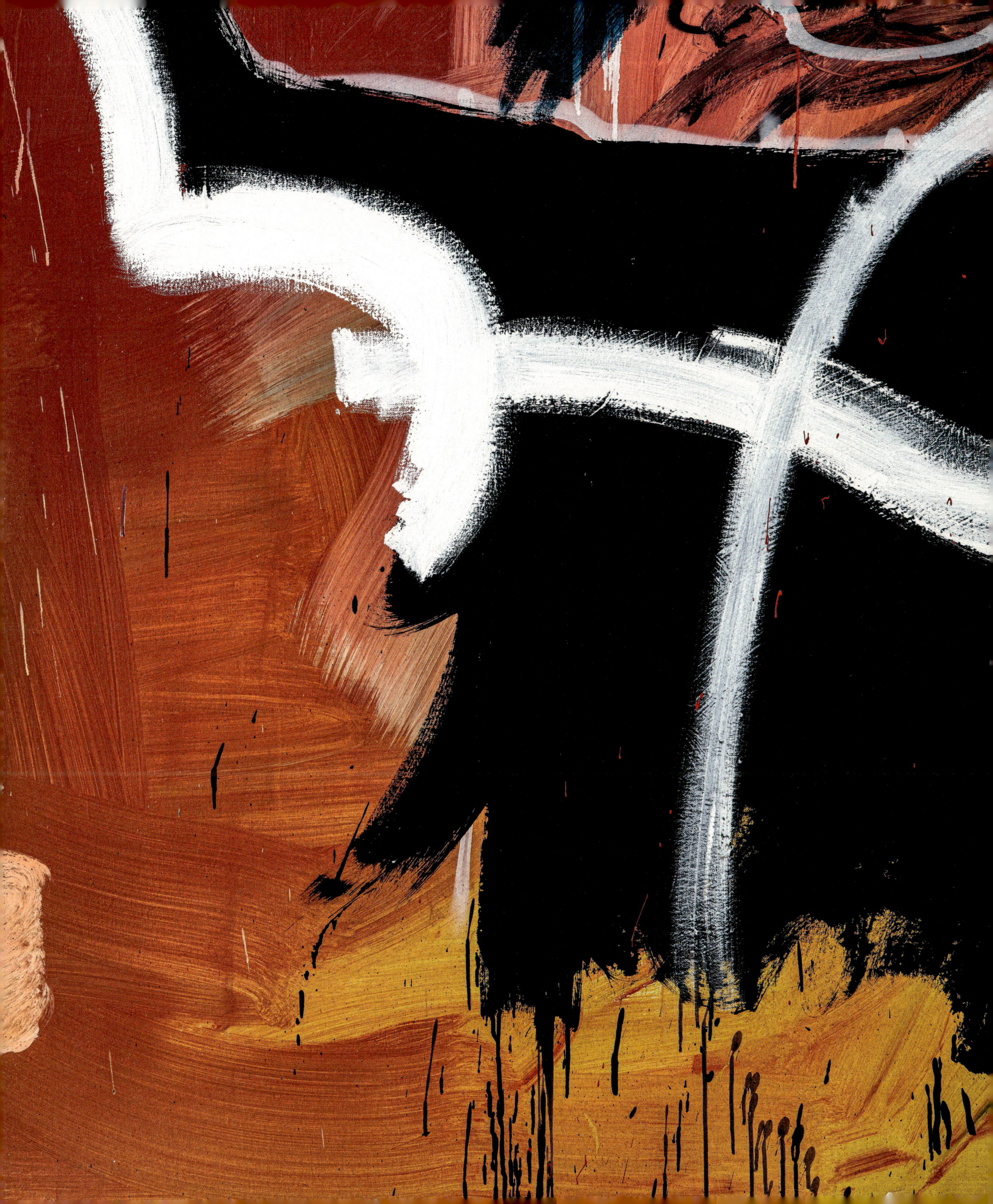

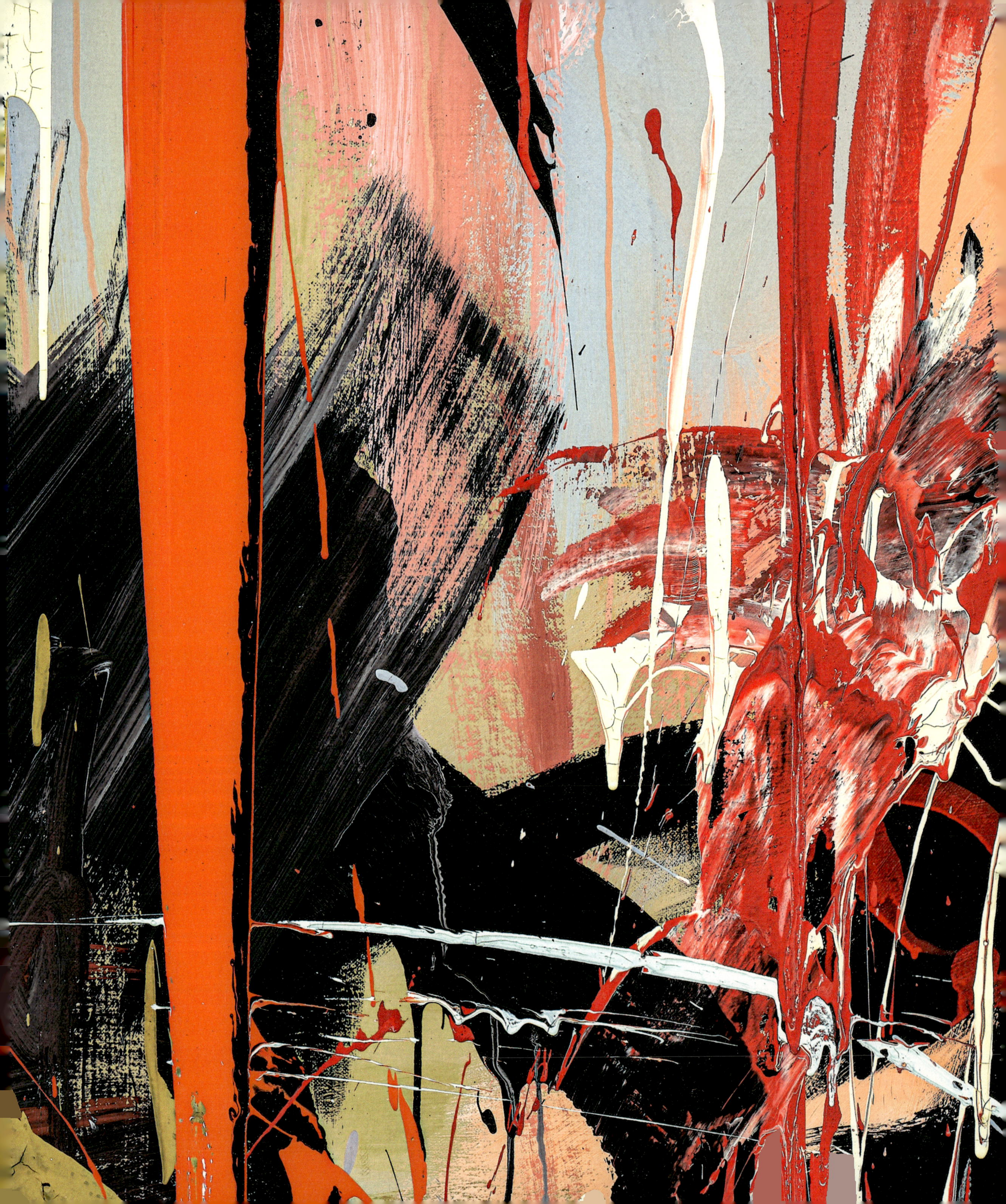

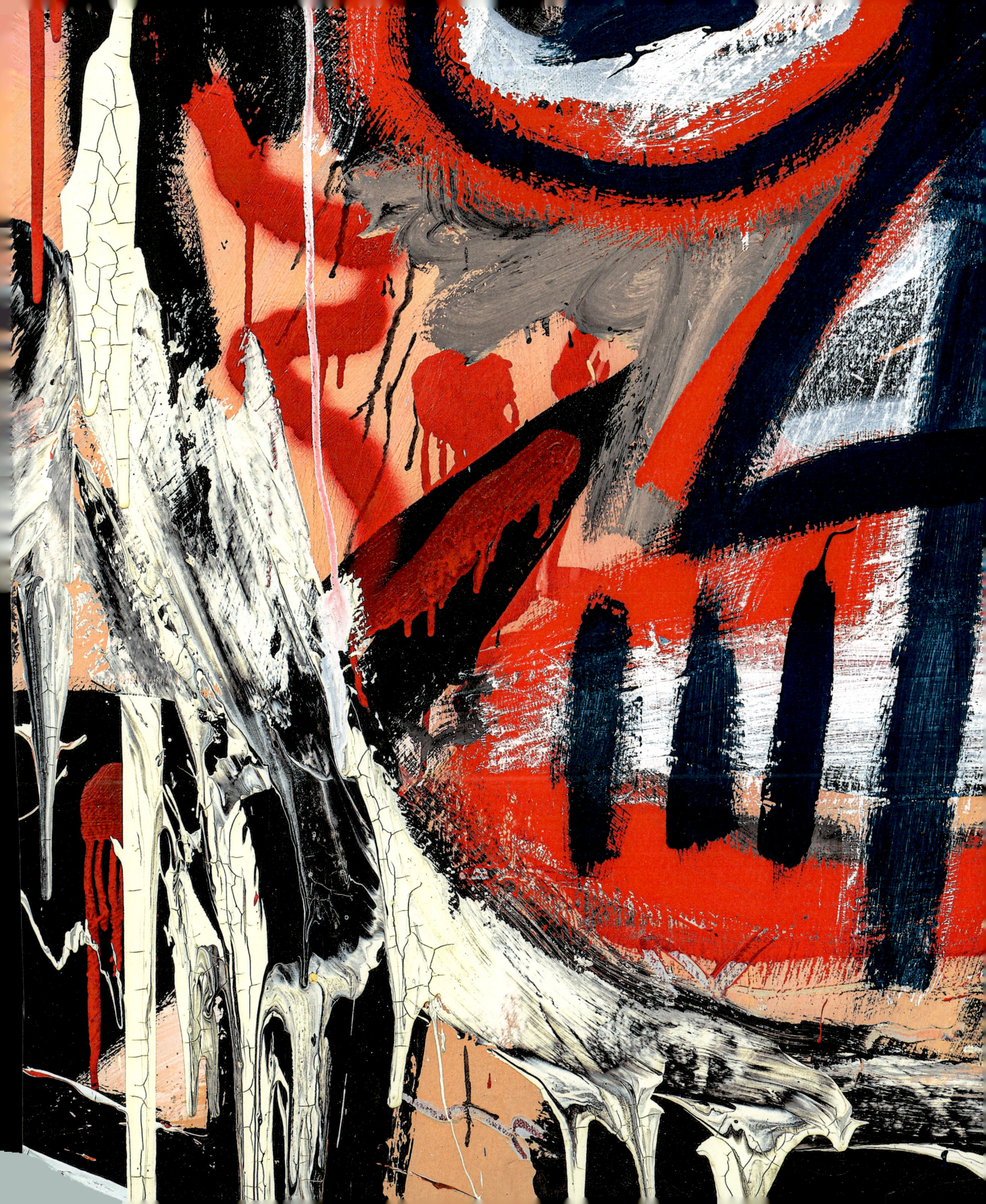

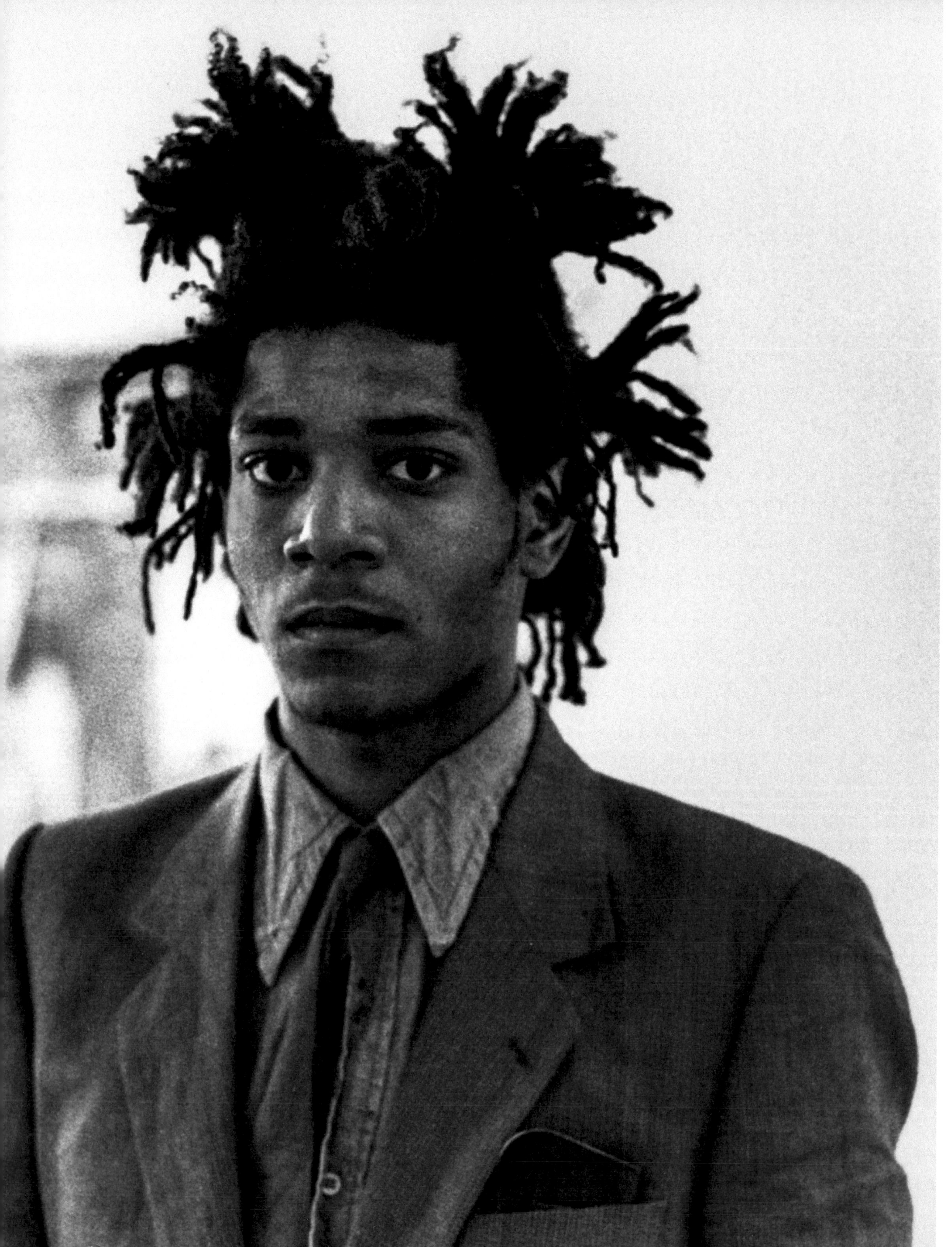

Jean-Michel Basquiat at the Galerie Bruno Bischofberger in Zurich, 1982, photographed by Beth Phillips